The

World's Greatest

BIBLE
TRIVIA
for Kids

The World's Greatest

BIBLE
TRIVIA
for Kids

The Who? The Where? The What?...
and MORE of Scripture!

Donna K. Maltese

BARBOUR BOOKS
An Imprint of Barbour Publishing, Inc.

ecpa Member of the
Evangelical Christian
Publishers Association

Printed in the United States of America.
06307 1118 OP

Contents

Introduction

Welcome to *The World's Greatest Bible Trivia for Kids—The Who? The Where? The What? and More of Scripture*. Within these pages, you will find more than five hundred trivia questions that will amuse and amaze you! The clues will test your Bible knowledge and give you a thirst to read more about heroes and heroines, kings and prophets, giants and troublemakers, reward and promise receivers, encounters with God and angels, fascinating Bible facts and stories, animal antics, powerful tools and weapons, places and perils, wacky weather, supernatural heroes, and so much more!

To help you come up with answers to multiple-choice, matching, fill-in-the-blank, and true-or-false questions, hints and scripture references are given throughout. And, of course, if you're really stumped, an answer key is found at the back of the book.

Turn to page 9 and begin having fun testing your Bible knowledge and discovering how romping with God through the pages of scripture is an amazing adventure!

Heroes and Heroines

- - - - - - -

The Bible is chock-full of men and
women, girls and boys (heroes and
heroines) who did some pretty amazing
things for God and in His power.
Maybe someday you will be one of them!

Which *one* of the following is *not* true about
Aaron?
   a. He was the older brother of Moses.
   b. He was Israel's first "high priest."
   c. He wore special robes.
   d. He had a sister named Ariel.
(Exodus 6:20; 15:20; 28:3)

Fill in the blank:
[The Lord said to Moses,] "Is not Aaron the
Levite your brother? I know he can speak
well. . . . He will be a _____ for you."

Exodus 4:14, 16 NLV

Hint: The answer rhymes with *south*.

True or false: Aaron did miracles with his staff.
(Exodus 7:9)

Which *one* of the following is *not* true about
Abigail?
   a. She was the wife of Nabal.
   b. She was the widow of Nabal.
   c. She married King David.
   d. She wasn't very wise.
(1 Samuel 25:2–3, 33, 38, 42)

One of the many things Abigail brought out to David's hungry and thirsty army was:

   a. manna
   b. raisin cakes
   c. grapefruit juice
   d. Fig Newtons

(1 Samuel 25:18)

Fill in the blank:
Then David said to Abigail, "Thanks be to the Lord God of Israel, Who sent you this day to meet me. May thanks be given for your _____, and thanks be to you. You have kept me this day from being guilty of blood."

                    1 Samuel 25:32–33 NLV
          Hint: The answer starts with w.

Which *one* of the following is *not* true about **Abraham**?

   a. He was also called "Abram."
   b. He was married to Sarah.
   c. His nephew's name was Isaac.
   d. He came from Haran.

(Genesis 12:5; 17:5, 15)

How old was Abraham when God told him to leave his home?

    a. 25
    b. 45
    c. 75
    d. 95

(Genesis 12:4)

True or false: Abraham did whatever God told him to do—even if it meant sacrificing his own son!
(Genesis 26:5)

True or false: Abraham was 100 and Sarah was 90 years old when their one and only son was born.
(Genesis 17:17; 21:5)

Match the following:

    1. Isaac   a. mother of Ishmael
    2. Ishmael   b. mother of Isaac
    3. Sarah   c. means "he laughs"
    4. Hagar   d. means "God hears"

(Genesis 16:11, 15; 21:1–3, 6)

True or false: Abraham was 86 years old when Ishmael was born and 100 years old when Isaac was born.
(Genesis 16:16; 21:3, 5)

Fill in the blank:
Abraham had faith. So he _____ God. God called him to go to a place he would later receive as his own. So he went. He did it even though he didn't know where he was going.

Hebrews 11:8

Hint: The answer starts with o.

Daniel was thrown into a lions' den because:
   a. he could interpret dreams.
   b. he prayed to God three times a day.
   c. he was from Judah.
   d. he knew too much.
(Daniel 6:12–16)

Which *one* of the following is *not* true about **David**?
   a. He was the apple of God's eye.
   b. He never disobeyed God.
   c. His son's name was Solomon.
   d. He led a team of 37 mighty men.
(Psalm 17:8; 2 Samuel 12:9; 5:13–14; 23:39)

Fill in the blank:
"God said, 'I have found David son of Jesse, a man after my own _____. He will do everything I want him to do.' "

Acts 13:22 NLT

Hint: The answer rhymes with *part*.

How many stones did David use to kill Goliath?
   a. 1
   b. 3
   c. 5
   d. 7
(1 Samuel 17:40, 49–50)

Deborah, a judge of Israel, led her people into battle because:
   a. she liked to fight.
   b. she was tired of sitting beneath a palm tree, settling people's arguments.
   c. her army commander, Barak, wouldn't lead the men unless she went along.
   d. her husband told her to.
(Judges 4:8–9)

Which *one* of the following is *not* true about **Esther**?
   a. She was an orphan.
   b. Her cousin's name was Morty.
   c. She married King Xerxes.
   d. Her courage saved her people.
(Esther 2:7, 17; 8:3–17)

Fill in the blank in this verse about Esther:
"If you keep quiet at a time like this, deliverance and relief for the Jews will arise from some other place, but you and your relatives will die. Who knows if perhaps you were made queen for just such a _____ as this?"

Esther 4:14 NLT
Hint: The word that fits appears earlier in this quote.

Which *two* of the following were *not* excuses that **Gideon** gave to God when He called him to lead the Israelites into battle?
   a. "My family is the weakest in its tribe."
   b. "I'm the least important member of my family."
   c. "I have a broken foot."
   d. "My mom said I can't go."
(Judges 6:15)

God knew Gideon was strong before Gideon knew it himself! What was it that made Gideon strong?

    a. his muscles
    b. the army he led
    c. the fact that God was with him
    d. eating oatmeal

(Judges 6:14–16)

Which *one* of the following is *not* true about **Jacob**?

    a. He was father of the 11 tribes of Israel.
    b. He married Leah, then Rachel.
    c. He wrestled with God—and won!
    d. He had a twin brother named Esau.

(Genesis 49:1, 28; 29:25–28; 32:24–28; 25:24–26)

Jael, the wife of Heber, killed Sisera, the commander of an army warring against the Israelites. What *one* thing was the commander doing at the time?

    a. eating and drinking
    b. driving his chariot
    c. coming to attack her
    d. sleeping

(Judges 4:21)

True or false: To save her son from being killed by the king's men, **Jochebed** put her baby Moses in a basket and hid him in the reeds of the Dead Sea.
(Exodus 2:1–3)

Which *one* of the following is *not* true about **John the Baptist**?
- a. His parents' names were Zechariah and Elizabeth.
- b. He was a cousin of Jesus.
- c. He pointed everyone to Jesus!
- d. His head was put on a post.

(Luke 1:57–60; 1:36; John 1:6–8; Mark 6:25–28)

Fill in the blanks:
John wore clothes made of _____ from camels. . . . His food was _____ and wild honey.

Matthew 3:4 NLV
Hint: The first answer rhymes with *pair* and the second with *focused*.

Fill in the blank:
Even though John the Baptist was an amazing hero, he said this about Jesus: "He must become more important. I must become _____ important."

John 3:30 NLV
Hint: The answer is more or less easy!

Which *one* of the following is *not* true about **Jonathan**?

   a.   His dad was King Saul.
   b.   He was stronger than a lion.
   c.   He risked his life to save David.
   d.   His sister's name was Tamar.

(1 Samuel 13:2; 20:12–13; 2 Samuel 1:23)

Fill in the blank:
The soul of Jonathan became one with the soul of David. Jonathan _____ him as himself.

                                 1 Samuel 18:1 NLV
      Hint: The answer is the opposite of *hated*.

Match the following feelings with the actions of **Joseph of Arimathea**:

   1. fearful   a. asked Pilate for Jesus'
                       body
   2. bold   b. put Jesus in his own
                       tomb
   3. giving   c. kept the fact that he
                       followed Jesus a secret

(Mark 15:43–46; John 19:38)

Lots of bad things happened to **Joseph**, the son of Jacob. Can you put them in the right order?

1. first   a. sold to traders
2. second   b. put in prison
3. third   c. bought as a slave
4. fourth   d. thrown in a pit

(Genesis 37:24, 28; 39:1, 20)

Which *one* of the following is *not* true about Joseph?

a. He wore a really colorful coat.
b. He told people what their dreams meant.
c. He became a great leader in Europe.
d. God kept blessing him.

(Genesis 37:3; 39:2–3; 41:12, 41)

Fill in the blank:
[Joseph said to his brothers,] "You planned to do a bad thing to me. But God planned it for _____, to make it happen that many people should be kept alive, as they are today."

Genesis 50:20 NLV
Hint: The answer rhymes with *hood*.

Which *one* of the following is *not* true about
Joshua, son of Nun?
   a. He was afraid of giants.
   b. He was Moses' helper.
   c. He led God's people into the promised
      land.
   d. He defeated 31 kings.
(Numbers 14:6–9; Joshua 1:1–5; 12:24)

Fill in the blanks:
Joshua said to the people, ". . . Choose today
whom you will _____ . . . . As for me
and my family, we will _____ the LORD."

Joshua 24:2, 15 NLT
Hint: The same word fits in each blank
and rhymes with *nerve*.

Mary Magdalene was the first to see Jesus
after His death. Which *one* of the following is
not true about her?
   a. Jesus chased seven demons out of her.
   b. She was with Jesus when He died on
      the cross.
   c. She spoke to two angels.
   d. She thought the risen Jesus was a
      winemaker.
(Mark 16:9; John 19:25; 20:11–16)

When the angel Gabriel told **Mary** she would
be the mother of Jesus, she was what *one*
thing?

    a.   worried
    b.   wrestling
    c.   willing
    d.   wary

(Luke 1:38)

Because he would worship no one but God,
Mordecai, Esther's cousin, refused to bow
down to one of the king's officials. What was
that official's name?

    a.   Xerxes
    b.   Haman
    c.   Susa
    d.   Hegai

(Esther 3:1–2)

Moses was a great hero of the Jewish people.
Which *one* of the following is *not* true about
him?

    a.   He was raised by Pharaoh's daughter.
    b.   He became a shepherd.
    c.   He parted the Red Sea.
    d.   He led his people to Pittsburgh.

(Exodus 2:8–10; 3:1, 7–8; 14:21–22)

When people were behaving badly, God decided to start over with good **Noah**. So He told him to build an ark. Noah was 600 years old when God flooded the earth. How old was he when he died?

    a.   600 years and 40 days
    b.   720 years
    c.   835 years
    d.   950 years

(Genesis 7:6; 9:29)

Fill in the blank:
Noah was a preacher of right living. He and his family of _____ were the only ones God saved.

2 Peter 2:5 NLV
Hint: The answer rhymes with *heaven*.

True or false: When **Paul** started working *for* Jesus instead of *against* Him, he wrote that because of what Jesus has done, nothing can ever separate us from God's love.
(Romans 8:39)

Simon Peter was not only a water walker but a great preacher. After a wonderful sermon, how many believers were added to the church?

    a. 1,000
    b. 2,000
    c. 3,000
    d. 4,000

(Acts 2:41)

Which *one* of the following is *not* true about **Rahab**?

    a. She had made poor life decisions that didn't glorify God.
    b. She saved the lives of Joshua's five spies.
    c. She had faith in God.
    d. She's in Jesus' family tree!

(Joshua 2:1–4; Matthew 1:5; Hebrews 11:31)

Methuselah had one claim to fame. What was it?

    a. He divided the Red Sea.
    b. He lived 969 years.
    c. He grew to be 10 feet tall.
    d. God picked him up in His chariot.

(Genesis 5:27)

Samson was a very strong man and a judge of Israel. Which *one* of the following things did he *not* do?

   a. kill a lion with his bare hands
   b. kill 1,000 Philistines with the jawbone of a donkey
   c. kill more Philistines at his death than in his life
   d. cut his hair

(Judges 14:6; 15:15; 16:17, 30)

The apostle **Stephen** was full of the Holy Spirit, did lots of miracles, and preached to many people. What did he cry out to God when he was being stoned to death?

   a. "Lord, save me!"
   b. "Sticks and stones may break my bones, but words will never hurt me!"
   c. "Lord! Don't hold this sin against them!"

(Acts 7:60)

Jesus' disciples were simple men who did extraordinary things. Which of the following were *not* Jesus' disciples?

   a. Simon Peter, Andrew, James, John
   b. Judas Iscariot, Bartholomew, Thomas, Matthew
   c. Jacob, Levi, Luke, Larry
   d. James (son of Alphaeus), Simon (the zealot), Thaddaeus, Philip

(Matthew 10:2–4)
Hint: There's only one answer.

Jesus sent out how many disciples as lambs among wolves?

   a. 12
   b. 42
   c. 72
   d. 102

(Luke 10:1–3 NLT)

Fill in the blank:
When the disciples returned to Jesus, they said: "Lord, even the demons obey us when we use your _____!"

Luke 10:17 NLT
Hint: The answer rhymes with *fame*.

True or false: **Deborah** was not just the only woman judge in Israel; she was also a wife, mother, prophet, and leader of an army that defeated King Jabin's 900 chariot drivers! (Judges 4:4–16)

Two midwives dared to disobey the king of Egypt, who told them to kill Jewish boys at birth. What were the *two* midwives' names?
    a. Shiphrah
    b. Puah
    c. Sarah
    d. Dinah
(Exodus 1:15–21)

Shadrach, Meshach, and Abednego refused to worship King Nebuchadnezzar's god. What did that god look like?
    a. 90 feet tall
    b. 9 feet wide
    c. made of gold
    d. made of silver
(Daniel 3:1)
Hint: Pick three.

Because Shadrach, Meshach, and Abednego disobeyed the king, they were thrown into a fiery furnace. How hot did the king make it?

   a.   three times hotter than usual
   b.   five times hotter than usual
   c.   seven times hotter than usual
   d.   nine times hotter than usual

(Daniel 3:19)

When the king looked into the furnace, he saw Shadrach, Meshach, and Abednego walking around in there with whom?

   a.   a person who looked like the Son of God
   b.   Daniel
   c.   Moses
   d.   an angel

(Daniel 3:25)
Hint: Pick one.

True or false: When the three men came out of the furnace, they were fine and didn't even smell like smoke!
(Daniel 3:27)

Because of all this, the king did what?

   a.   threw the men in the furnace again
   b.   jumped in the fire himself
   c.   praised God
   d.   dropped dead

(Daniel 3:28)

Which *one* of the following did **King Solomon** *not* do?

  a.   rule directly after King Saul
  b.   build God's temple
  c.   build his own palace
  d.   make a throne of ivory

(1 Kings 2:24; 6:14; 7:1; 10:18)

When evil Queen Athaliah was killing all the king's children, only Prince Joash was saved— by a woman named **Jehosheba**. She was his what?

  a.   aunt
  b.   mom
  c.   guard
  d.   neighbor

(2 Chronicles 22:10–11)

Where did Jehosheba hide Joash and his nurse until he was old enough to become king?

  a.   in a cave
  b.   in a forest
  c.   in the temple
  d.   in the palace

(2 Kings 11:3)

Prophets, Priests, Kings, and Judges

- - - - - - -

The greatest prophet, priest, king, and judge was, of course, Jesus. He fit all four bills. But for now, here are some other fascinating prophets, priests, kings, and judges you should know about.

Which *one* of the following is *not* true about **Deborah**?

    a. She's the only woman judge of Israel in the Bible.

    b. She was also a prophet.

    c. She judged while sitting under an oak tree.

    d. She was called a "mother for Israel."

(Judges 4:4–5; 5:7 NLT)

The prophet **Elijah** did lots of amazing things. And lots of amazing things happened to him! Which of the following is *not* one of them?

    a. He was fed by ravens.

    b. He heard God whisper.

    c. He went up to heaven in a chariot of fire.

    d. He appeared on a mountain with Aaron and Jesus in bright light.

(1 Kings 17:4; 19:12; 2 Kings 2:11–12; Matthew 17:1–3)

True or false: **Samuel** was born in answer to his mother, Anna's, prayer to God for a son. (1 Samuel 1:19–20)

Ezekiel was not just a prophet, priest, and book writer; he also was given dreams by God. What four faces were on each flying angel he dreamed of?

    a.   cherub, human, lion, eagle
    b.   ox, horse, tiger, raven
    c.   dog, cat, sparrow, cow
    d.   human, donkey, dog, lion

(Ezekiel 10:14)

Which *one* of the following things did the prophet **Jeremiah** *not* have happen to him?

    a.   held in a dungeon
    b.   put in a muddy pit
    c.   whipped and put in stocks
    d.   run over by a chariot

(Jeremiah 37:16; 38:7; 20:2 NLT)

Because the people didn't listen to his messages, the prophet Jeremiah was known as what?

    a.   the prophet who gave up
    b.   the ignored prophet
    c.   the weeping prophet
    d.   the peeved prophet

(Jeremiah 13:17)

Which *one* of the following is *not* true about **King Josiah**?

    a. He was the king of Judah.

    b. He was six when he was crowned.

    c. He fixed up God's temple.

    d. He read Moses' law to his people.

(2 Kings 22:1, 4; 23:2)

True or false: King Josiah followed God with all his heart, soul, and strength.

(2 Kings 23:25)

Because **King Saul** kept disobeying God, the Lord replaced him with whom?

    a. Asa

    b. Josiah

    c. David

    d. Hezekiah

(1 Samuel 16:1, 13)

Fill in the blank:

Men came from all nations to hear the

_____ of **[King] Solomon**.

1 Kings 4:34 NLV

Hint: The answer starts with a *w*.

Match the prophet with the deed:

1. Jonah   a. rebuilt Jerusalem's wall
2. Moses   b. told others the baby
                     Jesus was the Messiah
3. Nathan   c. led the Israelites into
                     battle—and won
4. Anna   d. parted the Jordan River
5. Deborah   e. dreamed of battling
                     skeletons
6. Elijah   f. was swallowed by a fish
7. Ezekiel   g. knew God face-to-face
8. Nehemiah   h. told David that God said
                     his throne would last
                     forever

(Jonah 1:17; Deuteronomy 34:10–11; 1 Chronicles 17:3–14; Luke 2:36–38; Judges 4:9, 14–16; 2 Kings 2:8; Ezekiel 37:7–10; Nehemiah 6:15)

Caiaphas talked other leaders into having Jesus arrested, tried, and killed. Fill in the blank of what he said to them about Jesus: Caiaphas, who was high priest at that time, said, "You don't know what you're talking about! You don't realize that it's better for you that _____ man should die for the people."

John 11:49–50 NLT
Hint: The answer is a number.

Ezra the priest wrote that after hearing God's words, all the people did what *one* thing?
   a. bowed down
   b. cried
   c. shook with fear
   d. ran away
(Ezra 9:4 NLV)

Which *one* of the following is *not* true about **Melchizedek**?
   a. He has no beginning or end.
   b. He met Moses.
   c. He was the king of Salem.
   d. He was a priest of God Most High.
(Hebrews 7:1–3)

True or false: When God wondered whom He could send to speak to His people, the prophet **Isaiah** said, "Here I am. Send me!"
(Isaiah 6:8)

God told the prophet, priest, and judge of Israel named **Samuel** to anoint (put oil on the head of) what *two* kings of Israel?

    a. Josiah
    b. David
    c. Asa
    d. Saul

(1 Samuel 10:1; 16:13)

Match the priest, prophet, king or queen, or judge with his/her spouse:

1. Zechariah   a. Bathsheba
2. Moses   b. Jezebel
3. David   c. Gomer
4. Esther   d. Lappidoth
5. Ahab   e. Elizabeth
6. Deborah   f. Xerxes
7. Hosea   g. Zipporah

(Luke 1:5; Exodus 2:21; 2 Samuel 12:24; Esther 2:16–17; 1 Kings 16:30–31; Judges 4:4; Hosea 1:3)

Fill in the blank: **Samson**, a judge of Israel, lost his strength when a woman cut off his

_____.

(Judges 16:17–19)
Hint: The answer rhymes with *fair*.

Which *one* of the following was *not* a judge of
Israel?
   a. Deborah
   b. Samuel
   c. Gideon
   d. Matthew
(1 Samuel 7:15; Judges 4:4; 8:28)

When surrounded by an enemy army that was
allowing no food or water to get into Jerusalem, **King Hezekiah** came up with an idea.
What was it?
   a. He called for takeout.
   b. He dug a pool and built a tunnel.
   c. He had supplies flown in.
   d. He prayed for manna and well water.
(2 Kings 20:20)

What was the name of the king of Persia who
let the captive Jews go home to Jerusalem?
   a. Nebuchadnezzar
   b. Xerxes
   c. Cyrus
   d. Jeshua
(2 Chronicles 36:23)

Dangerous People and Mistake Makers

- - - - - - -

You can read about quite a few dangerous people in the Bible. Some of them were also mistake makers. Here's your "giant" of a chance to see how much you know about them!

Fill in the blank: Samson fell in love with a dangerous Philistine woman named **Delilah**. But she was paid by the Israelites' enemies to find the secret of Samson's _____.

(Judges 16:4–5)

Hint: The answer rhymes with *length*.

King Herod the Great tried to get rid of baby Jesus by having boys two years old and younger killed. Who messed up his plans?

a. an angel
b. Joseph, Jesus' foster father
c. the wise men
d. the disciples

(Matthew 2:1–12)

Hint: Pick three.

Which disciple did **King Herod Agrippa** have killed with a sword?

a. James, son of Zebedee
b. Simon Peter
c. Andrew
d. Matthew

(Acts 12:1–2)

True or false: **King Herod Antipas** not only killed John the Baptist but had his head put on a platter because a young girl asked him to—and all this happened on Herod's birthday! (Mark 6:21–28)

Queen Jezebel was very wicked. Which *one* of the following is *not* true about her?
    a. She was the wife of evil King Ahab.
    b. She led her husband to worship false gods.
    c. She killed a lot of God's prophets.
    d. Her body was eaten by cats.
(1 Kings 16:31; 18:4; 2 Kings 9:10)

Haman got mad because Mordecai, a Jew, wouldn't bow down to him. So he planned to have all the Jews killed. What *two* things happened instead?
    a. Haman had to honor Mordecai.
    b. Haman was fired by the king.
    c. God smote Haman.
    d. Haman was hanged.
(Esther 6:10–11; 7:9–10)

The giant **Goliath** from Gath fought with the shepherd boy David—and lost. Which *three* of the following are true about Goliath?
    a.   He was over 9 feet tall.
    b.   His armor weighed 125 pounds.
    c.   His spear weighed 15 pounds.
    d.   His mom's name was Golly.
(1 Samuel 17:4–7)

Evil **Queen Athaliah** killed all the king's children except one. What was his name?
    a.   Jonas
    b.   Jonathan
    c.   Joash
    d.   Joe
(2 Chronicles 22:11)

Before Jesus set him straight, **Saul** (later known as **Paul**) killed a lot of Christians. He also gave the okay for people to stone whom?
    a.   Stephen
    b.   John
    c.   Barnabas
    d.   Nicodemus
(Acts 8:1)

Which *one* of the following did Jesus *not* do to set Saul/Paul straight?
  a. flashed him with light
  b. hit him with hail
  c. spoke to him from heaven
  d. blinded, then healed him
(Acts 9:3–19)

Fill in the blank to complete the verse that the changed Paul wrote:
God had mercy on me so that Christ Jesus could use me as a prime example of his great patience with even the worst _____.

                         1 Timothy 1:16 NLT
  Hint: The missing word rhymes with *winners*.

True or false: Before he became a hero for Jesus, **Peter** not only sank in the sea for lack of faith but later denied even knowing Jesus. (Matthew 14:29–30; 26:69–75)

The first people God made, **Adam and Eve**, made big mistakes while in the Garden of Eden. Which *two* are listed below?

    a.   listened to a snake's lies
    b.   killed animals for clothes
    c.   ate fruit God told them not to
    d.   cut down a tree

(Genesis 3:1–7)

True or false: Because Adam and Eve disobeyed God, sin was brought into the world.
(Romans 5:12)

When Moses' brother, **Aaron**, let others talk him into doing things that were against God's will, he got into trouble. One such time was when he made something for the people to worship instead of God. What was that something?

    a.   a statue of himself
    b.   a golden calf
    c.   an ark
    d.   the god Dagon

(Exodus 32:4)

Miriam was jealous of her brother Moses, so she spoke out against him. What did God give her that He later healed her of, thanks to Moses' prayer?
   a. demons
   b. sleeping sickness
   c. leprosy
   d. snakebites
(Numbers 12:9–10)

True or false: When God told **Jonah** to go to Nineveh, Jonah went down to Joppa instead and boarded a ship heading to Tarshish.
(Jonah 1:3)

Instead of going to Nineveh with a message for the people from God, Jonah ran away from God. Which of the following *three* things then happened to Jonah?
   a. He was thrown off a ship and into the sea.
   b. A sea creature swallowed him.
   c. He was spit up on dry land.
   d. He had to write 20 times, "I will obey God from now on."
(Jonah 1:15, 17; 2:10)

True or false: Even though **Moses** was a great leader for God, he still made some mistakes, such as killing an Egyptian, hiding his body, and then running away.
(Exodus 2:12–15)

David sinned in a few ways when it came to a certain bathing beauty. Which *one* of the following things did *not* happen?
- a. He wanted Bathsheba, Uriah's wife, for his own.
- b. He and Bathsheba were expecting a child.
- c. He killed her husband, Uriah.
- d. He refused to marry her.

(2 Samuel 11:1–5, 14–17, 27)

While making a big dinner at her house, **Martha**, the sister of Mary and Lazarus, was too *what* to sit at Jesus' feet and listen to Him?
- a. busy, worried, and upset
- b. angry, bored, and hungry
- c. lazy, upset, and thirsty
- d. mad, whiny, and lazy

(Luke 10:40–41)

Which *one* of the following is *not* true about
the disciple **Judas Iscariot**?
  a. He was keeper of the disciples' money
      bag.
  b. He never stole coins for himself.
  c. He was paid 30 silver coins for betray-
      ing Jesus.
  d. He later felt bad for what he had done.
(John 12:4–6; Matthew 26:15; 27:4–5)

What did Judas do so the soldiers would know
Jesus was the person to arrest?
  a. He pointed to Jesus.
  b. He yelled out Jesus' name.
  c. He kissed Jesus.
  d. He sent the soldiers a photo.
(Matthew 26:47–49)

The married couple **Ananias and Sapphira**
dropped dead when Peter told them they had
made this mistake:
  a. stolen money
  b. helped kill Jesus
  c. cheated their friend
  d. lied to the Holy Spirit
(Acts 5:1–10)

While the Roman governor **Pilate** was judging Jesus, his wife, who'd had a dream about Jesus, sent Pilate what message?
    a. "Jesus is innocent."
    b. "Jesus will save us."
    c. "Jesus should be beaten."
    d. "Come home! I'm tired!"
(Matthew 27:19)

Fill in the blank:
Pilate wanted to _____ the people. He. . .had Jesus beaten. Then he handed Him over to be nailed to a cross.

Mark 15:15 NLV
Hint: This word rhymes with *seize*.

What was the name of the murderer whom Pilate set free instead of Jesus?
    a. Barnabas
    b. Barabbas
    c. Barnaby
    d. Barney
(Matthew 27:26)

Thomas doubted that Jesus had risen from the grave. That's because he wasn't there when Jesus first appeared to the other disciples. How many days later did Jesus show up when Thomas *was* around?

    a. 3
    b. 4
    c. 8
    d. 10

(John 20:24–26)

Fill in the blanks:
Jesus said to him, "Thomas, because you have seen Me, you _____. Those are happy who have never seen Me and yet _____!"

John 20:29 NLV
Hint: The same word, which rhymes with *receive*, fits both blanks.

Zacchaeus was a greedy tax collector who cheated people. What *two* things did he promise to do after he met Jesus?

    a. give half his wealth to the poor
    b. give back four times the amount he had cheated people
    c. work seven years for those he cheated
    d. give Jesus all his money

(Luke 19:8)

Many years ago, when everyone spoke the same language, people in **Babel** began building a tower to reach heaven. To bring them back down to earth and show them that He's the highest power, God did what *two* things?
    a. struck them with lightning
    b. made it rain 40 days
    c. mixed up their language
    d. scattered them throughout the earth
(Genesis 11:9)

King Nebuchadnezzar of Babylon bragged about his great deeds, power, and palace. That's when God told him he would change into a beast that all but what *one* thing?
    a. ate grass like a cow
    b. had nails that looked like bird claws
    c. had hair as long as an eagle's feathers
    d. was slick with oil
(Daniel 4:29–33)

True or false: When Nebuchadnezzar came to his senses and began praising God instead of himself, he became a king again.
(Daniel 4:34–37)

True or false: Even though she started out living a life that didn't glorify God, **Rahab** saved the lives of Joshua's spies, her faith kept her from being killed, and she ended up being an ancestor of Jesus.
(Matthew 1:5; Hebrews 11:31)

Because he hung around a dangerous woman named Delilah, what *three* things did **Samson** lose?
   a. his hair
   b. his strength
   c. his eyes
   d. his mom
(Judges 16:4–5, 19–21)

Fill in the blank: Because **King Saul** made some pretty bad choices, God told him: "You haven't _____ the command the LORD your God gave you. . . . Now your kingdom won't last."

1 Samuel 13:13–14
Hint: The answer starts with an *o*.

Too impatient to wait for God's guidance, King Saul decided to get wisdom from a medium (a person who attempts to communicate with the dead) who lived where?

  a. Egypt
  b. Endor
  c. En Gedi
  d. Ephesus

(1 Samuel 28:7–8)

True or false: Because a man named **Achan** had taken things that didn't belong to him, Joshua and the Israelites lost the battle in Ai. (Joshua 7:1–5)

When God was destroying her home in the evil Sodom, angels told **Lot's wife** not to look back. But she did. What *one* thing happened to her?

  a. She caught on fire.
  b. She was hit by brimstone.
  c. She turned into a pillar of salt.
  d. She got a skin disease.

(Genesis 19:24–26)

Reward and Promise Receivers

When people faithfully obey and follow
God, God gives them promises and
rewards. Check out the amazing things
that were given to some pretty
amazing people who lived for God!

Job had lots of things and money. Then God let who test Job?
   a.   his wife
   b.   Satan
   c.   his children
   d.   his teacher
(Job 1:12; 2:6)
Hint: Pick one.

When Job lost his animals, land, children, and health, his wife gave him some bad advice. Fill in the blank to complete what she said:
"Do you still hold on to your faith? Curse God and _____!"

Job 2:9 NLV
Hint: The answer rhymes with *lie*.

No matter what bad things happened to him, Job kept trusting in and waiting on God. Knowing that, fill in the following blank:
People who don't give up are blessed. You have heard that Job was _____. And you have seen what the Lord finally did for him.

James 5:11
Hint: The answer starts with a *p*.

Fill in the blank: The name God gave him, **Abraham**, means "father of many _____," which God promised he would be.

Genesis 17:5

Hint: The answer rhymes with *stations*.

True or false: After God promised **Sarah** she would have a son in her old age, she laughed. God then asked her, "Is anything too hard for the Lord?"
(Genesis 18:14 NLV)

As God promised, Abraham and Sarah did have a son in their old age! What did they name him?
   a.   Ishmael
   b.   Isaac
   c.   Isaiah
   d.   Ichabod
(Genesis 21:1–3)

Fill in the blank: Because Abraham proved he would obey God, God made him some promises. And because God kept those promises, the Levites said to God:
"And you have done what you promised, for you are always true to your _____."

Nehemiah 9:8 NLT
Hint: The answer rhymes with bird.

Which *one* of the following did God *not* promise **Jacob**?
    a. "I will be with you."
    b. "I will never leave you."
    c. "You'll have lots of kids."
    d. "I'll leave my angel with you."
(Genesis 28:13–15)

Jacob was tricked into marrying **Leah**, whom he didn't love. Yet she kept trusting in God. So God rewarded her by letting her have children. Which *one* of the following pairs were *not* Leah's sons?
    a. Reuben and Simeon
    b. Levi and Judah
    c. Aaron and Moses
    d. Issachar and Zebulun
(Genesis 35:23)

Jephthah promised God that if He helped him win a battle, he would give God the first person who came out of his door to greet him afterward. Whom did Jephthah end up giving away to God?

- a. his wife
- b. his daughter
- c. his mother
- d. his servant

(Judges 11:29–35)

Hannah prayed to God with all her heart for a child. When God rewarded her with a son, what did she joyfully give God in return?

- a. her son Samuel and a prayer of thanks
- b. all the manna she could find
- c. gold and silver
- d. a bull, flour, and wine

(1 Samuel 1:24–28; 2:1–11)
Hint: Pick two of the four choices!

Fill in the blank in this promise that **Elisha** made to a rich woman who had been kind to him in Shunem:
"At this time next year you will hold a _____ in your arms."

2 Kings 4:16 NLV
Hint: The answer rhymes with *won*.

True or false: Because the widow **Ruth** promised never to leave her mother-in-law and trusted in God, she found a new husband and wound up in Jesus' family tree!
(Ruth 1:16–17; Matthew 1:5)

The king of Egypt told midwives **Shiphrah and Puah** to kill Jewish boys at birth. But because they loved God, they dared to disobey the king and let the boys live. Which *one* of the following did God do to reward them?
   a.   gave them a new car
   b.   made them queens of Egypt
   c.   gave them families of their own
   d.   blessed them with riches
(Exodus 1:15–21)

How did Jesus reward **Mary of Bethany** for pouring perfume on His feet and sitting at His feet to listen to Him?
   a.   He gave her money.
   b.   He said that what she did will always be remembered.
   c.   He patted her head.
   d.   He said, "Thank you."
(Matthew 26:13)

Miracle Makers

— — — — — —

The Bible contains a lot of stories
about miracles. And although the
miracles were done by a lot of praying
people, the miracle *power* came from
God. If you want to be a miracle maker,
keep praying, and God will answer
you with miracle-making power!

One day a woman looked for Jesus to heal her. For how long had she been badly bleeding?
   a.   5 years
   b.   12 years
   c.   19 years
   d.   26 years
(Mark 5:25)

What *one* thing had the woman *not* done before going to Jesus?
   a.   seen lots of doctors
   b.   changed her diet
   c.   spent all her money
   d.   gotten worse
(Mark 5:25–26)

What *two* things did the woman do when she saw Jesus?
   a.   joined the crowd following Him
   b.   pushed people out of her way
   c.   touched His clothes
   d.   grabbed His sandal
(Mark 5:27)

What did the woman say to herself as she reached out to Jesus?

    a. "I hope He can heal me."
    b. "I hope I don't get in trouble."
    c. "If I touch Him, I'll be healed."
    d. "If He heals me, I'll follow Him."

(Mark 5:28)

As soon as the woman connected with Jesus physically, what *two* things happened?

    a. She got in trouble.
    b. Jesus stopped walking.
    c. The crowd pushed her away.
    d. She stopped bleeding.

(Mark 5:29–30)

As soon as the woman connected with Jesus, what *two* things did Jesus realize?

    a. Power had gone out from Him.
    b. He had a bleeder on His hands.
    c. Someone had touched Him.
    d. She could not be healed.

(Mark 5:30)

When Jesus looked around at the crowd, the healed woman was filled with what *one* thing?
- a. fire
- b. fear
- c. love
- d. hope

(Mark 5:33)

What *one* thing did Jesus say had healed the woman?
- a. her courage
- b. her doctor
- c. her faith
- d. her hope

(Mark 5:34)

What *two* things did Jesus tell the now healed woman to do?
- a. "Go in peace."
- b. "You are free from sickness."
- c. "Don't ever touch Me again."
- d. "Come with Me."

(Mark 5:34)

Which of the following *three* things are true about **Lazarus**?
  a. He was the brother of Mary and Mona.
  b. Jesus loved him.
  c. Jesus cried when He heard Lazarus had died.
  d. He was in the grave four days before Jesus brought him back to life.
(John 11:1, 35–36, 39–44)

Fill in the blanks:
Jesus. . .said, "Lazarus's sickness will not end in death. No, it happened for the _____ of God so that the Son of God will receive _____ from this."

John 11:4 NLT
Hint: The same word—which rhymes with *story*—fits both blanks.

True or false: In Troas, Paul was preaching on and on while a man named **Eutychus** sat on a windowsill. But then he fell asleep and fell out the window—and died! But after Paul took him in his arms, Eutychus came back to life! (Acts 20:9–10, 12)

After thanking God for the food a little boy had, Jesus fed over 5,000 people with what?
- a. two loaves and five fish
- b. three loaves and four fish
- c. four loaves and one fish
- d. five loaves and two fish

(John 6:8–9)

How many baskets of leftovers were there after Jesus fed all the people?
- a. 3
- b. 6
- c. 12
- d. 18

(Matthew 14:20)

After making mud from dirt and spit and putting it on a blind man's eyes, Jesus told the man to wash where?
- a. Dead Sea
- b. Jordan River
- c. Pool of Siloam
- d. Sea of Galilee

(John 9:6–7)

The prophet **Elijah** was a major miracle maker!
Which of the following did he do through the
power of prayer?
   a. made flour and oil appear
   b. brought fire down from heaven
   c. stopped the Jordan River's flow
   d. raised people from the dead
(1 Kings 17:13–16, 21–22; 18:36–39; 2 Kings 2:8)

Elisha not only promised a woman she would
have a son but later brought the boy what *one*
thing?
   a. a bottle of oil that never ran dry
   b. a talking donkey
   c. a special fleece
   d. back to life
(2 Kings 4:31–35)

When a kind and giving woman named **Dorcas**
died, the apostle Peter prayed for her. Then he
said a few words and she opened her eyes and
rose up! What did Peter say?
   a. "Open your eyes, Dorcas!"
   b. "Your faith has healed you. Rise!"
   c. "Get up, Tabitha!"
   d. "Woman, take a breath!"
(Acts 9:39–41 NLT)

Match the place name with the miracle maker:
1. Cana   a. Elijah
2. Jordan River   b. Jesus
3. Marah   c. Elisha
4. Mount Carmel   d. Moses

(John 2:1, 6–9; 2 Kings 5:10–15;
Exodus 15:23–25; 1 Kings 18:20, 36–38)

Match the sick/dead person with the person who healed him or her.
1. Naaman   a. Peter
2. Bartimaeus   b. Paul
3. Eutychus   c. Elisha
4. Dorcas/Tabitha   d. Jesus

(2 Kings 5:9–10, 14; Mark 10:46–52;
Acts 20:9–10; 9:39–41)

Match the ailment with the miracle remedy:
1. leprosy   a. throwing in a stick
2. bitter water   b. applying mud made
                          with dirt and spit
3. blindness   c. washing in the Jordan
                          seven times

(2 Kings 5:9–10, 14; Exodus 15:23–25;
John 9:6–7)

Close Encounters of the Supernatural Kind

· — — — — — ·

God, Jesus, the Holy Spirit, and angels
are at work in the world today! Check
out these fun facts about how they
worked in the lives of people in Bible
days. Then think about how they
might be working in *your* life!

Abraham had courage. He stood in front of God and asked Him to rescue his nephew Lot before God destroyed what city?

    a. Babylon
    b. Sodom
    c. Philadelphia
    d. Nineveh

(Genesis 19:28–29)

The further Abraham's nephew **Lot** drifted away from God, the further he drifted into trouble. Yet God sent angels to rescue him because Abraham kept trusting God. How many angels did God send to save Lot?

    a. one
    b. two
    c. three
    d. four

(Genesis 19:1)

Fill in the blank:
God opened **Hagar's** _____. And she saw a well of water. She went and filled the leather bag with water and gave the boy a drink.

Genesis 21:19 NLV
Hint: The answer rhymes with *ties*.

Jacob dreamed about angels climbing up and down a ladder that reached from heaven to earth. Who was at the top of that ladder?

    a. Moses
    b. Jesus
    c. Gabriel
    d. God

(Genesis 28:13)
Hint: Pick one.

There was a man who walked so closely with God while on earth that he "was taken up to heaven without dying" (Hebrews 11:5 NLT)! What was the man's name?

    a. Noah
    b. Joseph
    c. Moses
    d. Enoch

After meeting up with an angel of God, **Manoah's wife** gave birth to a baby boy. What did she name him?

    a. Samson
    b. Manoah Jr.
    c. Atlas
    d. Hercules

(Judges 13:2–24)

Fill in the blank:
The Angel of the Lord showed Himself
to **Moses** in a burning fire from inside a

_____.

Exodus 3:2 NLV
Hint: The answer rhymes with *whoosh*.

Using His finger, God wrote the Ten Commandments on stone tablets and handed them
to **Moses**. See if you can put those rules in
God's order:

1. One   a. Don't use "God" as a
                             curse word.

2. Two   b. Don't murder.

3. Three   c. Don't steal.

4. Four   d. Honor Mom and Dad.

5. Five   e. Don't want someone
                             else's stuff.

6. Six   f. Have only one God.

7. Seven   g. Don't lie.

8. Eight   h. Rest on the Sabbath.

9. Nine   i. Stay faithful to your
                             spouse.

10. Ten   j. Make no idols.
(Exodus 20:1–17; 31:18)

What did **Samuel** say when God came to his bed, stood there, and called his name?
   a. "Shh! I'm sleeping!"
   b. "Speak. I'm listening."
   c. "Send me!"
   d. "Can You repeat that?"
(1 Samuel 3:10)

Fill in the blank with the name of a prophet: The LORD continued to appear at Shiloh and gave messages to _____ there.

1 Samuel 3:21 NLT

Hint: The answer rhymes with manual.

Because they refused to worship King Nebuchadnezzar's statue, **Shadrach, Meshach, and Abednego** were thrown into a fiery furnace. Who was it that the king saw walking with them in the flames?
   a. an angel
   b. Moses
   c. a firefighter
   d. a person who looked like the Son of God (Jesus)
(Daniel 3:25 NLV)

The angel Gabriel was 21 days late coming to visit **Daniel** because of what *one* reason?
    a.   God held him up.
    b.   He had to visit Mary.
    c.   The prince of Persia stood against him.
    d.   He got lost on the way.
(Daniel 10:13)

What did God ask first when He spoke to **Job** out of a whirlwind?
    a.   "Who made you king?"
    b.   "Who do you think you are?"
    c.   "What do you need?"
    d.   "How can I help?"
(Job 38:1–2)

Match the angel's message to the person who heard it:
1. "God has heard Ishmael crying."   a. Daniel
2. "Get up!"   b. Gad
3. "I give you wisdom!"   c. Mary
4. "God has blessed you!"   d. Peter
5. "Tell David to build me an altar."   e. Hagar
(Genesis 21:17; Acts 12:7; Daniel 9:21–22;
Luke 1:28; 1 Chronicles 21:18)

The angel Gabriel visited the priest **Zechariah** and told him that he and his wife would have a baby boy. Because Zechariah didn't believe Gabriel, what *one* thing did the angel take away from the priest until the baby was born?

   a. his riches
   b. his voice
   c. his wife
   d. his robe
(Luke 1:19–20)

True or false: The name of the angel who told **Mary** she would be the mother of Jesus was Gabriel.
(Luke 1:26–31)

Four times an angel of God told **Joseph**, Jesus' earthly father, in a dream, what to do to keep baby Jesus safe. Match the time of the visit with the angel's guidance to Joseph:

1. first visit	a. Take Jesus to Egypt.
2. second visit	b. Take Jesus to Israel.
3. third visit	c. Head to Galilee.
4. fourth visit	d. Marry the pregnant Mary.

(Matthew 1:20; 2:13, 19–20, 22)

Fill in the blank:
Joseph awoke from his _____. He
did what the angel of the Lord told him to do.

Matthew 1:24 NLV
Hint: The answer rhymes with *weep*.

Fill in the blanks with the names of two Old
Testament men who had a chat with Jesus:
[Jesus'] appearance was changed. His face
shone like the sun. His clothes became as
white as the light. Just then _____
and _____ appeared in front of
them. . .talking with Jesus.

Matthew 17:2–3
Hint: One name starts with *M*,
the other with *E*.

What *three* disciples were with Jesus when
He was transfigured, and again when he was
praying in the garden?
   a. James
   b. John
   c. Peter
   d. Paul
(Matthew 17:1–3; 26:36–37)

What were the names of *three* of the women who saw the angels in Jesus' tomb?
a. Mary Magdalene
b. Joanna
c. Dorcas
d. Mary, the mother of James
(Luke 24:1–10)

True or false: After He rose from the dead, Jesus appeared to two of His followers who were on the road to Emmaus.
(Luke 24:13–15)

An angel of God came to **Cornelius** in a dream because this army captain had done what?
a. worked hard
b. sung really well
c. prayed and given gifts to God
d. not eaten unclean meat
(Acts 10:3–4)
Hint: Pick one.

True or false: Gabriel and Michael are the only two angels the Bible names.
(Daniel 9:21; 10:21)

The angel told Cornelius to:
    a. take another nap for more instructions
    b. pray harder
    c. go to Egypt
    d. invite Simon Peter to his house
(Acts 10:5)

Fill in the blank: To get **Saul** (later known as the apostle **Paul**) going the right way, Jesus met up with him on the road and blinded him. When he was later being healed, "something like _____ fell from Saul's eyes."

Acts 9:18 NLT

Hint: The answer rhymes with *whales*.

One night in Corinth, the Lord spoke to the preacher Paul in a vision. Which of the following did God say?
    a. "Don't be afraid."
    b. "Keep on speaking."
    c. "Don't be silent."
    d. "I am with you."
(Acts 18:8–10)

Book Hooks

- — — — — — -

The books of the Bible are filled with stories about giants, strange animals, God followers, dangerous people, and so much more. Have fun seeing how much you know and remember about these special God-inspired books, the characters in them, and the people who wrote them!

The Bible has how many books?
   a. 26
   b. 46
   c. 66
   d. 86

Moses wrote the first five books of the Old Testament. Can you name them all—in order? Hint: They start with these letters: *G, E, L, N, D*

What are the names of the *four* books of the Gospel?
   a. Matthew and Mark
   b. Titus and Timothy
   c. Luke and John
   d. Peter and Philip
Hint: Pick two.

True or false: In **Genesis**, the first book of the Bible, God created the world in six days and rested on the seventh.
(Genesis 2:1–3)

God made Adam from what?
- a. air
- b. breath
- c. dirt
- d. a rib

(Genesis 2:7)

God made Eve from what?
- a. air
- b. breath
- c. dirt
- d. a rib

(Genesis 2:21–22)

The book of **Exodus** tells about Moses helping God's people escape from being slaves where?
- a. in England
- b. in Egypt
- c. in Ecuador
- d. in Emerald City

(Exodus 6:5–6)

How many plagues did God send on Egypt so their ruler would let God's people go?
- a. 4
- b. 7
- c. 10
- d. 12

(Exodus 7:14–11:10)

After the Israelites escaped Egypt, God led them night and day as what?
- a. a pillar of fire
- b. a pillar of cloud
- c. a small voice
- d. a strong wind

(Exodus 13:21)
Hint: Pick two.

While they were in the wilderness, God fed His hungry people with what?
- a. chicken fingers
- b. hamburger
- c. vegetables
- d. manna

(Exodus 16:31)

True or false: The book of **Leviticus** tells the people how to worship God.
(Leviticus 1)

True or false: The book of **Numbers** got its name because it starts by counting warriors.
(Numbers 1:1–4)

Numbers also tells how God's people wandered for how many years?
   a. 10
   b. 20
   c. 30
   d. 40
(Numbers 32:13)

In the book of **Deuteronomy**, all the people who escaped Egypt are dead except for which *three*:
   a. Joshua
   b. Aaron
   c. Moses
   d. Caleb
(Numbers 20:28; Deuteronomy 1:1, 35–38)

In the book of **Joshua**, where did Rahab hide two of Joshua's spies?

    a.   under bundles of flax
    b.   under blankets
    c.   in a cellar
    d.   in a well

(Joshua 2:6)

The book of **Judges** tells the story about Gideon and his wool what?

    a.   blanket
    b.   fleece
    c.   shirt
    d.   coat of many colors

(Judges 6:37 NLT)

Which *one* person is *not* a part of the story in the book of **Ruth**?

    a.   Boaz
    b.   Naomi
    c.   Samuel
    d.   Ruth

(Ruth 4:13–14)

True or false: In **1 Samuel**, God told Samuel His people didn't want Him (God) as king.
(1 Samuel 8:7)

The book of **2 Samuel** talks about a giant who had what?
    a. two heads
    b. three feet
    c. one eye
    d. 12 fingers and 12 toes
(2 Samuel 21:20)
Hint: Pick one.

Fill in the blank: The book called **1 Kings** tells the story of the _____ of Sheba, who visited King Solomon and was amazed at his wisdom and riches.

                            1 Kings 10:1
          Hint: The answer rhymes with *clean*.

In **2 Kings** the prophet Elisha and his servant are surrounded by an enemy army. What *one* thing did Elisha pray to God for so his servant would not be afraid?
    a. to open the servant's eyes
    b. to give the servant courage
    c. to send weapons
    d. to help them escape
(2 Kings 6:17)

When Elisha's prayer was answered, what was surrounding him and his servant?
   a.   horses and chariots of fire
   b.   God's angels
   c.   flaming swords
   d.   a secret door
(2 Kings 6:17)
Hint: Pick one.

True or false: In **1 Chronicles**, you can read about King David's mighty man Jashobeam who "killed 300 men with his spear at one time"!
(1 Chronicles 11:11 NLV)

In **2 Chronicles**, King Jehoshaphat and his people are surrounded by an enemy army. But thanks to his prayers and praise to God, God did what *one* thing?
   a.   sent flaming swords to the king's men
   b.   set traps so that the enemy armies destroyed each other
   c.   told the earth to swallow the enemy
   d.   washed the enemy away in a flood
(2 Chronicles 20:22–23)

Ezra, a priest and teacher, wrote in his book that God would keep him and the Jews safe in their travel back to Jerusalem, so he decided *not* to ask the king for what?

    a. shields and swords
    b. soldiers and horsemen
    c. bows and arrows
    d. armor and spears

(Ezra 7:12; 8:21–22)
Hint: Pick one.

Nehemiah, who was a Bible book writer, the king's wine taster, and a prophet, led the Jews to rebuild Jerusalem's wall. How many days did it take to rebuild the wall?

    a. 14
    b. 40
    c. 52
    d. 83

(Nehemiah 6:15)

Fill in the blank: The book of **Esther** is an amazing story about an orphan girl who becomes a _____ queen.

Esther 2:7, 16
Hint: The answer rhymes with *crave*.

The book of **Job** is about a man who was tested by Satan. What *one* thing did Job hang on to no matter what happened to him?
   a.   his children
   b.   his wealth
   c.   his animals
   d.   his trust in God
(Job 13:15)

True or false: At the end, Job, who had lost almost everything, was blessed with 10 more children and two times the number of animals he'd had before!
(Job 42:10, 13)

How many poems or songs are in the book of **Psalms**?
   a.   90
   b.   119
   c.   139
   d.   150

In one of the most famous psalms, David wrote that the Lord is his what?

a. King
b. Savior
c. Shepherd
d. Helper

(Psalm 23:1)

Fill in the blank in this well-known verse: Your word is like a _____ that shows me the way. It is like a light that guides me.

Psalm 119:105

Hint: The answer rhymes with *damp*.

The book of **Proverbs** teaches us how to live in a way that pleases God. Which *three* of the following people wrote some of them?

a. Agur
b. King Lemuel
c. King Ahab
d. King Solomon

(Proverbs 1:1; 30:1; 31:1)

Proverbs 31 was written by a king. It's all about things that who had taught him?
   a. God
   b. his mom
   c. his grandmother
   d. his pastor
(Proverbs 31:1)

True or false: King Solomon wrote the **Song of Songs**, the book of **Ecclesiastes**, and many psalms and proverbs.
(1 Kings 4:32; Song of Songs 1:1; Ecclesiastes 1:1)

In his book, the prophet **Isaiah** said he saw angels whom he called what?
   a. seraphim
   b. sallyforth
   c. Sarah
   d. Syracruse
(Isaiah 6:2 NLT)

Fill in the blank with a number: Isaiah said these angels had _____ wings.

Isaiah 6:2

Hint: The answer is a number that rhymes with *mix*.

Fill in the blanks to complete this wonderful quote from the book of the prophet **Jeremiah**: "For I know the _____ I have for you," says the Lord, "_____ for well-being and not for trouble, to give you a future and a hope."

Jeremiah 29:11 NLV
Hint: The same word—which rhymes with *tans*—fits both blanks.

Most people think the sad book of **Lamentations** was written by the man known as the weeping prophet. What was his name?
a. Isaiah
b. Jeremiah
c. Nehemiah
d. Obadiah

True or false: **Ezekiel**, who wrote the book of Ezekiel, was a prophet, priest, and prisoner who had visions of weird flying creatures and a skeleton army!
(Ezekiel 1; 37)

Fill in the blanks:
[God said to Ezekiel], "Son of man, eat this _____ that I give you and fill your stomach with it." So I ate it, and it was as sweet as _____ in my mouth.

Ezekiel 3:3 NLV

Hint: The first word rhymes with *hook* and the second rhymes with *sunny*.

What *one* story will you *not* find in the book of **Daniel**?
a. three men saved from a furnace
b. fingers writing a message on a wall
c. an angel shutting lions' mouths
d. a talking donkey

(Daniel 3:28; 5:5; 6:21–22)

Put in order the four books that come after Daniel in the Bible, all of which were written by prophets:
a. Joel
b. Obadiah
c. Amos
d. Hosea

In the book of **Jonah**, which *one* of the following does *not* happen to him after he disobeys God?
   a.   He is thrown into a stormy sea.
   b.   He battles an octopus.
   c.   He is swallowed by a giant fish.
   d.   He is spit up on dry land.
(Jonah 1:15, 17; 2:10)

True or false: At the end of the book of **Jonah**, God destroys the city of Nineveh.
(Jonah 3:10)

In his book, what *three* things does the prophet **Micah** say God wants you to do?
   a.   do what's right
   b.   love money
   c.   show kindness
   d.   walk without pride with God
(Micah 6:8)

True or false: Micah said that God told him a ruler and shepherd of God's people would be born in Nazareth someday.
(Micah 5:2–5)

Fill in the blank: The book of **Nahum** says:
"The LORD is slow to get _____."

Nahum 1:3 NLT

Hint: The answer starts with an *a*.

The prophet **Habakkuk** said the problem with
proud people is that instead of trusting in
God, they trust in what?
   a.   money
   b.   other people
   c.   horses and chariots
   d.   themselves
(Habakkuk 2:4)

True or false: In his book, **Zephaniah** said he
was the great-great-great-grandson of King
Hezekiah.
(Zephaniah 1:1)

The prophet **Haggai** wrote his book telling
Jews to take courage and finish what building
project?
   a.   the king's palace
   b.   Jerusalem's wall
   c.   God's house
   d.   a pyramid
(Haggai 1:14; 2:4)

In his book, **Zechariah** sees something flying. What is it?
   a. a scroll
   b. a carpet
   c. a monkey
   d. a sleigh
(Zechariah 5:1)

Fill in the blank in the following promise that God spoke through the prophet **Malachi**: "Return to me. Then I will _____ to you."
                                          Malachi 3:7
                     Hint: The word that fits the blank
                           is somewhere else in the quote.

Which *one* of the following is *not* true about **Matthew**, a follower of Jesus who wrote the Gospel of Matthew?
   a. He kept track of taxes.
   b. He was also known by the name Levi.
   c. Jesus ate at his house.
   d. He hesitated to follow Jesus.
(Mark 2:14–15)

True or false: In the Gospel of Matthew, Jesus said that if you keep asking, seeking, and knocking, you will receive what you ask for from God.
(Matthew 7:7)

Which *one* "person" does Matthew say rolled away the stone door on Jesus' tomb?

   a. God
   b. Goliath
   c. an angel
   d. Jesus

(Matthew 28:2)

Mark (John Mark), a follower of Jesus, wrote the Gospel of Mark. With whom did he go on a mission trip?

   a. Peter and Gabriel
   b. Saul and Barnabas
   c. Luke and John
   d. Amos and Andrew

(Acts 13:3–5)
Hint: Pick one.

Fill in the blank: Mark wrote that Jesus' family thought Jesus was _____.

Mark 3:21 NLV
Hint: The answer rhymes with *daisy*.

Fill in the blank: Luke wrote both of his Bible books (**Luke** and **Acts**) for his friend named

_____.

Luke 1:3–4
Hint: His name starts with a *T*.

Which *one* of the following is *not* true about Luke?
- a. He was a doctor.
- b. He took mission trips with Paul.
- c. He was a fact seeker.
- d. He worked for a newspaper.

(Colossians 4:14; 2 Timothy 4:11; Luke 1:3–4)

The apostle John wrote the **Gospel of John**, the **three letters of John**, and the book of **Revelation**. In his Gospel, John calls himself what?
- a. the best disciple ever
- b. Mary's adopted son
- c. the one who walked on water
- d. the disciple Jesus loved

(John 19:26)

Fill in the blank to complete John's most famous verse:

"God so _____ the world that He gave His only Son."

John 3:16 NLV
Hint: The answer rhymes with *gloved*.

In the book of **Acts**, Luke wrote that Jesus told His followers they would receive power when what *one* thing came into their lives?
- a. more vegetables
- b. more meat
- c. the Holy Spirit
- d. prayer

(Acts 1:8)

Which is the only one of Jesus' miracles that can be read about in all four Gospel books—Matthew, Mark, Luke, and John?
- a. feeding many with loaves and fishes
- b. walking on water
- c. turning water into wine
- d. raising Lazarus from the dead

(Matthew 14:13–21; Mark 6:30–44; Luke 9:10–17; John 6:1–15)

Fill in the blank with the name of a Bible book writer:
Paul said, "The Holy Spirit spoke the truth to your early fathers through the early preacher _____."

Acts 28:25 NLV
Hint: His name starts with an *I*.

The apostle Paul wrote many books of the Bible. They are made up of the letters he wrote to whom?
  a. his mother
  b. churches
  c. his sister
  d. his diary
Hint: Pick one.

The book of **Romans** mentions which things that cannot separate us from God's love?
  a. death, life, or angels
  b. leaders or powers
  c. things now or later
  d. the world above or below
(Romans 8:38–39)
Hint: Pick more than one.

Fill in the blank:
The three most important things to have are faith, hope and _____. But the greatest of them is _____.

1 Corinthians 13:13
Hint: The same word—which rhymes with *dove*—fits in both blanks.

In **2 Corinthians**, Jesus told Paul that His power works best when people are what *one* thing?

a. strong
b. weak
c. big
d. little

(2 Corinthians 12:9)

Fill in the blank:
God is able to do much more than we ask or think through His _____ working in us.

Ephesians 3:20 NLV
Hint: The answer rhymes with *hour*.

True or false: Peter wrote letters to churches in **Colossae**, **Corinth**, **Ephesus**, **Galatia**, **Philippi**, and **Thessalonica** that later became books in your Bible!
(Colossians 1:2; 1 Corinthians 1:1; 2 Corinthians 1:1; Ephesus 1:1; Galatians 1:1; Philippians 1:1; 1 Thessalonians 1:1; 2 Thessalonians 1:1)

Fill in the blank:
_____ for money causes all kinds of evil.

1 Timothy 6:10
Hint: The answer rhymes with *of*.

Fill in the blank:
God has _____ life into all Scripture.
2 Timothy 3:16
Hint: The answer rhymes with *wreathed*.

True or false: The Bible books named **Timothy** and **Titus** were originally letters Paul sent to friends and pastors.
(1 Timothy 1:1; Titus 1:1)

True or false: The Bible book **Philemon** is really a letter Paul wrote to Philemon whose slave Onesimus had run away.
(Philemon 1:1, 15–16)

Hebrews 13:2 says we should be kind to strangers and invite them to our homes because they might be what *one* thing?
   a.   long-lost relatives
   b.   Jesus
   c.   the Spirit
   d.   angels
(But only invite people into your home if Mom and Dad are with you.)

Fill in the blank in the following verse from the book of **James**:

The _____ of a godly person is powerful.

James 5:16

Hint: The answer rhymes with *hair*.

Fill in the blank: Peter wrote two letters (**1 and 2 Peter**) that are part of your Bible. About Peter, Jesus said:

"I tell you that you are Peter. On this _____ I will build My church."

Matthew 16:18 NLV

Hint: The answer rhymes with *dock*.

In his Bible book, **Jude** says the devil and the head angel, Michael, argued over the body of what *one* person?

   a. Abraham
   b. Moses
   c. Jesus
   d. Joseph

(Jude 1:9)

In John's book **Revelation**, he begins writing about Jesus' message to the seven churches and ends the book talking about what *one* thing?

   a. a war in heaven
   b. a beast from the sea
   c. a beast from the earth
   d. a new heaven and a new earth

(Revelation 21:1)

Parables

- - - - - - -

Parables are stories or word pictures
that use ordinary things to teach
extraordinary lessons. Jesus told lots
of parables so that people could
understand what He wanted them to
learn. Let's see how much Jesus has
taught *you* as you answer these questions
about some of the stories He's told.

In Jesus' story about a **rich man** in hell and the beggar Lazarus in heaven, the rich man cries for help from whom?

    a. God
    b. an angel
    c. Jesus
    d. Father Abraham

(Luke 16:23–24)
Hint: Pick one.

In the parable of the **good Samaritan**, who walks right by an injured man lying on the road?

    a. two disciples
    b. two women
    c. two religious leaders
    d. two farmers

(Luke 10:31–32 NLT)
Hint: Pick one.

What *one* thing does the good man from Samaria *not* do to help the injured man?

    a. He soothes the man's wounds with olive oil and slime.
    b. He bandages the man's wounds.
    c. He puts the man on his donkey.
    d. He takes him to an inn and cares for him.

(Luke 10:34)

Fill in the blank: After telling the good Samaritan story, Jesus asked:
"Which of these three do you think was a _____ to the man who was beaten by the robbers?"

Luke 10:36 NLV

Hint: The answer begins with the letter *n*.

True or false: The lesson Jesus wants you to learn from the good Samaritan story is that you are to show kindness to everyone—no matter who they (or you) are!
(Luke 10:36–37)

The **prodigal son** parable is a story about a father and two sons. Which son asks his dad for his share of the family's money?
  a. the oldest
  b. the strongest
  c. the youngest
  d. the weakest
(Luke 15:12)

After getting his money, this son goes away, spends all his money, and ends up getting what *one* job?

a. mucking out horse stalls
b. plucking chickens
c. herding sheep
d. feeding pigs

(Luke 15:15)

Starving from hunger, the son decides to go home, tell his dad he made a mistake, and ask him for what *one* thing?

a. more money
b. a job
c. food
d. clothing

(Luke 15:19)

When the son is still a long way off, his father does what *one* thing?

a. runs to him and hugs him
b. chases him away
c. yells at him
d. gives him a time-out

(Luke 15:20)

The lesson of the prodigal son parable is what *one* thing?
   a. When you feel lost, God will welcome you home.
   b. Save your money.
   c. Never leave home.
   d. Get a good job.
(Luke 15:32)

Fill in the blank:
In the **parable of the two builders,** Jesus said:
"Everyone who hears my _____ and puts them into practice is like a wise man."
                                          Matthew 7:24
          Hint: The answer rhymes with *birds*.

The wise man builds his house on what *one* thing?
   a. sand
   b. earth
   c. cement
   d. rock
(Matthew 7:24)

The foolish man builds his house on what *one* thing?

 a. sand
 b. earth
 c. cement
 d. rock

(Matthew 7:26)

Fill in the blanks: When the rains come down and the water comes up, the _____ man's house does not fall, but the _____ man's house comes crashing down.

Matthew 7:25, 27
Hint: The words that fit here appear
in the two questions above.

What's the *one* lesson of the parable of the two builders?

 a. Be careful how you build your house.
 b. Move out if it rains.
 c. Live in the desert.
 d. Build your life on what Jesus says.

(Matthew 7:24)

Animal Antics

- - - - - - -

The animals in this world are amazing creatures. But some Bible animals and the roles they played in God's plan are even *more* amazing! As you answer the next questions, you will find out how and why!

True or false: After running away from God, Jonah was swallowed by a giant sea creature. He was in its stomach for three days and three nights.
(Jonah 1:17)

Fill in the blank in the following instructions God gave to Noah:
"You are to bring into the large boat _____ of every kind of living thing of all flesh, to keep them alive with you."

Genesis 6:19 NLV
Hint: The answer is a number that rhymes with *boo*.

What was the first bird Noah sent out of the ark 40 days after the rain stopped?
    a.   raven
    b.   crow
    c.   dove
    d.   eagle
(Genesis 8:6–7)

What bird did Noah keep sending out to see if the floodwaters had gone down?
a. raven
b. crow
c. dove
d. eagle
(Genesis 8:8–12)

What amazing animal opened up the magician Balaam's eyes and ears to God's will and way?
a. a sparrow that fed him
b. a donkey that talked to him
c. a giant fish that walked on land
d. a spider that spun gold
(Numbers 22:28–31)

Fill in the blank with the name of an animal: [The Lord told Elijah], "You will drink from the river. And I have told the _____ to bring food to you there."

1 Kings 17:4 NLV
Hint: The answer rhymes with *havens*.

Fill in the blank: Samson not only killed a lion with his bare hands but killed people with the jawbone of a _____.

Judges 14:6; 15:15
Hint: The answer rhymes with *wonky*.

Who shut the mouths of the lions that were about to eat Daniel?
   a. Daniel
   b. an angel
   c. the king
   d. a lion tamer named Lionel
(Daniel 6:22)

John the Baptist called Jesus the *what* of God who would take away the sins of the world?
   a. Lamb
   b. Lion
   c. Wolf
   d. Dove
(John 1:29)

Jesus chased out of God's house people who were selling what *one* kind of animal?
   a. chickens
   b. turkeys
   c. doves
   d. sparrows
(John 2:15–16)

After Jesus rose from the dead, some of His followers went fishing but couldn't catch anything. But when Jesus told them where to put down their nets, how many fish did they catch?
   a. 103
   b. 133
   c. 153
   d. 173
(John 21:11–12)

What did Jesus ride into Jerusalem five days before He went to the cross?
   a. a horse
   b. a mule
   c. a camel
   d. a donkey
(John 12:14–16)

Fill in the blanks:
Jesus replied, "_____ have dens.
_____ have nests. But the Son of
Man has no place to lay his head."

Luke 9:58
The first answer rhymes with *boxes*
and the second with *words*.

Jesus sent out the 72 disciples as what?
  a. doves among vultures
  b. dogs among foxes
  c. lambs among wolves
  d. worms among fish
(Luke 10:3)

What did King Solomon ride on when he was
named king of Israel?
  a. a horse
  b. a mule
  c. a donkey
  d. a lion
(1 Kings 1:33–38)

When the people asked Aaron to make them a new god, he made what animal out of gold?
- a. a cow
- b. a calf
- c. a bull
- d. a horse

(Exodus 32:8)

Moses told the Israelites who were slaves in Egypt to sprinkle the blood of what young animal on their doorposts?
- a. a bull or cow
- b. a horse or donkey
- c. a dove or pigeon
- d. a sheep or goat

(Exodus 12:5)

Another name for the devil or Satan is what?
- a. serpent or snake
- b. snail or worm
- c. lion or wolf
- d. fang or tooth

(2 Corinthians 11:3)
Hint: Pick one.

What four kinds of animals did the rich man Job have?

    a. sheep and camels

    b. oxen and donkeys

    c. horses and mules

    d. goats and llamas

(Job 1:3)

Hint: Pick two.

True or false: Lamentations 5:18 says that one day either foxes, jackals, or wild dogs will be running all over Mount Zion (Jerusalem).

Daniel had a vision of four beastlike animals. Match what animal the beast looked like with what it had:

1. lion
2. bear
3. leopard
4. iron-toothed beast

a. ten horns
b. four wings and four heads
c. two eagle wings
d. three ribs in its mouth

(Daniel 7:2–7)

Fill in the blank:

The devil. . .prowls around like a roaring _____, looking for someone to devour.

                1 Peter 5:8 NLT

         Hint: The answer rhymes with *Zion*.

True or false: Adam, the man God created in His image, named all the animals.
(Genesis 2:19–20)

The prophet Habakkuk wrote that the horses of the Babylonians were faster than which *one* of the following?
    a. greyhounds
    b. ostriches
    c. roadrunners
    d. leopards
(Habakkuk 1:8 NLV)

True or false: While shipwrecked on the island of Malta, Paul was bitten by a poisonous snake and died.
(Acts 28:3–5)

Fill in the blank: In Revelation, Jesus is called the "_____ of the tribe of Judah."
Revelation 5:5 NLT
Hint: The answer rhymes with *Brian*.

True or false: The prophet Isaiah wrote that one day the wolf and the lamb would hang out together in peace.
(Isaiah 11:6)

Match the animal with the event:

1. rooster
2. dove
3. big fish
4. ravens
5. donkey
6. snake
7. lions
8. mule

a. Elijah is fed.
b. King Solomon takes a ride.
c. Daniel is saved by an angel.
d. Paul is bitten.
e. Peter denies Jesus.
f. Jonah is swallowed.
g. Balaam is preached to.
h. Jesus is baptized.

(Matthew 26:75; Matthew 3:16; Jonah 1:17; 1 Kings 17:5–6; Numbers 22:28–31; Acts 28:3–5; Daniel 6:22; 1 Kings 1:33–38)

True or false: In the book of Revelation, John wrote about a red dragon with 7 heads, 7 crowns, and 10 horns.
(Revelation 12:3)

Tools and Weapons

— - — - — - — .

God can help people do remarkable and powerful things with the tools and weapons He gives them. Some tools and weapons can be physical things—like swords and bows. Or they can be nonphysical things—like prayer and praise. Keep that in mind as you answer the next set of trivia questions!

The prophet **Elijah** used an unusual tool to divide the waters of the Jordan River so he could cross on dry ground. What was that *one* tool?

    a. a stick
    b. his staff
    c. his hand
    d. his coat

(2 Kings 2:8)

Elijah often used another tool—prayer—to help people. Fill in the blanks with the same word to make clear what he did for this boy: "LORD my God, give this boy's _____ back to him!" The LORD answered Elijah's prayer. He gave the boy's _____ back to him. So the boy lived.

1 Kings 17:21–22

Hint: The answer rhymes with *wife*.

True or false: **King Jehoshaphat** used the twin tools of prayer and praise to defeat the armies that came against him.
(2 Chronicles 20:6–17, 21–24)

Sometimes tools can be used as weapons. That's what happened when **Jael**, the wife of Heber, killed Sisera, the commander of an army warring against the Israelites. What *two* tools or weapons did she use?

a. a rope and a ladder
b. a tent stake and a hammer
c. a knife and a fork
d. a saw and a strap

(Judges 4:21)

After **Jonah** used this power tool, "the Lord spoke to the fish, and it spit Jonah out onto the dry land." What was the power tool Jonah used?

a. a hammer
b. a jack
c. sweet talk
d. prayer

(Jonah 2:1, 10 NLV)

Fill in the blanks to name two tools **Moses** used to part the Red Sea:

[The LORD said to Moses,] "Pick up your _____ and raise your _____ over the sea. Divide the water so the Israelites can walk through the middle of the sea on dry ground."

Exodus 14:15–16 NLT
Hint: The first answer rhymes with *laugh* and the second with *band*.

What *one* "tool" did Moses use to turn Marah's water from bitter to sweet?
- a. his staff
- b. a stick
- c. a hammer
- d. his coat

(Exodus 15:25)

In the wilderness, **Jesus** used what one powerful weapon to defeat the devil's temptations?
- a. His power
- b. a sword
- c. God's Word
- d. holy water

(Luke 4:1–13)

Faith in Jesus and focus on (eyes on) Him are very powerful tools. For it was both of these that kept Peter doing what *one* thing?
- a. fishing on his boat
- b. walking on water
- c. pulling up the anchor
- d. riding out of the storm

(Matthew 14:25–32)

Fill in the blank: One of the ways we can keep from making mistakes is to hide God's _____ in our hearts.

Psalm 119:11

Hint: The answer rhymes with *curd*.

The Bible says God's Word is alive and powerful, that it's sharper than what *one* thing?
    a. a sword with two edges
    b. a spear
    c. an arrow
    d. a knife
(Hebrews 4:12)

It's so sharp, God's Word can cut between what?
    a. soul and spirit
    b. joints and marrow
    c. love and hate
    d. mind and body
(Hebrews 4:12)
Hint: Pick two.

What *two* tools did God tell **Moses** to use to get water to gush from a rock at Kadesh?

    a. his staff

    b. his rope

    c. his sword

    d. his words

(Numbers 20:1, 8)

What did **Rahab** use to help spies escape and later to let soldiers know where she lived so her household would be safe?

    a. a white sheet

    b. a red rope

    c. a yellow cord

    d. a green curtain

(Joshua 2:15–18)

Goliath was a giant! But the shepherd boy David brought him down with one rock. What was *not* one of the weapons Goliath had when he faced David?

    a. a sword

    b. a spear

    c. a bow and arrow

    d. a javelin

(1 Samuel 17:45)

You Are There

- — — — — — •

The world is filled with some pretty amazing places. Check out these locations where people came up against giants, angels, flames, armies, strange stairways, and so much more!

In the city of **Anab**, Joshua met up with *one* fierce race of giants from the family of whom?

    a. Anak
    b. Goliath
    c. Jolly Green
    d. Cyclops

(Joshua 11:21 NLT)

In the **Garden of Eden**, God told Adam and Eve not to eat from the tree of the knowledge of what?

    a. people and places
    b. time and space
    c. love and laughter
    d. good and evil

(Genesis 3:5)

After Adam and Eve ate from that tree, God kicked them out of the Garden of Eden so that they would not eat from what other *one* tree?

    a. the tree of death
    b. the tree of three
    c. the tree of life
    d. the tree of love

(Genesis 3:22)

After God drove Adam and Eve out of the garden, He set up what to guard the path to that special tree?

a. angels
b. a flaming sword
c. a burning shield
d. a maze

(Genesis 3:24)
Hint: Pick two.

True or false: God's people will be able to eat fruit from that special tree when they are in paradise.
(Revelation 2:7)

During a battle in **Aphek**, the ark of God was captured and two of God's priests were killed. What were their names?

a. Isaac and Esau
b. Hophni and Phinehas
c. Wily and Coyote
d. Joseph and Benjamin

(1 Samuel 4:11)

The Philistines put the ark of God in **Ashdod**'s temple where there was a statue of their god Dagon. What *one* thing happened to Dagon's statue after they did that?

    a.   It fell on its face.
    b.   It burned up.
    c.   It turned to dust.
    d.   It turned green.

(1 Samuel 5:4)

True or false: The final battle between Christ and wicked people will be fought in **Armageddon**. And Christ will win!
(Revelation 16:16)

Paul preached a really good sermon in **Athens** on a rocky hill. The mound, named after the Roman god of war, was called what?

    a.   Venus's View
    b.   Pluto's Platte
    c.   Mars' Hill
    d.   Saturn's Soil

(Acts 17:22 NLV)

Fill in the blank:
So the name of the city was _____,
because there the Lord mixed up the language
of the whole earth.

Genesis 11:9 NLV
Hint: The answer rhymes with *dabble*.

When Daniel was taken to **Babylon**, what
three friends went with him?
    a. Abednego
    b. Belteshazzar
    c. Shadrach
    d. Meshach
(Daniel 1:7)

True or false: King Og, a giant from **Bashan**,
slept in an iron bed that was more than 13
feet long and 6 feet wide!
(Deuteronomy 3:11)

Where did David fight the giant Goliath?
    a. Elah Valley
    b. Mount Moreb
    c. the Colosseum
    d. Jezreel Valley
(1 Samuel 21:9)

True or false: In **En Gedi**, King Saul went into a cave, not knowing David was hiding out in there.
(1 Samuel 24:1–3)

Lot's wife turned into a pillar of salt when she looked back at her home in **Sodom**. What was the name of Sodom's sister city that was destroyed on the same day?
- a. Galilee
- b. Gethsemane
- c. Gomorrah
- d. Golgotha

(Genesis 19:24–26)

What did Jacob name the place where he dreamed of a stairway to heaven with angels going up and down it?
- a. Bethlehem
- b. Bethel
- c. Broadway
- d. Babylon

(Genesis 28:12, 19)

Where was the giant Goliath from?
    a. Gettysburg
    b. Guam
    c. Gath
    d. Gaza
(1 Samuel 17:4)

Fill in the blank:
This was the first powerful work Jesus did. It
was done in _____ of Galilee.

John 2:11 NLV

Hint: The name of this place
rhymes with *Dana*.

Match the prophet with the place he was sent
or taken:
    1. Jonah   a. Canaan
    2. Moses   b. Babylon
    3. Daniel   c. Nineveh
    4. Abraham d. Egypt
(Jonah 1:1–2; Exodus 3:11–12; Daniel 1:1–6;
Genesis 12:1, 5)

True or false: While he was traveling down the road to **Damascus**, Saul (who later became Paul) was stopped by Jesus with a bright light. (Acts 9:3–5)

Fill in the blank: After his hair was cut off and his eyes cut out, _____ was put in prison in Gaza.

Judges 16:20–21
Hint: The answer starts with a "strong" *S*.

True or false: Philip, Andrew, and Peter were from the town of **Bethsaida**. (John 1:44)

Where were the followers of Jesus first called Christians?
- a. Antioch, Syria
- b. Christiana, Delaware
- c. Jerusalem, Israel
- d. Bethlehem, Pennsylvania

(Acts 11:26)

Match the place with the event in Jesus' life:
1. Bethlehem   a. Jesus made His home
                           here.
2. Nazareth   b. Jesus died.
3. Jordan River   c. Jesus rose to heaven.
4. Gethsemane   d. Jesus grew up here.
5. Golgotha   e. Jesus prayed in the
                           garden.
6. Mount of Olives   f. Jesus was born.
7. Capernaum   g. Jesus was baptized.
(Matthew 2:1; Luke 4:16; 3:2–3, 21-22; Matthew 26:36–44; John 19:17–18; Acts 1:11–12;
Mark 2:1)

True or false: In the book of Revelation,
Jesus has a message for the seven churches
in **Ephesus**, **Smyrna**, **Pergamum**, **Thyatira**,
Sardis, **Philadelphia**, and **Laodicea**.
(Revelation 2:1, 8, 12, 18; 3:1, 7, 14)

Match the place name with its meaning:
1. Beer Lahai Roi   a. place of the skull
2. Bethel   b. bitter
3. Ebenezer   c. struggle with God
4. Golgotha   d. house of God
5. Israel   e. sent
6. Marah   f. well of God who sees
7. Siloam   g. stone of help
(Genesis 16:13–14; 28:17–19; 1 Samuel 7:12;
John 19:17–18 NLT; Genesis 32:26–28; Exodus
15:23; John 9:7)

Match the place with the event:
1. Jordan River   a. Moses dies.
2. Marah   b. Naaman is healed.
3. Mount Carmel   c. Job lives here.
4. Mount Nebo   d. Abraham is born and
                          raised.
5. Island of Patmos   e. Moses sweetens bitter
                          water.
6. Ur   f. Elijah prays down fire.
7. Uz   g. John receives a
                          revelation.
8. Garden of Eden   h. Ezekiel has a vision of
                          this place.
9. Dead Sea   i. Eve gives in to a
                          snake.

(2 Kings 5:14–15; Exodus 15:23–25; 1 Kings 18:20,
36–38; Deuteronomy 34:1, 5–6; Revelation 1:9;
Nehemiah 9:7; Job 1:1; 2 Corinthians 11:3; Ezekiel
47:8–9)

Match the place with the event:
1. Mount Sinai or Horeb a. The Holy Spirit comes
                            down on Jesus' followers.
2. Red Sea   b. Peter raises Dorcas
                            from death.
3. Island of Malta   c. King Saul and Jona-
                            than are killed.
4. Sea of Galilee   d. Paul is bitten by a
                            snake.
5. Jericho   e. Peter walks on water.
6. Jerusalem   f. A bush burns.
7. Joppa   g. Walls come down.
8. Mount Gilboa   h. Moses parted this.

(Exodus 3:1–2; 14:21–22; Acts 28:1–3; Matthew
14:22–30; Joshua 6:1, 15–20; Acts 1:4–5; 9:38–42;
1 Samuel 31:1–7)

Wacky Weather and Notable Nature

- - - - - - -

God has control over *everything*,
including the weather and nature—and
you! Turn the page to find out more about
the power of God and some freaky ways
He works to get His message across!

True or false: When people were behaving badly, God decided to start over with Noah and his family. To get rid of everyone else, God made it rain for three days and three nights. (Genesis 7:1–4)

Fill in the blank: After the Flood, God promised that He would never let it rain so much again. The sign of His promise is a _____.

Genesis 9:15–16
Hint: The answer is something you may see in the sky after a storm.

To help Joshua and the Israelites cross the flooding Jordan River, God made the waters back up in what town?
   a.   Adam
   b.   Eve
   c.   Edom
   d.   Jerusalem
(Joshua 3:16)

Fill in the blank: When Jesus rode into Jerusalem on a donkey, the cheering people threw _____ branches onto the road.

John 12:13
Hint: The answer rhymes with *calm*.

Fill in the blank: Jesus wants you to be the
_____ of the earth.

Matthew 5:13
Hint: The answer rhymes with malt.

True or false: To help the Israelites win a battle
in Aijalon, God answered Joshua's prayer and
made the sun and moon stand still!
(Joshua 10:12)

Fill in the blank: When you trust in God,
you will be as strong and healthy as an
_____ tree.

Psalm 52:8
Hint: The answer is the first half of the name
of Popeye's girlfriend! (If you don't know
who Popeye is, ask your parent!)

True or false: A short man named Zacchaeus
climbed an oak tree so he could get a better
look at Jesus.
(Luke 19:3–4)

Fill in the blank: Jesus said you can move a
mountain if you have faith even as small as a
_____ seed.

Matthew 17:20
Hint: The answer rhymes with custard.

Fill in the blanks: The promised land flowed with _____ and _____.

Exodus 3:17

Hint: The first answer rhymes with *silk* and the second with *funny*.

A man named Korah said that he was better than Moses. What happened to him?
   a. Wind swept him away.
   b. He died on the spot.
   c. The earth swallowed him.
   d. A shark attacked him.
(Numbers 16:31–32)

When King Hezekiah was sick, he wanted a sign that God would heal him. So God made what one thing go back ten steps?
   a. the sun
   b. the moon
   c. the earth
   d. a shadow
(2 Kings 20:8–10)

True or false: God talked to Job out of an earthquake.
(Job 38:1 NLT)

Words, Words, Words

- - - - - - - ·

The Bible is filled with many different words. Now is your chance to see how much you know about those words and phrases (bunches of words) and some of the amazing ones people used.

Which of the following statements are true about the beings called **angels**?

    a. They rescue people.
    b. They deliver messages.
    c. They guard people.
    d. They worship God in heaven.

(Genesis 19:10; Luke 1:11–13; Psalm 91:11–12; Revelation 7:11)

Hint: Pick more than one.

Fill in the blank: "Do for other people whatever you would like to have them do for you" is called the _____ Rule.

Matthew 7:12 NLV

Hint: The answer rhymes with *hold in*.

Match the words with their meaning:

1. Gospel
2. angel
3. disciple
4. manna
5. tomb
6. abba
7. alpha
8. omega
9. Christ

a. anointed one
b. what is it?
c. messenger
d. daddy
e. beginning
f. burial place
g. end
h. follower
i. good news

(Galatians 4:6; Revelation 1:8)

Fill in the blank: Children's _____ are always in God's presence.

Matthew 18:10
Hint: The answer begins with *a* and ends with *s*.

Anointing is when what *one* thing is poured on someone or something for a special reason or use?
   a. water
   b. oil
   c. wine
   d. lemonade
(Psalm 23:5)

The **ark of the covenant** was a symbol of God's presence. What *three* things were in it?
   a. manna
   b. Aaron's rod
   c. stone tablets of the Ten Commandments
   d. Joseph's coat
(Hebrews 9:4)

The **armor of God** is the spiritual clothing God's people are to wear. Match the item you "wear" with the spiritual strength or protection it gives you:

1. belt
2. chest plate
3. shoes
4. shield
5. helmet
6. sword
(Ephesians 6:14–17)

a. faith
b. God's Word
c. truth
d. salvation
e. peace
f. God's goodness

When people do something bad to us, we are not to pay them back with evil but with what *one* thing?

a. a time-out
b. a talking-to
c. a blessing
d. money

(1 Peter 3:9)

The first recorded words of God were what?

a. "Let there be light."
b. "Let us make people."
c. "Let there be plants."
d. "Let there be toys."

(Genesis 1:3)

Faith means to trust in or believe in someone or something. When you have faith in God, what is the *one* thing Jesus said you can move?

    a. a building
    b. a heavy rock
    c. an iron giant
    d. a mountain
(Mark 11:23)

Jesus said that with faith, you not only can move that big thing but can do what *other* thing with it?

    a. crush it
    b. punch it
    c. throw it
    d. burn it
(Mark 11:23)

But to move that big thing above, you must not what?

    a. be too little
    b. doubt
    c. be too young
    d. disobey your parents
(Mark 11:23)
Hint: Pick one.

What is the **ark** that Noah built?
   a. a wooden box
   b. a curved stick
   c. a place where kids play
   d. a large boat
(Hebrews 11:7 NLT)

Forgiveness means letting go of a wrong that someone has done to us. How many times does Jesus say we are to forgive?
   a. 4 times 4 times
   b. 7 times 7 times
   c. 40 times 40 times
   d. 70 times 7 times
(Matthew 18:21–22 NLT)

True or false: The **fruit of the Spirit** are the good ways people act or behave when the Holy Spirit is running their lives.
(Galatians 5:22)

Which of the following are *not* fruits of the Spirit?
- a. love, joy, peace, not giving up
- b. being kind, good, and gentle
- c. having faith and being boss over our desires
- d. apples, peaches, oranges

(Galatians 5:22–23)

Hint: Pick one.

A **Gentile** is a person who is what *one* thing?
- a. not Jewish
- b. kind
- c. soft-spoken
- d. from Genoa

(Galatians 3:28)

In the Bible, what is **grace**?
- a. a girl's name
- b. love and kindness from God
- c. a free gift from God
- d. a follower of Jesus

(Ephesians 2:8–9)

Hint: Pick two.

When you're happy in the Lord, He will give you the desires of your what?

a. heart
b. parents
c. teacher
d. mind

(Psalm 37:4)
Hint: Pick one.

Heaven is high above the clouds where Jesus and God live. That's where Jesus said we are to store our what?

a. love
b. ideas
c. treasures
d. loved ones

(Matthew 6:19–21 NLT)
Hint: Pick one.

Fill in the blank:
Faith is being sure of what we _____ for.

Hebrews 11:1
Hint: The answer rhymes with *rope*.

What is an **idol**?
  a. something you can't see
  b. someone or something you worship instead of God
  c. something that just sits there
  d. someone who doesn't work
(Exodus 20:4–5)
Hint: Pick one.

Fill in the blank:
God created human beings in his own

_____.

Genesis 1:27 NLT
Hint: The answer rhymes with *scrimmage*.

Mercy is what *one* thing?
  a. the French word for "thanks"
  b. not being punished even though you should be
  c. grumbling
  d. a Roman god
(Psalm 103:8, 10)

True or false: **Passover** is when the death angel passed over the homes of the Israelites when they were slaves in Egypt.
(Exodus 12:1–27)

What *one* thing did Moses command the people to sprinkle on their doorposts to keep the Passover?

    a. oil from an olive
    b. water from the Nile
    c. the blood of a lamb
    d. wine from the vine

(Hebrews 11:28)

What *one* thing did the Passover sprinkling keep the angel of death from doing in a person's house?

    a. killing the firstborn son
    b. striking down evil people
    c. making the animals sick
    d. filling it with dirt

(Hebrews 11:28)

The **promised land** was the land God said He would give to whom?

    a. Adam and Eve
    b. Noah and his children
    c. Abraham, Isaac, and Jacob
    d. people who kept promises

(Numbers 32:11–12)
Hint: Pick one.

The only *two* of Moses' followers who entered the promised land were who?
   a.   Aaron and Miriam
   b.   Moses and Aaron
   c.   Caleb and Moses
   d.   Joshua and Caleb
(Numbers 32:11–12)

Only those two got to see the promised land because they followed God with what?
   a.   their whole minds
   b.   their whole hearts
   c.   their whole riches
   d.   their whole strength
(Numbers 32:11–12)
Hint: Pick one.

Jesus taught His followers which *one* of the following listed below?
   a.   the New Testament
   b.   how to read
   c.   how to speak Hebrew
   d.   how to pray
(Matthew 6:9–13)

A **parable** is what *one* thing listed below?
    a. a picture-story used to help people understand a truth
    b. a gymnastic bar
    c. someone who can't move
    d. a kind of fish
(Mark 4:30 NLV)

Jesus gave people an awesome message of how to be happy and live for God. That message is called what?
    a. the Sermon on the Mount
    b. the Lord's Prayer
    c. the Twelve Commandments
    d. the Apostles' Creed
(Matthew 5–7)

Fill in the blank: In that message, Jesus told us to _____ those who hate us.
                            Matthew 5:43–44
            Hint: The answer rhymes with *shove*.

The **Trinity** is made up of which *three* beings?
a. Jesus
b. Moses
c. Holy Spirit
d. God
(Matthew 28:19)

Fill in the blank: God wants you to **trust** Him, which means to count on Him for everything. When you do, the Bible says you will have perfect _____.

Romans 15:13
Hint: The answer rhymes with *fleece*.

True or false: If you ask God for **wisdom**, He will freely give it to you.
(James 1:5)

True or false: **Spiritual gifts** are the gifts the Holy Spirit gives believers to serve Him and others.
(1 Peter 4:10)

True or false? **Pagans** are people who worship things other than God.
(1 Corinthians 12:2 NLT)

The **tabernacle** was a tent where God's children met Him in the early days of Israel's history. To which *one* person did God give the plans as to how it was to be built?
   a. Abraham
   b. Jacob
   c. Moses
   d. Joshua
(Acts 7:44)

Years ago, the **temple** was the house of God that King Solomon built. Where is God's temple now?
   a. in Jerusalem
   b. in Bethlehem
   c. in Jesus
   d. in you
(1 Corinthians 3:16–17)
Hint: Pick one.

True or false: The lid on the ark of God was called the mercy seat.
(Exodus 25:21 NLV)

Match the words with who said or wrote them:
1. "Let there be light."   a. Nehemiah
2. "I will go where you go."   b. Solomon
3. "The LORD is my shepherd."   c. Job
4. "LORD, open his eyes!"   d. David
5. "Give me a heart
        that understands."   e. Mordecai
6. "We'll start rebuilding
        the walls."   f. God
7. "Perhaps you were made
        queen for such a
        time as this."   g. Ruth
8. "No matter what,
        I'll trust God."   h. Elisha
(Genesis 1:3; Ruth 1:16 NLV; Psalm 23:1; 2 Kings 6:17 NLT; 1 Kings 3:9; Nehemiah 2:20; Esther 4:14 NLT; Job 13:15)

Fill in the blank in this quote by King Solomon:
Love is like a blazing _____. . . .
No amount of water can put it out.

Song of Songs 8:6–7
Hint: The answer rhymes with *tire*.

True or false: The **body of Christ** is made up of all the people at your church and all other churches who follow Jesus.
(1 Corinthians 12:27)

Some words in the Bible aren't defined there but are ones you should know. Match the word you should know with its meaning:

1. adopt
2. anoint
3. baptize
4. believer
5. Bible
6. blessing
7. blood
8. chosen people

a. people picked by God
b. liquid that flows in a living person or animal
c. to raise a child as one's own
d. the Holy Word of God
e. a good thing given
f. to dip in water
g. to pour oil on someone for a special purpose
h. someone who has faith in Jesus

(Romans 8:15; Psalm 23:5; Galatians 3:27; Acts 9:36; 2 Timothy 3:16; 1 Peter 3:9; Ephesians 2:13; 1 Peter 2:9)

Fill in the blank:
Christ is the _____ of the church which is His body.

Colossians 1:18 NLV
Hint: The answer rhymes with *said*.

True or false: The City of David is another name for the town of Bethlehem.
(Luke 2:4)

Here are some more words you should know. Match them with their meaning:

1. Christian   a. a group of believers
2. church   b. something made
3. compassion   c. a promise or agreement
4. cornerstone   d. a place with no light
5. covenant   e. feeling sorry for some one
6. creation   f. someone who follows Jesus
7. darkness   g. when the heart stops beating
8. death   h. a stone put on the corner of a building

(1 Peter 4:15–16; 1 Corinthians 14:12; Matthew 14:14; Isaiah 28:16; Hebrews 9:15; 2 Corinthians 5:17; 1 John 2:10–11; Hebrews 2:14)

Fill in the blank:
Jesus saw the huge crowd. . .and he had compassion on them and healed their _____.
Matthew 14:14 NLT
Hint: The answer rhymes with *pick*.

Fill in the blank to complete what Jesus said:
"_____ the Kingdom of God above all else. . .and he will give you everything you need."

Matthew 6:33 NLT
Hint: The answer rhymes with *peek*.

Here are some more words and phrases you should know. Match them with their meaning:
1. devil   a. where God isn't
2. eternal life   b. God's bright presence
3. evil   c. when water covered earth
4. furnace   d. a bad thing
5. the Flood   e. a spirit against God
6. God's glory   f. Jesus has come!
7. Good News   g. living forever
8. hell   h. a very hot place
(James 4:7–8; Matthew 25:46; Romans 12:17–18; Daniel 3:6; Hebrews 11:7; Revelation 21:10–11; Mark 15:15–16; Revelation 1:17–18)

True or false: When people are living in the **kingdom of God**, it means they are living in God's power.
(1 Corinthians 4:20)

True or false: God has put His law into your mind and written it on your heart.
(Jeremiah 31:33)

Here are some more words and phrases you should know. Match them with their meaning:

1. high priest
2. holiness
3. Holy Spirit
4. I AM
5. joy
6. judgment
7. kingdom of God
8. Last Supper

a. God
b. being happy
c. the last meal Jesus ate with His followers
d. the invisible Spirit of God
e. loving God and following His laws
f. top Hebrew priest
g. an opinion on how people act
h. God's peace and power to believers

(Hebrews 6:20; 12:10; Acts 8:39–40; Exodus 3:14; Matthew 5:22; 6:33; 1 Corinthians 4:20; Luke 22:7)

Fill in the blank:
Christ is the visible image of the _____ God.
Colossians 1:15 NLT
Hint: The answer is the opposite of the word *visible*.

Fill in the blank:
"You are the _____ of the world—like a city on a hilltop that cannot be hidden."

Matthew 5:14 NLT

Hint: The answer rhymes with *sight*.

Here are some more words and phrases you should know. Match them with their meaning:

1. Law of Moses   a. bread God made
2. light of the world   b. Savior of God's people
3. love   c. God's messenger
4. manna   d. when dead people are raised back to life

5. Messiah   e. first five Bible books
6. prophet   f. to give up something
7. resurrection   g. what God is
8. sacrifice   h. God, Jesus, and you

(Acts 13:39; Isaiah 60:19; John 8:12; Matthew 5:14; 1 John 4:8; Exodus 16:4; John 20:31; 1 John 4:1; John 11:25–26; Romans 12:1)

True or false: Jesus said He was the meat of life—that you will never be hungry with Him in your life.
(John 6:35)

True or false: Your body is a holy sacrifice that is pleasing to God.
(Romans 12:1)

Here are some more words and phrases you should know. Match them with their meaning:

1. salvation
2. Second Coming
3. temptation
4. truth
5. worship
6. zeal

a. what is true
b. to show love to something or someone
c. showing a passion for something
d. when Jesus returns
e. being rescued from sin
f. wanting to give in to something not good for you

(Philippians 2:12; Hebrews 9:28; 1 Corinthians 10:13; John 16:13; Matthew 2:11; 1 Corinthians 14:12)

Your good deeds are to shine out for all people to see so that what?
   a. you will get a reward
   b. everyone will praise God
   c. your parents will be happy
   d. your teacher will praise you
(Matthew 5:16)
Hint: Pick one.

Fill in the blank:
God is faithful. He will not allow the temptation to be more than you can _____.

1 Corinthians 10:13 NLT
Hint: The answer rhymes with *hand*.

The **Ascension** is when what happened?
- a. Moses climbed a hill.
- b. Jesus went up to heaven.
- c. Jacob climbed a ladder.
- d. Jesus was transfigured.

(Acts 1:9–11)
Hint: Pick one.

An **author** is someone who writes something. True or false: Jesus is called the Author of your faith because He has written a story of how you can live right with God!
(Hebrews 12:1–3)

A **bridegroom** is someone who loves and marries his wife. Jesus is called the Bridegroom to what *one* thing or person?
- a. the church
- b. Eve
- c. the temple
- d. the tabernacle

(Ephesians 5:31–32)

Odds and Ends

· — — — — — — ·

Here is where you will find lots of
questions about names, numbers—odds
and evens—relatives, jobs, and more!
You might want to do this section last
since you will find most answers to these
questions in the rest of this trivia book!

Hint: To find the right answer for the trivia
questions where you match people with
the Bible books that hold their stories,
try matching the bold letter that appears
in a person's name with the same bold
letter that appears in his or her Bible book!

See if you can match each number with the clue it is tied to.

1. Abraham's age when God told him to leave home   a. 31
2. Times Daniel prayed to God each day   b. 7
3. Stones David used to kill Goliath   c. 12
4. Tribes of Israel   d. 3
5. Kings Joshua defeated   e. 1
6. Demons Jesus chased out of Mary Magdalene   f. 75

(Genesis 12:4; Daniel 6:12–16; 1 Samuel 17:40, 49–50; Genesis 49:28; Joshua 12:24; Mark 16:9)

True or false: Rachel was the mother of Joseph and Benjamin.
(Genesis 35:24)

What were the names of the twin boys of Isaac and Rebekah?
    a. Perez
    b. Esau
    c. Zerah
    d. Jacob
(Genesis 25:24–26)

Which *one* of David's sons tried to take over his throne?

a. Absalom
b. Ammon
c. Nathan
d. Adonijah

(2 Samuel 15:10)

See if you can match each number with the clue it is tied to.

1. Abraham's age when
   Isaac was born   a. 900
2. Noah's age when he died   b. 72
3. Disciples Jesus sent
   out two by two   c. 100
4. Enemy chariots Deborah
   went to war against   d. 950
5. Midwives who disobeyed
   the king of Egypt   e. 3
6. Men who lived through
   fire in a king's furnace   f. 2

(Genesis 21:5; 9:28–29; Luke 10:1; Judges 4:4–16; Exodus 1:15–21; Daniel 3:26)

What were the names of the *three* children of Jochebed and Amram?

a. Moses
b. Samuel
c. Aaron
d. Miriam

(Numbers 26:59)

True or false: The followers of Jesus named Andrew, Simon Peter, and James and John (sons of Zebedee) were fishermen. (Matthew 4:18, 21)

Here's a list of not-so-odd jobs and the people who had them. Match the work with the worker:

1. seller of cloth
2. tax collector
3. shepherd
4. Italian army captain
5. maker of clothes
6. king's wine taster
7. teacher
8. tentmaker
9. servant
10. field worker
11. midwife
12. carpenter

a. Joseph
b. Shiprah
c. Ruth
d. Rhoda
e. Paul
f. Nehemiah
g. Nicodemus
h. Dorcas
i. Cornelius
j. Moses
k. Matthew
l. Lydia

(Acts 16:14; Mark 2:14; Exodus 3:1; Acts 10:1; 9:39; Nehemiah 1:11; John 3:9–10; Acts 18:3; Acts 12:13; Ruth 2:23; Exodus 1:15; Matthew 13:55)

True or false: Priscilla and her husband Apollos made tents with the apostle Paul.
(Acts 18:1–3)

Match each word with its meaning:
1. crucifixion   a. someone who gives a message or a sermon
2. living water   b. someone who helps you learn
3. Lord of peace c. the Spirit who enters believers in Jesus
4. nativity   d. when Jesus was nailed to the cross
5. preacher   e. Jesus' birth
6. teacher   f. one of Jesus' names
(Galatians 2:20; John 7:37–38; 2 Thessalonians 3:16; Luke 2:6–7; 2 Timothy 4:2; Matthew 23:9–10)

Fill in the blank:
[Nicodemus]. . .came to Jesus at _____.
John 3:2 NLV
Hint: The answer rhymes with *light*.

Match the parents with the child:
1. David and Bathsheba   a. John the Baptist
2. Hannah and Elkanah   b. Perez
3. Zechariah and Elizabeth c. Obed
4. Ruth and Boaz   d. Samuel
5. Jochebed and Amram   e. Boaz
6. Mary and Joseph   f. Moses
7. Judah and Tamar   g. Solomon
8. Salmon and Rahab   h. Jesus
(2 Samuel 12:24; 1 Samuel 1:19–20; Luke
1:57–60; Ruth 4:13, 17; Exodus 6:20; Matthew
1:3, 5, 16)

Match the name with its meaning:
1. Moses   a. heard of God
2. Eve   b. to praise
3. Barnabas   c. rock
4. Samuel   d. to give life
5. Peter   e. to lift out
6. Judah   f. Lord
7. Yahweh   g. Son of Encouragement
(Exodus 2:10; Genesis 3:20; Acts 4:36;
1 Samuel 1:20; Matthew 16:18 NLT;
Genesis 29:35 NLT)

Match the name of the disciple by what he was
also known by or what he was known to be:
1. Peter   a. betrayer
2. John   b. nothing false in him
3. Simon   c. son of Alphaeus
4. Thomas   d. son of Zebedee
5. James   e. Simon, the rock
6. Andrew   f. son of James
7. Judas   g. brother of Peter
8. Judas Iscariot   h. tax collector
9. Matthew   i. the zealot
10. Philip   j. the doubter
11. Nathanael   k. the disciple Jesus loved
12. James   l. inviter of Nathanael
(Matthew 9:9–13; 16:18; John 1:45–47; 19:26;
20:24–29; Luke 6:13–16)

After getting Jesus' body after the crucifixion,
Nicodemus and Joseph wrapped it in cloth and
added what?
    a. 75 pounds of mixed spices
    b. glue
    c. cornstarch powder
    d. a small jar of perfume
(John 19:39–40)
Hint: Pick one.

Even though some people had ordinary jobs, there was still something special about them. Match the person with the "something special."

1. First Christian in Europe   a. Priscilla
2. Wrote a Gospel book   b. Peter
3. Parted the Red Sea   c. Matthew
4. Walked on water   d. Moses
5. Almost died for Paul   e. Lydia

(Acts 16:12–15; Exodus 14:21; Matthew 14:29–30; Romans 16:3–4)

See if you can match each number with the clue it is tied to.

1. Age when Josiah was crowned   a. 21
2. People Jesus fed   b. 12
3. Baskets of food left over   c. 10
4. God's commandments   d. 2
5. Jesus' commandments   e. 8
6. Days Gabriel was held up
   by prince of Persia   f. 5,000

(2 Kings 22:1; John 6:8–10; Matthew 14:20; Exodus 20:1–17; Matthew 22:36–40; Daniel 10:13)

Match the people with the Bible book where you will find the beginning of their story:

1.	Adam	a.	Judges
2.	Aaron	b.	Luke
3.	Boaz	c.	Ruth
4.	David	d.	Exodus
5.	Samson	e.	Numbers
6.	Anna	f.	Acts
7.	Balaam	g.	1 Samuel
8.	Barnabas	h.	Genesis

(Genesis 2; Exodus 7; Ruth 2; 1 Samuel 16; Judges 13; Luke 2; Numbers 22; Acts 4)

See if you can match each number with the clue it is tied to.

1.	Times an angel visited Joseph (Jesus' earthly dad) in a dream	a. 2
2.	Disciples who saw Jesus transfigured	b. 10
3.	Men Jesus met on the road to Emmaus	c. 4
4.	Books in the Bible	d. 40
5.	Plagues on Egypt	e. 3
6.	Years the Israelites wandered	f. 66

(Matthew 1:20; 2:13, 19–20, 22; 17:1–3; Luke 24:35; Exodus 7:14–11:10; Numbers 32:13)

Match the people with the Bible book where you will find the beginning of their story:

1.	Abraham	a.	1 Kings
2.	Jochebed	b.	2 Samuel
3.	Jezebel	c.	Mark
4.	Abigail	d.	Judges
5.	Deborah	e.	Genesis
6.	Bathsheba	f.	Acts
7.	Saul/Paul	g.	1 Samuel
8.	Bartimaeus	h.	Exodus

(Genesis 12; Exodus 2; 1 Kings 19; 1 Samuel 25; Judges 4; 2 Samuel 11; Acts 9; Mark 10)

See if you can match each number with the clue it is tied to.

1.	Disciples with Jesus in the Garden of Gethsemane	a.	2
2.	Angels named in the Bible	b.	3
3.	Bible books Moses' wrote	c.	4
4.	Total Gospel books	d.	5

(Matthew 26:36–37; Daniel 9:21; 10:21)

True or false: Moses never got to enter the promised land.
(Numbers 27:12–14)

Match the fathers with their sons:
1. Abraham
2. Isaac
3. Jacob
4. Judah
5. Salmon
6. Jesse
7. David
8. Solomon
(Matthew 1:2–7)

a. Solomon
b. Isaac
c. Boaz
d. David
e. Perez
f. Judah
g. Rehoboam
h. Jacob

How many times did King Saul throw a spear at David and try to kill him?
   a. one time
   b. two times
   c. three times
   d. four times
(1 Samuel 18:11; 19:10)

Jonathan and David were great what?
 a. brothers
 b. cousins
 c. friends
 d. enemies
(1 Samuel 18:3)
Hint: Pick one.

Match the people with the Bible book where you will find the beginning of their story:

1. Jacob   a. Luke
2. Joshua   b. Numbers
3. Caleb   c. Joshua
4. King Og   d. Genesis
5. Rahab   e. Acts
6. Jael   f. Deuteronomy
7. Mary   g. Judges
8. Cornelius   h. Exodus

(Genesis 32; Exodus 17; Numbers 13; Deuteronomy 3; Joshua 2; Judges 4; Luke 1; Acts 10)

Fill in the blank: When King Saul was killed in battle, David became _____ of Judah.
                              2 Samuel 2:2–4
          Hint: The answer rhymes with *sing*.

True or false: When King Solomon died and his son Rehoboam became king, the nation of Israel split into two kingdoms called Judah and Israel.
(1 Kings 12)

Match the people with the Bible book where you will find the beginning of their story:
1. **S**arah
2. H**a**nnah
3. Absa**l**om
4. Quee**n** of Sheba
5. J**e**hoshaphat
6. Xerxes
7. B**e**lshazzar
8. G**o**mer

a. H**o**sea
b. Genesi**s**
c. 1 **S**amuel
d. 2 Samue**l**
e. 1 Ki**n**gs
f. 2 C**h**ronicles
g. Esther
h. Danie**l**

(Genesis 11; 1 Samuel 1; 2 Samuel 14; 1 Kings 10; 2 Chronicles 20; Esther 1; Daniel 5; Hosea 1)

In the book of Esther, Jews celebrate the first feast of what *one* holy day?
  a. Passover
  b. Sabbath
  c. Lent
  d. Purim
(Esther 9:26)

Fill in the blank: In his book, the prophet Joel wrote about locusts eating all the farmers' _____.

Joel 2:25

Hint: The answer rhymes with *drops*.

See if you can match each number with the clue it is tied to.

1. Women who saw angels at Jesus' tomb	a. 2
2. Spies Rahab hid	b. 3
3. Giant's total toes	c. 52
4. Men killed by Jashobeam with one spear	d. 150
5. Days it took for Jerusalem's wall to be rebuilt	e. 12
6. Total psalms in the Bible	f. 300

(Luke 24:1–10; Joshua 2:1–4; 2 Samuel 21:20; 1 Chronicles 11:11; Nehemiah 6:15)

True or false: In the book of Esther, Esther's relative Mordecai saved King Xerxes's life! (Esther 2:21–23)

Match the people with the Bible book where you will find the beginning of their story:

1. Hagar   a. Haggai
2. Delilah   b. Acts
3. Elijah   c. Judges
4. King Jehoiakim   d. Luke
5. Zerubbabel   e. 2 Chronicles
6. Wise men   f. Genesis
7. Zachariah   g. 1 Kings
8. Damaris   h. Matthew

(Genesis 16; Judges 16; 1 Kings 18; 2 Chronicles 36; Haggai 2; Matthew 2; Luke 1; Acts 17)

See if you can match each number with the clue it is tied to.

1. Abraham's age when
   Ishmael was born   a. 2
2. Noah's age when God
   flooded the earth   b. 969
3. Philistines Samson killed
   with a donkey's jawbone c. 3,000
4. Believers Peter's message
   added to the church   d. 600
5. Age when Methuselah died e. 1,000
6. Moses' siblings   f. 86

(Genesis 16:16; 7:6; Judges 15:15; Acts 2:41; Genesis 5:27; Exodus 15:20)

The people who lived in Edom were the off-spring of this man who was Jacob's twin:
   a. Ezekiel
   b. Esau
   c. Eddie
   d. Ezra
(Genesis 36:8)

See if you can match each number with the clue it is tied to.
1. People aboard Noah's ark   a. 6
2. Faces on angels in Ezekiel's vision   b. 9
3. Height (in feet) of Goliath   c. 8
4. Coins Judas got for betraying Jesus   d. 12
5. Years a woman bled before
     being healed by Jesus   e. 30
6. Sisters Lazarus lived with   f. 4
7. Wings of each angel in Isaiah's vision g. 2
(2 Peter 2:5; Ezekiel 10:14; 1 Samuel 17:4; Matthew 26:15; Mark 5:25; John 11:1; Isaiah 6:2)

Match the people with the Bible book where you will find the beginning of their story:

1. Joseph
2. Moses
3. Naomi
4. Mordecai
5. King Saul
6. Gideon
7. Elizabeth
8. Dorcas

a. Judges
b. Luke
c. Esther
d. 1 Samuel
e. Acts
f. Genesis
g. Exodus
h. Ruth

(Genesis 37; Exodus 2; Ruth 1; Esther 1; 1 Samuel 9; Judges 6; Luke 1; Acts 9)

See if you can match each number with the clue it is tied to.

1. Bible books written by Luke
2. Days Jonah was inside a big fish
3. Days of great flood rain
4. Fish disciples caught with Jesus' help
5. Golden calves Aaron made
6. Kinds of animals Job had

a. 1
b. 4
c. 3
d. 40
e. 2
f. 153

(Luke 1:1; Acts 1:1; Jonah 1:17; Genesis 7:12; John 21:11–12; Exodus 32:1–4; Job 1:3)

Joanna was a follower of Jesus. Her husband Chuza had a job running whose household?

a. Martha's
b. Caiaphas's
c. Herod's
d. Luke's

(Luke 8:3)

See if you can match each number with the clue it is tied to.

1. Beastlike animals Daniel saw   a. 7
2. Birds Noah sent out of ark   b. 6
3. Red dragon's heads John
   saw in Revelation   c. 2
4. Length (in feet) of giant
   King Og's iron bed   d. 10
5. Width (in feet) of King Og's bed   e. 13
6. Steps God made the shadow
   go back for Hezekiah   f. 4

(Daniel 7:2–7; Genesis 8:6–12; Revelation 12:3; Deuteronomy 3:11; 2 Kings 20:8–10)

Fill in the blank: During Jesus' day, Caiaphas was the high _____.

John 11:49

Hint: The answer rhymes with *creased*.

The Bible book called Leviticus talks about what to do during what *two* special holy days?
   a. Christmas
   b. Sabbath
   c. Easter
   d. Passover
(Leviticus 23)

See if you can match each number with the clue it is tied to.
1. Red dragon's horns John saw in Revelation   a. 10
2. Priests killed by Philistines who captured ark of God   b. 2
3. God's armor items   c. 6
4. Weight (in pounds) of Goliath's armor   d. 125
5. Day God rested from creation   e. 7
6. Members of the Trinity   f. 3
(Revelation 12:3; 1 Samuel 4:11; Ephesians 6:14–17; 1 Samuel 17:4–7; Genesis 2:2; Matthew 28:19)

True or false: The word *holy* appears in the book of Leviticus 150 times!

What were the names of the twin boys of
Judah and Tamar?
- a. Perez
- b. Esau
- c. Zerah
- d. Jacob

(Matthew 1:3)

See if you can match each number with the
clue it is tied to.
1. Days before Jesus rose
   from the dead   a. 12
2. Loaves Jesus used to feed 5,000   b. 490
3. Fish Jesus used to feed 5,000   c. 3
4. Disciples Jesus called   d. 2
5. Times Jesus said to forgive someone   e. 5

(1 Corinthians 15:4; Matthew 14:19; 10:2–4;
18:21–22 NLV)

Hundreds of years before it ever happened,
the prophet Zechariah predicted who would
be pierced by the spear of a soldier?
- a. David
- b. Daniel
- c. Jesus
- d. Paul

(Zechariah 12:10; John 19:36–37)

Supernatural Superheroes

— - — - — - — -

The supernatural superheroes are, of course, God, Jesus, and the Holy Spirit. In this section, you will find lots of trivia questions about this Holy Threesome that will boggle your mind! May those Three be with you as you take on this last challenge!

Fill in the blank: In the book of Revelation, Jesus calls Himself "the Alpha and the Omega," which means "the First and the _____."

Revelation 22:13

Hint: The answer rhymes with *fast*.

True or false: Jesus went up to heaven and will one day return the same way.
(Acts 1:9–11)

Sometimes when the Holy Spirit appears, He shows up as which of the following?
    a. a dove
    b. a strong wind
    c. a flame
    d. a calf
(Matthew 3:16; Acts 2:1–4)
Hint: Pick three.

Who did the Holy Spirit lift out of water and put down in another city?
    a. Peter
    b. Paul
    c. Philip
    d. Pilate
(Acts 8:39–40)

As soon as Jesus told the former blind man Bartimaeus that his faith had healed him, what one thing did Bartimaeus do?

    a.   follow Jesus down the road
    b.   clap his hands
    c.   go tell his mom and dad
    d.   sit down in wonder

(Mark 10:51–52)

True or false: After blessing the disciples near Bethany, Jesus was taken up to heaven.
(Luke 24:50–52)

Which *three* of the following are part of the commission (job) Jesus gave to His disciples?

    a.   make disciples of all nations
    b.   baptize them
    c.   teach them to obey
    d.   write down these words

(Matthew 28:18–20)

Fill in the blank: Jesus is the solid _____
on which you can build your life. That is why
He is called your cornerstone.

> Ephesians 2:19–22
> Hint: The answer rhymes with *dock*.

True or false: Jesus Christ not only made the
heavens and the earth but made everything
that is seen and things that are not seen.
(Colossians 1:16–17)

Fill in the blank:
Our old life, our old sinful self, was nailed to
the _____ with Christ.

> Romans 6:6 NLV
> Hint: The answer rhymes with *moss*.

Jesus is more powerful than the devil, whom
He called the father of what *one* thing?

   a. Judas
   b. bad people
   c. lies
   d. killers

(John 8:44)

Before Jesus was arrested, He washed and dried His followers' feet. He did that to show what *one* thing?

    a. We should stay clean.
    b. We should serve one another.
    c. We should keep dry.
    d. We should clip our toenails.

(John 13:14–16)

Who were the *three* disciples with Jesus when He prayed so hard He dripped blood in the Garden of Gethsemane?

    a. Philip
    b. Peter
    c. James
    d. John

(Matthew 26:36–37)

Fill in the blank: After suffering and _____ on the cross in Golgotha, Jesus came back to life!

Mark 15:22; 16:6
Hint: The answer rhymes with *lying*.

Fill in the blanks:
[Jesus said,] "I am the Good _____.
The Good _____ gives His life for the
sheep."

John 10:11 NLV
Hint: The same word—which rhymes
with *leopard*—fits in both blanks.

The first greatest rule Jesus wants you to fol-
low is to love God with what?
    a. all your heart
    b. all your soul
    c. all your mind
    d. all your strength
(Mark 12:30)
Hint: Pick more than one.

Fill in the blank: The second greatest rule
Jesus wants you to follow is to love your
_____ as yourself.

Mark 12:31
Hint: The answer rhymes with *labor*.

When Jesus went back to heaven, He sent the
Holy Spirit to be what *three* things for you?
    a. Helper
    b. Advocate
    c. Friend
    d. Brother
(John 14:26 NLV, NLT, NIrV)

As Jesus was dying on the cross, which *one* person did He tell to take care of His mom, Mary?

    a. Peter
    b. James
    c. Paul
    d. John

(John 19:26–27)

Fill in the blank:
Jesus said, ". . .You need to change and become like little _____. If you don't, you will never enter the kingdom of heaven."

Matthew 18:3
Hint: You are one of these.

At the last meal Jesus ate with His followers, He said the bread they ate and the wine they drank stood for what?

    a. His body and blood
    b. manna and living water
    c. food and drink
    d. yeast and juice

(Matthew 26:26–28)
Hint: Pick one.

Fill in the blank:
[Jesus said,] "I am the _____ of the world. Anyone who follows Me will not walk in darkness."

John 8:12
Hint: The answer rhymes with kite.

When Jesus was born, there was no room for Him and His family in an inn. So He was born in a what?
    a. hotel
    b. stable
    c. field
    d. day care
(Luke 2:6–7)

True or false: By not believing in Jesus, you can shut off His miracle-working power.
(Mark 6:1, 5–6)

Fill in the blank: Don't forget to pray, because Jesus said:
"My Father will give you whatever you ask in My _____."

John 16:23 NLV
Hint: The answer rhymes with game.

True or false: The name of the man who helped Jesus carry His cross to Golgotha was Simon of Cyrene.
(Luke 23:26)

After Jesus died on the cross, God raised Him back to life after how many days?
   a. 1
   b. 2
   c. 3
   d. 4
(1 Corinthians 15:4)

What was the first thing the risen Jesus said to the two men walking on the road to Emmaus?
   a. "You're going the wrong way."
   b. "Don't I know you?"
   c. "I'm back!"
   d. "Peace be with you."
(Luke 24:35–36 NLT)

Which *three* of the following names was Jesus called?
   a. Son of David
   b. Son of God
   c. Son of Man
   d. Son of Jesse
(Matthew 1:1; 3:16–17; Luke 9:58)

True or false: After His baptism, Jesus was full of the Spirit and was led by the Spirit into the desert where the devil's food tempted Him.
(Luke 4:1–2)

How long did Jesus go without food while the devil tempted Him?
   a. 10 days
   b. 20 days
   c. 40 days
   d. 80 days
(Luke 4:1–2)

What were the *three* things the devil tried to get Jesus to do?
 a. doubt Father God's care
 b. worship the devil alone
 c. test God's protection
 d. eat manna
(Luke 4:3–8)

Fill in the blank:
Jesus said to the devil, "Get _____ Me, Satan!"

Luke 4:8 NLV
 Hint: The answer is the opposite of *in front*.

Which *one* of the following did Jesus say to one of the two thieves hanging on the cross next to Him?
 a. "Don't steal ever again."
 b. "Today you will be with Me in Paradise."
 c. "I'll be back!"
 d. "I don't feel so good."
(Luke 23:42–43 NLV)

Because God is the Gardener and Jesus is the Vine, when you live in Him you can do what *one* thing?
- a. grow grapes
- b. make juice
- c. bear fruit
- d. never go sour

(John 15:4–5)

Fill in the blank:
[Jesus said,] "Apart from me you can do
_____."

John 15:5 NLT

Hint: The answer is the opposite of *something*.

What *one* thing did Peter say to Jesus when he saw Him walking on the water?
- a. "Are You a ghost?"
- b. "Tell me to come to You."
- c. "How do You do that?
- d. "Where's Your boat?"

(Matthew 14:28 NLV)

What *one* thing did Jesus say in answer to
Peter's question?
    a. "No, I'm not a ghost."
    b. "Yes, come."
    c. "I'm God. I can do anything!"
    d. "I don't need a boat."
(Matthew 14:29 NLT)

Peter began to sink when what *one* thing
happened?
    a. A big wave hit him.
    b. He lost his footing.
    c. A whale swam by.
    d. He took his eyes off Jesus.
(Matthew 14:30)

What *one* thing did Jesus do when the sinking
Peter yelled, "Save me, Jesus"?
    a. He sank down with Peter.
    b. He jumped into the boat.
    c. He immediately grabbed Peter.
    d. He rode away on a whale.
(Matthew 14:31)

Match what Jesus is with its meaning:

1. the Way   a. right and honest
2. the Truth   b. spiritual birth
3. the Life   c. road to God

(John 14:5–6)

The wise men brought which *three* gifts to Jesus when He was born?

a. gold
b. diapers
c. frankincense
d. myrrh

(Matthew 2:11–12)

What *one* thing did God do to warn the wise men not to go back to King Herod (who wanted to know where Jesus was so he could kill Him)?

a. God met them on the road.
b. God warned them in a dream.
c. God sent an angel with a message.
d. God sent word through Joseph.

(Matthew 2:12)

Jesus is called the Word because He was with God when He spoke to create the earth and heavens. What is true about the Word?

a. He was in the beginning.
b. He was with God.
c. He was God.
d. He became human.

(John 1:1–2, 14)
Hint: Pick more than one.

Jesus is the Rock on which you should build your life. In fact, He is called what *one* thing listed below?

a. a stone in Rockwood
b. a stone in Israel
c. a stone in Zion
d. a stone in Blarney

(1 Peter 2:6)

True or false: Jesus not only has power over both the wind and the waves but can walk on water!
(Matthew 14:22–30; Luke 8:22–24)

True or false: Jesus not only is all-powerful but made all the powers of heaven!
(Colossians 1:16)

Fill in the blank: Even when you don't know what to pray for or how, the Holy Spirit prays for you, "through _____ too deep for words."

Romans 8:26
Hint: The answer rhymes with *moans*.

Jesus said the Holy Spirit is the Spirit of what *one* thing listed below?
   a. life
   b. light
   c. truth
   d. power
(John 15:26)

Which *three* of the following things did Jesus say will get you a reward from heaven?
- a. loving your enemies
- b. doing good to your enemies
- c. lending without expecting to get anything back
- d. tying your shoes right

(Luke 6:35)

Jesus said He was which of the following:
- a. the Bread of Life and the True Vine
- b. the Light of the World
- c. the Good Shepherd and the Door
- d. the Resurrection and the Life
- e. the Way, the Truth, and the Life
- f. the Answer and the Question

(John 6:35; 8:12; 10:7, 11; 11:25; 14:6; 15:1)
Hint: Choose all but one!

True or false: Heaven is where God and Jesus are now. It's also where the souls and spirits of Christians go after they die.
(Mark 16:19; 2 Corinthians 5:6–9)

Answer Key

Heroes and Heroines

Page 10: d; mouth; true; d
Page 11: b; wisdom; c
Page 12: c; true; true; 1 (c), 2 (d), 3 (b), 4 (a)
Page 13: true; obeyed; b; b
Page 14: heart; a; c
Page 15: b; time; c, d
Page 16: c; a; d
Page 17: false—it was the Nile River; d; hair, locusts; less
Page 18: d; loved; 1 (c), 2 (a), 3 (b)
Page 19: 1 (d), 2 (a), 3 (c), 4 (b); c; good
Page 20: a; serve; d
Page 21: c; b; d
Page 22: d; seven; true
Page 23: c; b; b
Page 24: d; c
Page 25: c; c; name
Page 26: true; a, b; a, b, c
Page 27: c; a; true; c
Page 28: a; a; c

Prophets, Priests, Kings, and Judges

Page 30: c; d; false—her name was Hannah
Page 31: a; d; c
Page 32: b; true; c; wisdom
Page 33: 1 (f), 2 (g), 3 (h), 4 (b), 5 (c), 6 (d), 7
   (e), 8 (a); one
Page 34: c; b; true
Page 35: b, d; 1 (e), 2 (g), 3 (a), 4 (f), 5 (b), 6
(d), 7 (c); hair
Page 36: d; b; c

Dangerous People and Mistake Makers

Page 38: strength; a, b, c; a
Page 39: true; d; a, d
Page 40: a, b, c; c; a
Page 41: b; sinners; true
Page 42: a, c; true; b
Page 43: c; true; a, b, c
Page 44: true; d; a
Page 45: b; c; d
Page 46: a; please; b
Page 47: c; believe; a, b
Page 48: c, d; d; true
Page 49: true; a, b, c; obeyed
Page 50: b; true; c

Reward and Promise Receivers

Page 52: b; die; patient
Page 53: nations; true; b
Page 54: word; d; c
Page 55: b; a, d; son
Page 56: true; c; b

Miracle Makers

Page 58: b; b; a, c
Page 59: c; b, d; a, c
Page 60: b; c; a, b
Page 61: b, c, d; glory; true
Page 62: d; c; c
Page 63: all; d; c
Page 64: 1 (b), 2 (c), 3 (d), 4 (a); 1 (c), 2 (d), 3 (b), 4 (a); 1 (c), 2 (a), 3 (b)

Close Encounters of the Supernatural Kind

Page 66: b; b; eyes
Page 67: d; d; a
Page 68: bush; 1 (f), 2 (j), 3 (a), 4 (h), 5 (d), 6 (b), 7 (i), 8 (c), 9 (g), 10 (e)
Page 69: b; Samuel; d
Page 70: c; b; 1 (e), 2 (d), 3 (a), 4 (c), 5 (b)
Page 71: b; true; 1 (d), 2 (a), 3 (b), 4 (c)
Page 72: sleep; Moses, Elijah; a, b, c
Page 73: a, b, d; true; c; true
Page 74: d; scales; all

Book Hooks

Page 76: c; Genesis, Exodus, Leviticus,
  Numbers, Deuteronomy; a, c; true
Page 77: c; d; b
Page 78: c; a, b; d
Page 79: true; true; d; a, c, d
Page 80: a; b; c
Page 81: true; d; queen; a
Page 82: a; true; b
Page 83: b; c; brave
Page 84: d; true; d
Page 85: c; lamp; a, b, d
Page 86: b; true; a; six

Book Hooks (continued)

Page 87: plans; b; true
Page 88: book, honey; d; d, a, c, b
Page 89: b; false; a, c, d; false—Bethlehem
Page 90: angry; d; true; c
Page 91: a; return; d; true
Page 92: c; b; crazy; Theophilus
Page 93: d; d; loved
Page 94: c; a; Isaiah
Page 95: b; all; love
Page 96: b; power; false—Paul wrote them;
  Love
Page 97: breathed; true; true; d
Page 98: prayer; rock; b; d

Parables

Page 100: d; c; a—he used oil and wine
Page 101: neighbor; true; c
Page 102: d; b; a
Page 103: a; words; d
Page 104: a; wise, foolish; d

Animal Antics

Page 106: true; two; a
Page 107: c; b; ravens
Page 108: donkey; b; a
Page 109: c; c; d
Page 110: Foxes, Birds; c; b
Page 111: b; d; a
Page 112: a, b; true; 1 (c), 2 (d), 3 (b),
   4 (a); lion
Page 113: true; d; false—he lived; Lion
Page 114: true; 1 (e), 2 (h), 3 (f), 4 (a), 5 (g), 6
(d), 7 (c), 8 (b); true

Tools and Weapons

Page 116: d; life; true
Page 117: b; d; staff, hand
Page 118: b; c; b
Page 119: Word; a; a, b
Page 120: a, d; b; c

You Are There

Page 122: a; d; c
Page 123: a, b; true; b
Page 124: a; true; c
Page 125: Babel; a, c, d; true; a
Page 126: true; c; b
Page 127: c; Cana; 1 (c), 2 (d), 3 (b), 4 (a)
Page 128: true; Samson; true; a
Page 129: 1 (f), 2 (d), 3 (g), 4 (e), 5 (b), 6 (c),
    7 (a); true; 1 (f), 2 (d), 3 (g), 4 (a), 5 (c),
    6 (b), 7 (e)
Page 130: 1 (b), 2 (e), 3 (f), 4 (a), 5 (g), 6 (d),
    7 (c), 8 (i), 9 (h); 1 (f), 2 (h), 3 (d), 4 (e),
    5 (g), 6 (a), 7 (b), 8 (c)

Wacky Weather and Notable Nature

Page 132: false—it rained 40 days and 40 nights; rainbow; a; palm

Page 133: salt; true; olive; false—he climbed a sycamore-fig tree; mustard

Page 134: milk, honey; c; d; false—God talked to Job out of a whirlwind.

Words, Words, Words

Page 136: all; Golden; 1 (i), 2 (c), 3 (h), 4 (b), 5 (f), 6 (d), 7 (e), 8 (g), 9 (a)

Page 137: angels; b; a, b, c

Page 138: 1 (c), 2 (f), 3 (e), 4 (a), 5 (d), 6 (b); c; a

Page 139: d; c; b

Page 140: d; d; true

Words, Words, Words (continued)

Page 141: d; a; b, c
Page 142: a; c; hope
Page 143: b; image; b; true
Page 144: c; a; c
Page 145: d; b; d
Page 146: a; a; love
Page 147: a, c, d; peace; true; true
Page 148: true; c; d
Page 149: true; 1 (f), 2 (g), 3 (d), 4 (h), 5 (b),
    6 (a), 7 (e), 8 (c); fire
Page 150: true; 1 (c), 2 (g), 3 (f), 4 (h), 5 (d),
    6 (e), 7 (b), 8 (a); head
Page 151: true; 1 (f), 2 (a), 3 (e), 4 (h), 5 (c),
    6 (b), 7 (d), 8 (g); sick
Page 152: Seek; 1 (e), 2 (g), 3 (d), 4 (h), 5 (c),
    6 (b), 7 (f), 8 (a); true
Page 153: true; 1 (f), 2 (e), 3 (d), 4 (a), 5 (b),
    6 (g), 7 (h), 8 (c); invisible
Page 154: light; 1 (e), 2 (h), 3 (g), 4 (a), 5 (b),
    6 (c), 7 (d), 8 (f); false—Jesus is the Bread
    of Life
Page 155: true; 1 (e), 2 (d), 3 (f), 4 (a), 5 (b),
    6 (c); b
Page 156: stand; b; true; a

Odds and Ends

Page 158: 1 (f), 2 (d), 3 (e), 4 (c), 5 (a), 6 (b);
    true; b, d
Page 159: a; 1 (c), 2 (d), 3 (b), 4 (a), 5 (f),
    6 (e); a, c, d
Page 160: true; 1 (l), 2 (k), 3 (j), 4 (i), 5 (h),
    6 (f), 7 (g), 8 (e), 9 (d), 10 (c), 11 (b), 12 (a)
Page 161: false—Priscilla's husband's name
    was Aquila; 1 (d), 2 (c), 3 (f), 4 (e), 5 (a),
    6 (b); night
Page 162: 1 (g), 2 (d), 3 (a), 4 (c), 5 (f), 6 (h),
    7 (b), 8 (e); 1 (e), 2 (d), 3 (g), 4 (a), 5 (c),
    6 (b), 7 (f)
Page 163: 1 (e), 2 (k), 3 (i), 4 (j), 5 (c), 6 (g),
    7 (f), 8 (a), 9 (h), 10 (l), 11 (b), 12 (d); a
Page 164: 1 (e), 2 (c), 3 (d), 4 (b), 5 (a); 1 (e),
    2 (f), 3 (b), 4 (c), 5 (d), 6 (a)
Page 165: 1 (h), 2 (d), 3 (c), 4 (g), 5 (a), 6 (b),
    7 (e), 8 (f); 1 (c), 2 (e), 3 (a), 4 (f), 5 (b), 6 (d)
Page 166: 1 (e), 2 (h), 3 (a), 4 (g), 5 (d), 6 (b),
    7 (f), 8 (c); 1 (b), 2 (a), 3 (d), 4 (c)
Page 167: true; 1 (b), 2 (h), 3 (f), 4 (e), 5 (c),
    6 (d), 7 (a), 8 (g); b
Page 168: c; 1 (d), 2 (h), 3 (b), 4 (f), 5 (c),
    6 (g), 7 (a), 8 (e); king
Page 169: true; 1 (b), 2 (c), 3 (d), 4 (e), 5 (f),
    6 (g), 7 (h), 8 (a); d
Page 170: crops; 1 (b), 2 (a), 3 (e), 4 (f), 5 (c),
    6 (d); true
Page 171: 1 (f), 2 (c), 3 (g), 4 (e), 5 (a), 6 (h),
    7 (d), 8 (b); 1 (f), 2 (d), 3 (e), 4 (c), 5 (b),
    6 (a)

Supernatural Superheroes

Keep the Fun Going with. . .

999 Super Fun, Head-Scratching, Brain-Boosting Bible Trivia Questions for Kids

Kids love to learn about the Bible—and here's a fantastic collection of 999 Bible trivia questions especially for 6- to 12-year-olds! Compiled and edited *by* kids *for* kids, you can be sure this is a collection of trivia that young readers will enjoy and share—with anyone who will listen!

Paperback / 978-1-68322-560-7 / $4.99

Ross was silent for a moment before he said, "You are certain that he did it?"

The words seemed to have no immediate effect. Detective Chief Inspector Callum stared into the fire and said quietly, "The circumstantial evidence against him is overwhelming. His fingerprints are all over the cottage. He knew the layout. The murder weapon belonged to him. I take it, Superintendent, that you don't agree."

"I'm afraid not. I don't think the profile of this crime fits anything spontaneous. I think it was carefully planned, by someone who cut the phone line to the farm. By someone who knew that the Lassiters and the Halls would be in that cottage." He leaned forward and rested his elbows on his knees, fixing his gaze on Callum's. "It doesn't make sense otherwise. If this Danny Blaine wanted to make a few quid by robbing the cottage, why not do it when they were gone? Unless, of course, you really believe that he simply went berserk and killed them."

"Apparently he did," said Callum.

Ross looked at him for a moment. "I don't think he could have. . . ."

**Praise for Lucretia Grindle's
First Inspector Ross Mystery,
*THE KILLING OF ELLIS MARTIN***

"An extremely satisfying book. . . . A good whodunit, just a hint of romance, believable motivations, characters to care about—how can this miss?"

—*Criminal Record* (Denver, CO)

"Sensational. . . ."

—*Murder & Mayhem*

Books by Lucretia Grindle

The Killing of Ellis Martin
So Little to Die For

Published by POCKET BOOKS

SO LITTLE TO DIE FOR

AN INSPECTOR ROSS MYSTERY

LUCRETIA GRINDLE

POCKET BOOKS

New York   London   Toronto   Sydney   Tokyo   Singapore

This book is a work of fiction. Names, characters, places and incidents are products of the author's imagination or are used fictitiously. Any resemblance to actual events or locales or persons, living or dead, is entirely coincidental.

An *Original* Publication of POCKET BOOKS

POCKET BOOKS, a division of Simon & Schuster Inc.
1230 Avenue of the Americas, New York, NY 10020

ISBN: 0-671-74846-7

First Pocket Books printing October 1994

10 9 8 7 6 5 4 3 2 1

POCKET BOOKS and colophon are registered trademarks of Simon & Schuster Inc.

Cover design and art by Marc Burckhardt

Printed in the U.S.A.

With special thanks to Chief Inspector Barker-McCardle of the Kent County C.I.D. And to the staff of the Gleneagles Hotel, particularly the staff of the shooting school.

Prologue

She woke up suddenly, every muscle in her body alert, stiff with tension. In the stillness of the room she could hear nothing but her own breathing, and yet she knew a sound had been there. It lingered just at the edge of the late afternoon silence. And with it there was the feeling, the hand on the back of her neck, the prickle across her scalp, that told her she was not alone.

Slowly, with the precise, controlled movements that hold off panic, she sat up, swung her legs over the side of the bed and placed her stockinged feet on the floor. Summer light filtered through the worn curtains, and as she sat staring toward the open door, a cloud moved across the sun, dulling the shadows.

Her footsteps made no sound in the hallway as she moved slowly past the bathroom, with its rose-patterned wallpaper and dripping tap, past the closed doors of the other bedrooms. At the foot of the stairs she paused, willing her breathing to be quiet, half afraid to step into the downstairs passage for fear of what she would see and what she would not see.

It was always the same. At least it had been, the two times it happened before. Always she was alone in the cottage and always it was daylight, which made it worse. The first time, the others had gone up to the post office while she stayed behind to read. The second time, a few days later, all of them had gone down to the loch to fish, and she walked back early, alone. She'd been sitting in the kitchen when it happened.

Today the others were out walking.

It was as if someone invisible had walked into the room. And after leaving, when she was alone again, the presence would linger, drifting slowly away like a scent on the air.

Now she stood in the sitting room and felt her breath leave her. It had gone, of course; she'd known it would. Something was always gone, missing, misplaced, never found. Ordinary things. A glove. A book of matches. A glasses case. Today it was her headband, the blue velvet one she'd taken off just before going upstairs to sleep. She ran her hand back and forth across the top of the cheap false mantel where she'd left the headband not an hour ago.

The panic rose and she whimpered; a small stupid sound made over the loss of a headband in a rented cottage.

She swung around suddenly, bumping into the sofa, catching sight of herself in the heavy wood-framed mirror that hung on the opposite wall. The face that looked back at her was pinched and white, the black hair disheveled. Hecate, she thought. Ophelia. *The Three Sisters.* I am going mad.

And she watched as the tears came, welled up, and spilled over. In the dull four o'clock light the color seemed to drain from the picture until the face was black and white, a photograph.

"Oh Christ," Claudia Furnival said aloud. "I wish we'd never come here."

1

The shot rang out across the moor, echoing back into the stillness of the summer afternoon. Ross lowered the shotgun and indulged himself in a few moments of satisfaction. He was a good marksman, though it was a skill he neglected more often than not. Guns, he told himself, were not meant for pleasure. Like all good soldiers, Ross bore a deep and abiding loathing for the weapons of war.

Now, on an August afternoon in the Scottish highlands, Ross allowed himself the rare pleasure of sport for sport's sake. He had just completed the senior command course at the Police College at Bramshill, and decided to spend ten days in Scotland, at Gleneagles, where he planned to get in a few days fishing on the Spey. This morning, however, he'd walked up to the hotel's shooting range and spent a satisfying hour and a half obliterating clays as they flew overhead in a variety of alarming configurations.

It had been three years since Ross had taken a vacation, and he was alarmed that it was coming so easily to him. After the death of his wife, he'd turned to work as an acolyte turns to the hope of God, desperate to believe that he could somehow stanch the flow of pain threatening to overwhelm him. But as time passed, the desperation had passed with it. In recent months, he found himself contemplating the art of casting the perfect line, playing the salmon as it danced through white water, appreciating the fish's fine, glassy eye when the battle was done.

Even so, Ross was surprised that he now felt no compunction to pick up the telephone and check on the goings-on in his office. He was not fretting over unfinished paperwork that might be piling up on his desk, nor feeling depleted and lonely because he was not mired in the thick of a homicide investigation. As he walked back down the drive toward the hotel, he was instead preoccupied with the decision as to whether to spend the afternoon hiking up Glendevon or reading by the croquet lawn.

In the end he chose Glendevon, and by the time he settled himself at a table in the hotel's dining room for dinner, he was feeling more than justified in his decision to order himself a very large steak and a more than reasonable bottle of claret.

Her face was familiar, but he didn't recognize her at first. The dining room was crowded, and he hadn't realized that she was approaching until she stood beside the table, half apologetically, and stretched out her hand.

"Chief Inspector Ross, isn't it?" she asked.

He got to his feet as she spoke. He did not correct her, saying he was Detective Chief Inspector, since he worked for the Criminal Investigation Department, better known as the CID. In any case, it was Detective Superintendent, since he had recently been promoted.

She was not so much small as delicate. Her bones stood out like a framework under the translucent skin. A pair of almond-shaped green eyes dominated her face, which was turned up toward him. A batwing of black hair was tied with a ribbon at the nape of her neck, giving her both an otherworldly and oddly childish appearance. When he took her hand, he noticed that the fingers were long and fragile. She was smiling.

"I'm sure you don't remember me at all," she said, "but I knew your wife, through the RSC. My name is Claudia Furnival."

Even as she said it, he did remember her. Kendal had been involved in fund-raising for the Royal Shakespeare Company, and on several occasions they entertained various actors at their house in London. Though now she was quite well-known, Claudia Furnival had been little more than a bit player with the RSC then. He vaguely remembered that there had been some excitement about her, and something else remarkable, other than her appearance. He attempted to recall it, then it came to him: she was a twin, one of an identical pair of green-eyed, black-haired sisters. Now she stood in the Gleneagles dining room, holding his hand and looking up at him.

"I was terribly sorry to hear about your wife," she said. "She was very lovely."

"Thank you," Ross said.

"I don't mean to be annoying, and you must say so if I am." Claudia dropped his hand and waved down the room. "But I'm here with my husband and sister and some friends, and we wondered if there was any chance that you might like to join us for dessert and coffee?"

"I should like that very much," Ross replied, and he was vaguely surprised to realize that he meant it.

The others were sitting at a round table in the corner of the conservatory that opened off of the dining room. As Ross and Claudia approached, the men got to their feet. A waiter bustled behind to bring an extra chair and make room for a seventh place setting. Ross was struck by the appearance of these people. Each of the six was young and beautiful. He had the distinct impression that he'd stumbled into one of those BBC television plays that are exclusively concerned with handsome members of the upper classes who go to Oxford or Cambridge, where they form lifelong and not particularly complex bonds.

When they were all sitting down again and engaged in a discussion of the dessert trolley, Ross had a chance to observe them more closely. The men were essentially similar and of a type. In their early to mid-thirties, they had already done well for themselves in both their marriages and their professions, and now had a slightly pompous air of public goodwill about them.

Tarquin Lassiter, Claudia Furnival's husband, was the youngest of the three men; a dark young man whose rather fierce demeanor made a complementary and romantic counterpoint to the fragility of his wife. The other two, Edward Hall and Anthony Derringham, were blond and conventionally handsome. But Ross thought he detected, beneath their flawless exteriors, a hint of less appropriate, and therefore more interesting, tension between the two. They have a bone to pick with one another, he thought. And his policeman's mind could not help wondering what it was.

The remaining two women were perhaps equally predictable, but rather more interesting. Juliet Furnival was the identical twin to her sister, and there the similarity ended. In looking at them, Ross found himself thinking of two paintings, each of the same model, each by a master, each with the same palette, composition, and light. Identical, with an entirely different interpretation. There was no hint of frailty to Juliet Furnival. Like her twin, she had almond-shaped eyes, the peculiarly long and graceful neck, the hands of a Modigliani; yet there was no sense of vulnerability in this woman. Unless he was much mistaken, Ross thought—and given his powers of observation and his profession, that was rare—Juliet Furnival was honed, polished, and tempered of steel.

Angela Derringham, on the other hand, reminded him of liquid glass. She was as tall and fair and pale as a Renaissance madonna, a lovely woman with a quick smile and worried eyes. She leaned toward him and laughed.

"You'll have to excuse our manners, Inspector," she said. "You probably feel as if you've just been tipped into the middle of a rather raucous children's outing."

"Which is precisely what it is," her husband said. "We've escaped for the evening."

"Escaped?" Ross asked.

"Oh, come along," Edward Hall said, turning back to the table after making his choice from the trolley. "It's not all that bad."

"Oh yes, it bloody well is!" The last was contributed by Claudia Furnival, and, having said so, she turned away from the table to continue her examination of the cakes and fruit tarts and inevitable custard flan.

"I guess it is," Edward Hall said, smiling. "Mea culpa. Let's have a bottle of champagne to kiss it better."

"What we are referring to," Angela Derringham said to Ross, "is the cottage we've been staying in. You see, Claudia's been in *Macbeth* at the festival in Edinburgh, and it was Edward's brilliant idea that we rent a cottage up here afterward, for a holiday."

"Not a bad idea in itself," Edward added.

"No," she agreed. "Just a bloody awful cottage."

There was a general burst of laughter, followed by the sharp pop of a champagne cork. Claudia Furnival turned back to the table. She sat directly across from Ross, and through the glitter of the candlelight, her eyes seemed hidden in a mask from the Biannale, the only living things in a perfect porcelain face.

"It's haunted," she said quietly. The champagne was poured and one of the men raised a glass.

"To . . . to what?"

"To Claudia." It was her husband speaking. "To *Macbeth.*"

"It is," she reiterated. She spoke directly to Ross now, as if the rest of the group, the rest of the room, did not exist. "There's something there. I can feel it. You can't see it, but it's there. Things disappear." The rest of the table had become quiet.

"They do," Claudia Furnival insisted. "Matches, a lighter. Not the expensive kind. Just . . . just things. A pen. Sunglasses. A headband."

Her voice had grown rapid, though her face remained immobile. Only the trapped eyes were alive. This is what they talk about, Ross thought suddenly, this is what she does on the stage that is so extraordinary.

"Darling." Her husband reached out and covered her hand with his own. Claudia paused for a moment and looked down at her plate.

"Well, they do," she said quietly. "You know they do and you know I hate it." She turned and fixed herself on him. "Why do we have to stay there?" she asked. "Why can't we just go home? Or check in here? Why can't we check in here for the rest of the week?"

"Come on, Clu, don't be silly," Edward Hall said. "You've been seeing witches for too long. It's not as bad as all that."

"Too many weird sisters," Angela Derringham said. Ross glanced at her troubled face as she watched Claudia and Tarquin Lassiter across the table.

"Tell me, Inspector," Juliet Furnival said, "do you believe in ghosts?"

The group looked to him, smiling, relieved to turn the attention away from Claudia.

"I don't know," Ross said. "I suppose not, but one can never really be sure, can one?"

"What is a ghost anyway?" Angela asked. "Sometimes I

think they're more of, I don't know, a memory. An energy. An echo of a life."

"You mean rather than something that runs around in a bed sheet going bump in the night?" her husband asked. ·

"Yes," Angela replied. "And that's why, I think, some of us hear them and some of us don't. We don't all remember the same things after all, do we?"

Indeed we do not, Ross thought as he reached for his glass.

The energy at the table had dissipated, and it was not long afterward that the party broke up.

"Back to beautiful Balnacairn," Tarquin Lassiter said, putting his arm around his wife as they walked across the wide lobby of the hotel.

"Oh, it's pretty pastoral, really," Angela said. "Just a bit too atmospheric, that's all."

The night was soft and alive with stars as they stood in the gravel forecourt. Ross could feel the bulk of Glendevon rising before them into the summer dark.

"Come on," Anthony said. "We've all got to pile back into the clown car."

"We've got another one," Edward said, turning to Ross and shaking his hand, "but no sooner did we rent the bloody thing than it ended up in the garage."

"Never mind," Angela said, "we'll all pile into this. I suppose that up here one really ought to call it a 'shooting brake,' but now we've gone all American and call them 'station wagons.'"

"Careful, Angie," Edward said. "Next thing you know, you'll be stooping to Burger King. And wouldn't that be a fall from grace?"

She looked to Edward, and Ross was startled to find himself thinking that what passed between them looked momentarily like hatred. It's the night, he thought. Perhaps the wine.

"Inspector." Claudia Furnival was reaching her hand

out to him again. "Thank you for joining us." Again he felt the birdlike bones, the unexpected strength of her grip.

"I'm sorry I don't know, but what role have you been playing in *Macbeth?*"

"Can't you guess?" she asked with a smile.

"Go on, Clu," her sister said. "Do it for us." Juliet looked at Ross. "Hecate," she said. "The queen of the night, the dark spirit that one meets at the crossroads."

As Juliet spoke, Claudia Furnival stepped away from them into the courtyard. The dark mass of hills rose somewhere behind her, and the lights from the hotel shone on her face. It seemed to grow whiter and more abstract against the backdrop of the highland night. She half turned and then raised her arms, facing them again, and her voice, when she began to speak, was changed: bitter and dangerous as broken glass.

> "Have I not reason, beldams as you are?
> Saucy and overbold, how did you dare
> To trade and traffic with Macbeth
> In riddles and affairs of death;"

No one moved as she stepped back and continued.

> "And I the mistress of your charms,
> The close contriver of all harms,
> Was never called to bear my part,
> Or share the glory of our art?"

As she went on, Ross remembered the superstitions surrounding what some theater people will only call the "Scottish play." Watching Claudia Furnival become Hecate, he was moved to recall that there were those who believed that Macbeth was cursed, that the witches spell that Shakespeare wrote was not, in fact, his own, but a real spell, an incantation of true evil let loose in each performance.

Claudia was ending, and her words came clearly out into the night.

> "Your vessels and your spells provide,
> Your charms and everything beside.
> I am for the air; this night I'll spend
> Unto a dismal and a fatal end."

2

The next day Ross fished. The water was low on the Spey and he could sense the salmon lying sluggishly at the bottom of the still, dark pools. An otter appeared and disappeared amongst the low-lying underbrush at the far side of the river. Ross was predisposed to think of this as a hopeful sign, since otters are infinitely wiser than men when it comes to the whereabouts of fish. Toward sunset his optimism was rewarded. A bite resulted in an appropriately picturesque battle in the lower rapids as a hardy salmon took, ran and played the line. In the end Ross landed him with the help of the ghillie and was rewarded with a perfectly respectable catch that would, in the morning, be dispatched to the smoker in Auchterarder. As they walked back toward the Land Rover, Ross adjusted his rod case and contemplated his fish fondly, thinking largely in terms of capers and thinly sliced rye.

He was still in this slightly giddy state of postfishing euphoria upon their arrival back at Gleneagles. A soft and singularly Celtic rain had begun to fall, misting down from Glendevon and wrapping the hotel in a damp and rosy August evening light that might be described as "gloaming." As he ran his bath he felt an overwhelming desire to hum "Loch Lomond." This, he realized, was too much. The next step could be interjecting "auch" into sentences and whistling "Scotland the Brave" on the way to breakfast. The situation was getting out of hand. It would sober him up to watch the news.

They had not got back from fishing until quite late, and his table in the dining room was reserved for half past nine. He could just catch the nine o'clock news while he dressed. The television was discreetly hidden in a cabinet that also housed his sock drawer. The resulting effect was such that, while he selected his socks, he came face-to-face with Kate Adie reporting live from Beirut. Ross, in common with ninety percent of the men in the U.K., was hopelessly smitten with Kate Adie. He stepped back to get a better look at her, to take in the sharp intelligence of that face, the cheekbones, red hair, and sincere, sad eyes. He sat on the end of his bed holding his socks, utterly pixilated by the way she had turned up the collar of her shirt. He hoped that she was not cold, and then remembered that it was August in the Mideast and that this would, therefore, be unlikely.

The picture flashed from Kate Adie to a complex map of the region, of the sort the BBC savored, with lots of moving symbols and lines and arrows. Ross returned his attention to his socks. It was odd, he thought, smiling to himself, that for all of his adoration of Ms. Adie, he could not imagine having dinner with her. He could only see her, hear her, reporting against the backdrop of famine, strife, and danger. If she were to have dinner with him, it would be a tense affair. She would be wearing her trench coat, possibly holding a microphone, and he would spend the entire meal expecting half of the dining room to blow up behind them.

He was lost in this peculiarly enjoyable idiocy when the news broadcast switched back to the domestic scene, causing all thoughts of Kate Adie to fly from his head. He got to his feet and stood staring at the television as an announcement was made that late that afternoon the bodies of the actress Claudia Furnival, her sister Juliet, and their husbands—the Right Honorable Tarquin Lassiter and Mr. Edward Hall—had been found in a holiday cottage in Scotland. It appeared, the announcer added, that they had been the victims of violent death and that the Royal Scottish Constabulary were treating the case as murder.

Ross stood staring at the television as the picture cut away to location footage. There was a murky shot of the front of a cottage, its facade lit garishly with police floodlights which glowed and refracted in the light rain. Off camera a blue police light was flashing, and it lit the side of the local correspondent's face as he turned toward the camera.

"The bodies were found here," he said, "in a remote holiday cottage in Balnacairn at approximately half past five this afternoon. They were discovered by friends of the victims who had spent the day sightseeing in Edinburgh. Claudia Furnival had recently appeared in *Macbeth* at the Edinburgh Festival and was due to begin rehearsals for her first leading role in Britain's National Theatre in a production of *The Caucasian Chalk Circle* later this month. The police are treating the case as murder, but as of yet have divulged no information concerning the nature of the crime. Detective Chief Inspector Andrew Callum, the senior officer in charge of the investigation, spoke to us a few minutes ago."

The camera cut away to Chief Inspector Callum, a youngish, rugged-looking man in a Barbour jacket. If he had not been standing on the site of a quadruple murder, thought Ross, one might have taken him to be an instructor at the shooting school. His accent, when he spoke, was local.

"The police arrived here at Balnacairn approximately an hour ago after receiving a 999 call. The scene-of-crime officer is still inside, and when he's finished, I'll have a formal statement for you. In the meantime, this area has been sealed and an incident room is being set up at Blairlochie. This was an exceptionally brutal crime and we're asking anyone who had contact with any member of this party or thinks that they may have anything useful to tell us to ring in to the incident room at Blairlochie."

"Do I understand that you do not have a suspect at this time?" the correspondent asked.

"That is correct," Callum said.

"Were they shot, Chief Inspector?"

Callum shook his head. "I'll be making a more detailed statement from Blairlochie later tonight."

The camera cut away and returned to the studio, where the announcer repeated the incident-room number as it was flashed onto the screen. Ross reached for a pen on the desk and scrawled the number across the top of a postcard he had forgotten to mail to his sister.

It was after eleven o'clock when the phone rang in Ross's room. He had been waiting for the call, and as he reached out to lift the receiver, he knew that it would be Chief Inspector Andrew Callum. On the phone Callum's accent was slightly thicker than it sounded on television. It was a rolling Scots brogue, appropriate to his sandy-colored hair and generally Highland demeanor.

"Superintendent, good evening, sir. I'm sorry to be so long in getting back to you."

"Don't worry, Chief Inspector," Ross said, "I wasn't asleep."

"My notation here says that you knew the victims?"

"Yes," Ross replied. "In a manner of speaking. In fact I had dinner with them last night." Was it possible? he wondered. Could it have been just over twenty-four hours ago that they sat in the dining room drinking a bottle of champagne that was going to "kiss it better"? He shook his head slightly; Callum was speaking again.

"Last night?" he asked.

"I met them in the dining room here at Gleneagles."

"I see," Callum said. "And you knew them previously, did you, sir?"

"I had met Claudia Furnival several years ago. I didn't know them. No. I joined them for a drink and spent, oh, perhaps an hour with them."

"I see," Callum said again. "And what time would that have been, sir?"

Ross thought for a moment. "I would say from approximately nine to perhaps half past ten at the latest."

"Yes," Callum said. Ross could sense him thinking on the other end of the phone. "I think perhaps we should have a word in person," he said slowly. "Perhaps . . ." He let the sentence drift off, and Ross had a sudden image of the chaos that surrounds the first hours of a homicide investigation. The last thing that the senior officer was likely to have time to do was drive over to Gleneagles to interview a probably not very important witness, even if he were a superintendent.

"If it would be of any help," Ross found himself saying, "I could come to you."

"It would be helpful," Callum said slowly. "I have to be back there tomorrow morning quite early, if you can manage it."

Ross realized that Callum was speaking not of the Blairlochie police station, but of the crime site itself. As he wrote down the directions Callum dictated, he could not help feeling a small, instinctive surge of professional curiosity.

Later that night Ross sat in the armchair beside the large casement window of his room and stared out toward the dark shadow of Glendevon. He was not watching the stars or the faint glow of northern light on the horizon. Instead he was watching Claudia Furnival. He could see her clearly, arms raised and outstretched, hands reaching, becoming not fingers, but talons, eyes black and full. Hecate, the darkest of all dark spirits. The one that stands at the crossroads. Never again would she touch the earth. Under which sky now, he wondered, was she flying, through which dismal night?

3

A single lane ran along the eastern edge of the loch. It rose and fell with the folds of the shoreline until all sign of civilization was out of sight, lost behind the trees and thickening hedgerows. At the loch's edge a tangle of baby oak and briar ran down to the still, brown water.

It was beautiful in its wild way, Ross thought as he crept slowly up the next hill and around the corner. On his right there was a passing place, a shallow dent cut into the hedgerow. They were spaced every two hundred yards or so and were not generous. Meeting another car would require some clever reversing. Ross could not help thinking what unutterable chaos there must have been last night, the narrow lane clogged with police cars, ambulances, and the press.

This morning it did not appear that he would have to test his reversing skills. Since he had entered the lane at

Balquhidder, he hadn't seen a soul. At the top of the lane he had passed a few driveways and had noticed a small church and several rather pretty houses perched above the loch. But that had been some time ago. For the last several miles there had been no evidence of habitation of any kind. The hedgerows had grown thicker and wilder, closing off the view behind him; he felt as if he were entering his own private world.

Just as he had begun to wonder if he had, after all, got it wrong and if this loch was in fact a river that he might follow aimlessly forever, he turned a corner and realized the end was in sight. Below him the loch abruptly ended, its waters coming up to a muddy stretch of beach that faded away into a bog. The glen continued on, however, and a little way up there lay a farm. From where he sat in his rental car, Ross could see a small squad of police vans spread among the buildings.

There was nothing picturesque about the cluster of barns that lay straggled across the bottom of the valley. Even from a distance Ross could sense the meanness of their proportions, the peeling paint, the sense, not just of hard times, but of neglect. A certain aura of bitterness, of hopes betrayed, rose from the farm and hung above the low cow sheds and muddy yards. As he let out the clutch and moved down the hill, Ross thought that it was, quite literally, the end of the road.

The gate was metal, set in a wire fencing. Once, a very long time ago, it might have been dark green. Now it was mud-spattered and mottled in rust. In place of a latch there was only a loop of chain and, dangling from it, a padlock that looked incongruously new and shiny. Luckily, the padlock was not in use. The gate stood open and Ross drove in without hesitating.

The paved drive, where there was any paving left at all, was pitted with holes and frost heaves. In places the tarmac had fallen away altogether, leaving large stretches of rutted dirt track. Well, Ross thought, at least his embarrassingly shiny new Avis-try-harder car would return to Gleneagles looking suitably muddied. It would appear that he had been out huntin' and shootin' and fishin' in the true spirit of a sportsman, instead of offering himself as a witness at a quadruple murder.

The drive led him directly into the main farmyard, flanked on two sides by sheds and on the third by a farmhouse. Beyond the yard was a row of long, low aluminum cow barns. The drive passed these and, after crossing a small stream, turned up the hillside toward two identical cottages. The cottages stood some distance apart along the side of the hill, one slightly above the other. They were perhaps a quarter of a mile from the main yard. It didn't take great powers of deduction to guess which of them must have been the holiday rental.

A neon yellow band of police tape had been strung around the property, looped through the newly painted green wicket fencing that encircled the small garden. Two panda cars and an unmarked police car were parked in the drive. A forensics van had pulled onto the nettled verge on the far side of the garden.

Ross stopped behind the panda cars and rolled down his window to speak to the approaching uniformed constable.

"I'm sorry, sir, this is a closed police site," the constable said, leaning down to Ross's open window. Ross handed him his identification wallet. The constable looked at it quizzically. It was true that Ross was a superintendent with the Kent County CID, but he was a long way from his jurisdiction.

"DCI Callum requested I meet him here," Ross offered by way of explanation.

"I see, sir." The constable handed the wallet back and looked up. He was spared any further conversation by the arrival of Callum, who had come out of the front door of the cottage and was making his way toward Ross's car.

Ross recognized him from the television and got out to greet him. A light rain felt cool on his face and hands after the stuffiness of the car.

"Superintendent Ross, I presume," Callum said, smiling. "Thank you for coming all the way out here. As you may gather, we've quite a little mess on our hands."

"I don't know how much help I can be, Chief Inspector," Ross said. "You do understand that I simply met them by chance in the Gleneagles dining room."

Callum nodded. "That I do. However," he continued, "with the exception of the friends who found them, Angela and Anthony Derringham, we now believe that you may have been the last person to see them alive." Callum glanced up at the sky, which was low and gray and promising more rain. He gestured toward a blue Range Rover and smiled. "Shall we get out of the rain a bit?"

Settled comfortably in the front of the Range Rover, Ross told Callum his story. In repetition, he thought as he spoke, it sounded inconsequential and rather odd.

At the end of his recitation, Callum looked at him and then stared abstractedly out of the window for a moment before he asked, "And what else?"

Ross smiled. Now, he thought, we come to the real issue.

"Tension," he said, recalling the faces lit with candlelight, the civilized and soothing sounds of the dining room beyond, the sense that an argument lingered, poking its lethal tip into the gathering like the icebergs all sailors fear.

"Between?" Callum asked.

"Edward Hall and Derringham, most noticeably. And Edward Hall and Angela Derringham, as well. Juliet Furnival and everyone, I would have said."

"And Claudia Furnival?"

Ross thought for a moment. The word that came to mind instantly was fear, but that seemed both ridiculous and melodramatic, and he was not sure that he would have thought of it if she were not now dead.

"Wrought up," he said carefully. "Very edgy."

"Drunk? Drugs?"

Ross thought for a moment and shook his head. "I don't think so," he said. "No. I think it was just temperament. The others, in particular Angela Derringham and her husband, Lassiter, were protective."

"Was she afraid?"

Ross thought carefully before answering. "She certainly hated this place," he said. "As a rest cure, I would have said that it was a miserable failure."

Callum looked at him out of the corner of his eye. "Yes," he said. He reached for the door handle. "I wonder if you'd mind, Superintendent, having a look inside. I wouldn't mind the benefit of your opinion. Off-the-record, of course."

"Of course," Ross replied.

The cottage had been recently painted. In the sun it might have looked pristine, possibly even cheerful, but in the August rain the dark green trim looked almost black and the whitewash appeared to be running down the brick in a thin, soured coat.

The two men went through the gate and up the muddy and slick flagstone path. The garden was mown, and an unenthusiastic line of begonias ran along the wall under what Ross presumed to be the kitchen window. Callum handed Ross a pair of latex gloves before pushing open the front door.

"This is the only entrance," he said. "The shooter came in this way, and there was no sign of the door being forced. I'm sorry," he said when he saw the look on Ross's face. "I didn't tell you. They were shot, with a shotgun, a twenty-bore I should think, from the spread."

Ross felt a familiar twisting in his gut. There was a particular sense of carnage to shotgun killings that he had always found especially nauseating. He followed Callum through the door and into a small glassed-in front entry. Several pairs of gum boots sat on the rush matting. A Barbour and a Puffa vest hung from hooks along the back wall, as well as a well-used rod case and an umbrella. A second glass-paneled door led into the kitchen. Two forensics men in coveralls were on their knees dusting the insides of the cabinets, the front of the aging gas stove, the space under the sink. The oak laminate kitchen table was already covered in a thin layer of fingerprint dust. One of the men was carefully bagging and labeling a notepad that had hung on the front of one of the upper cabinets. He looked up at Callum and smiled.

"Lo, guvnor," he said. "Small bits and bobs are out of the sitting room. We're ready to move the furniture on your say-so."

"Yeah, all right," Callum said. "They've done what they have to. You can take it anytime." He turned to Ross. "This room was undisturbed. As best as we can make out, he walked right through here and into the hallway." He stepped toward the door leading to the hall and Ross followed. The light was on and Ross could see a narrow stone-floored passage that ran along the side of the small house. To the left a set of steep stairs went up to the bedrooms. The walls had been papered in a chintzlike print of overblown pink and green roses. A few not very nice watercolors hung along the passageway; they were the standard pastoral scenes of lochs and highland moors. Ross followed them down the passage to the back wall, where the wallpaper was peppered and ripped with shot, stained with a huge brown smear instantly recognizable as human blood. Another watercolor lay broken, smashed against the floor. As he looked up, Ross could see smatterings along the top of the ceiling.

"That was Claudia Furnival," Callum said from behind him. "As far as we can make out, she must have heard a noise in the kitchen, come out into the passage to see who it was." He stepped past Ross into the hallway. "The others were in here, in the sitting room," he said.

The room was not overly large, but seemed even smaller because of its low ceiling and its scattered furniture. A picture window took up most of the far wall. It had been shattered. Shards of glass still stuck out from the frame and sills. The two men stood just inside the doorway. A cheap nylon-covered couch had been pushed back against the wall at a forty-five-degree angle, as if someone had tried to shove it toward the door for protection. Two side tables were toppled. The television screen had been shot out. Two matching armchairs, one on either side of the false mantel that housed a gas fire, were still in place. There was blood everywhere. Despite air through the shattered window, the room still smelled like an abattoir.

"Edward Hall was in the far corner," Callum said, nodding toward the sofa, "Juliet Furnival in the far armchair. Never even got to her feet. They were having tea by the looks of it," he added.

"Tarquin Lassiter?" Ross asked. He knew the answer before Callum spoke.

"Here," Callum said, pointing to the center of the floor where the carpeting was soaked in brown. Of course, Ross thought. He was moving toward the passage. He was trying to protect his wife.

"The tea things, smaller pieces, have been bagged and removed," Callum said. "We'll get the furniture out of here today. The telephone line had been cut about a quarter of a mile back up the loch road." He turned and stepped out of the room.

"May I see the upstairs?" Ross asked.

Callum nodded. "It was undisturbed as far as we could tell," he said. "Three bedrooms, one bath." He led the way up the narrow stairs to the above hallway.

At the head of the stairs they faced the bathroom door,

propped open, its white panels covered in the telltale dust of the fingerprinters. Ross could see a large claw-footed tub, a single porcelain washbasin, and a toilet made of molded pea-green plastic. There was a carpet on the floor that echoed the same large pattern of roses. On a stand by the tub there was a dish of tiny soaps in the shape of rosebuds. Blue and lavender and pink, the kind one found in the cheaper sort of gift shop where the smell of potpourri stifled the air.

The bedrooms were at either end of the hallway, with one in the middle facing backward, away from the farm and into the hills. All three rooms had double beds with slightly sagging mattresses and white-painted iron bedposts. They might have been picturesque in a Victorian sort of way, but they weren't. The huge wardrobes in each of the three rooms dwarfed almost everything else. Two of the rooms had bureaus. In one, a cheval glass stood, slightly cockeyed, in the corner.

Ross had a sudden sense of claustrophobia. How on earth had they come to be here? Callum was already making his way back down the narrow staircase. Ross turned and followed him, glad to be leaving this place that still held the slightly acrid tinge of gunpowder, almost echoed with the sound of shot, the reverberation of slaughter.

"I've got to go along and see the Derringhams," Callum said as they stepped out onto the pathway. "They're at a hotel halfway up the loch, on the far side. He was utterly hysterical last night, a total basket case. Do you know them?"

"I met them at dinner," Ross said. "That's all."

"You can follow me up if you'd care to," Callum said. "She might appreciate a familiar face." He gestured back toward the cottage. "Any thoughts?"

"I would have thought it was a professional job."

"The phone line?"

"That and the general efficiency of it. And the method. People who aren't accustomed to killing probably wouldn't use a shotgun. They'd prefer cleaner methods so their nerve wouldn't fail."

Callum stared at his Range Rover for a moment before replying. "On the other hand, shotguns are very easy to get ahold of." He looked at Ross for a moment. "We've found some latents, rather a lot of them in fact. Fingerprints all over the place, including upstairs. So far not the victims', nor the Derringhams'. You can follow me if you like."

"Right," Ross said, and he watched as Callum opened the door and climbed in behind the wheel.

The rain wasn't cold, and by the time Ross got to his car it had built up in a fine film on his cheeks and hair. As he turned the ignition and started to follow Callum, he noticed that they were not turning around but going straight on along the drive, running away from the cottages and along the side of the hill above the farm toward the loch. He supposed that it must form a separate entrance, joining up with the lane farther along, making it unnecessary for anyone coming to the cottages to pass through the farmyard. He watched as the blue rear end of Callum's Range Rover disappeared over a rise. He hoped he did not end up with his rental car in the bog.

He had let the clutch out and was just moving off down the drive when he caught the movement in the rearview mirror. He braked sharply as he stared into the mirror. A figure stood on the hill above the cottage. He could see her quite clearly, an old woman dressed in black, standing still on the side of the hill in the rain. He couldn't make out her face through the streaked back window of the car, but he could tell from the way she stood that she was old. He could also feel her watching him.

Ross felt a peculiar tingle run down the back of his neck. Slowly he let out the clutch again and began to move down the drive. She did not move. He could still see her hunched black figure against the gray receding hill.

I saw him today, the tall man. He comes because the women who had one face and their men are dead. They died when the loch turns white, when the hawks go out across the moor, when the fox is sleeping. But not me. I see everything.

I saw him too, and her. He knew I was there, but he could not see me. He went to their place and she came too, but this time she was crying. She was crying and he talked to her, but still she cried. She cried and cried and clung to him. And he said, "Now, the time is now." And she said, "I am afraid."

4

The hotel where Angela and Anthony Derringham were staying, from which they had called the police the night before, was at the top end of the loch, just across the water from the church Ross had noticed as he drove into Balquhidder Glen. It took ten minutes to get there from the holiday cottage. The drive was dark and narrow, flanked by rhododendrons, to Ross's mind a peculiarly Victorian ornament, like yew and cyprus, all of which reminded him of Bram Stoker and Dickens and William Wilkie Collins. As he unfolded himself from the depths of his rental car and stepped onto the inevitable gravel courtyard, he wondered if he wasn't going a little batty.

The house that rose up before him was undoubtably Victorian. It was all gray stone, peaked gables with ornamental tiling, and mullioned windows surrounded by dark red trim. He was certain the bedrooms were decorated in plaid and had names like "Ballantrae" and "Flora Mac-Donald." There would be a large barnlike dining room where the gentlemen of the house would have paced back and forth before the fireplace eating salted porridge and shouting at their children. It was very much the sort of thing calculated to appeal to Americans.

As Ross crossed the courtyard to join Callum, waiting for him under the wide and ivy hung porch, he was startled by the very un-Victorian sound of a moped. It was actually two mopeds, and they came whizzing down the drive at something close to breakneck speed. They swerved wildly to miss Ross as they first careened into the courtyard, and then disappeared down a service drive to the left. As he watched them go, Ross smiled. One moped was red and the other was yellow, and they were obviously very new. He hadn't been able to see the faces of the riders, given their trendy helmets, but from the size of them he would have guessed they were twelve or thirteen. He joined Callum on the hotel steps, and as they went inside he noticed that the RAC sign discreetly mounted to the right of the door announced that the establishment's name was the Rob Roy. It was only then that he remembered why it was that the name Balquhidder had been so familiar to him. It was here, in this very glen, that the aging robber baron had holed up against the forces of British law some two hundred years before.

The entrance hall stretched away before them with the sort of downscale baronial splendor popular for the middle-class hunting lodges of the period. There was a stone fireplace with the requisite antlers above. A massively ugly dark staircase ran both ways along the back of the hall. It framed a dark stained-glass window whose colors clashed with the yards upon yards of Wilton carpet. A reception desk was to the right of the stairs. Behind it hung the inevitable "Monarch of the Glen." Not a particularly inviting place to come for comfort, Ross thought, when one had just found the bodies of one's friends blown to pieces with a shotgun. But then, where would be?

Detective Chief Inspector Callum was about to ring the brass bell marked Service on the reception desk when Ross heard a woman speak his name. Both men looked up to see Angela Derringham standing on the landing.

She wore a pair of dark green suede trousers and what looked to be a man's pullover. Her hair did not look particularly well-brushed, and she was even paler than Ross remembered.

"Chief Inspector," she said. "Superintendent. I wondered when you'd come." She came down the stairs toward them hesitantly. As she approached, Ross realized that her tentative quality was due more to exhaustion than timidity. She seemed both keyed up and ready to collapse. Hardly surprising in the circumstances, Ross thought, and probably clinically describable as shock. Andrew Callum clearly thought the same thing. He rang the bell at his elbow decisively.

"I was hoping, Mrs. Derringham," he said kindly, "that you might be ready to talk to us now? But perhaps we ought to get some coffee first?"

"Thank you," she said. "Yes. Of course. My husband Anthony's asleep still. They called a doctor last night and he gave him something, Halcyon or something. Can you do with just me for the moment?"

Callum rang the bell again, and while no one remotely resembling hotel staff appeared, a WPC did. She was a thick-set girl with red hair and dimples. She resembled a milkmaid rather more than a detective sergeant.

"Jane," Callum said, "find us someone to get some coffee, would you? This is Superintendent Ross, from Kent. He's a friend of Mrs. Derringham's and he'll be joining us. Mrs. Derringham's ready to make a statement, I think. Superintendent, Detective Sergeant Trew." With that by way of an introduction, Callum turned and led the way across the hall to a sitting room.

It was ten minutes before Sergeant Trew joined them in the sitting room. She was followed by a small, dark-haired woman bearing a tray of coffee cups. To Ross's eye, she was unmistakably a Londoner. As she put the tray down, there was the sound of running footsteps in the hallway. Ross turned in time to see two young boys streak through, giggling and banging the brass bell as they went.

"David! Colin!" the dark woman shouted. "I am sorry," she said, turning back to them and arranging the tray on a side table. "Those two will be the death of me, I swear. Just ring if you'd like some hot. I'll shut the doors—shall I?—and that way you won't be disturbed."

"Thank you, Mrs. Coley," Jane Trew said. Ross took his cup and moved away, sitting slightly back, away from Angela and the two police officers. Sergeant Trew had notebook and pen out, Andrew Callum was stirring his coffee, staring absently into the cup as if he might read his fortune there. Angela Derringham held her cup and saucer carefully, taking automatic sips like an obedient child or someone in a Nescafé commercial.

Andrew Callum finally put his cup down and looked up at her. "I wonder, then, Mrs. Derringham," he said, "if you'd like to tell me what happened?"

Angela looked almost surprised, as if she had forgotten why they were all sitting there. "Yes," she said, putting her cup down. "Of course. Where would you like me to start?"

"You arrived here when?" Callum asked.

"About a week ago. They'd been here a bit longer. A few days before us. We flew up from London and joined them."

"You rented a car at the airport?"

"That's right. It broke down almost immediately. Anthony, my husband, was furious. We made Hertz pay, to have it repaired here. Actually we collected it yesterday morning. Tarquin drove us to the garage. Then we went on to Edinburgh."

"I see," Callum said. He looked thoughtfully at his jacket cuff and then smiled at Angela Derringham again. "Before we get to that, to yesterday," he said, "could we just back up a bit? You came up for a holiday, did you?"

"Yes," Angela replied. "We'd planned it ages ago, back in the spring. The festival—the Edinburgh Festival, I mean—is always very hard on the actors. It's a long haul, lots of performances back to back. And Claudia would be going straight down to London afterward, next week, to start rehearsals. So they thought this would be a good time for a bit of a break. They asked us if we'd like to come up. We're old friends," she added.

"I see," Callum said, "and when you got here, what did you do?"

"Nothing really. That was the point. I don't know. We went for walks, visited the distillery, the one up the road, poked about old churches, went to Glamis. Claudia did her witch's bit on the ramparts there—it was rather good actually. We talked about going to the Falls of Shin, but no one had the energy. We went to Gleneagles for supper instead." She looked up at Ross and smiled quickly.

"And then yesterday," Callum said, "you went to Edinburgh for the day. Just you and your husband?"

"Yes," she said. "We hadn't had much time alone together so we . . . we decided to do that."

"And could you tell us, Mrs. Derringham, what you did during the day?" She nodded. "As precisely as you can." Callum said, smiling.

"Well, we got there at about eleven, I should think."

"Where did you park?"

"In a lot. One of those high-rise places just off Princes Street, I believe. And then we walked most of the day. We went up to the castle. And then we had lunch in an Italian sort of place, Bertoni's or something, I think it was called.

It's just below the castle. And then we took a taxi to Holyrood and did that in the afternoon. We'd not been to Edinburgh before, so we wanted to do the touristy things."

"And after Holyrood?"

"Well, it was getting late. We took a taxi back to the Caledonian. It was about half past three. We stopped at Waterstone's, the bookshop."

"Buy anything?"

She shook her head. "No, I wanted the new biography of Edwina Mountbatten, but they didn't have it. It was sold out. So we thought we'd better get on. We'd told the others we'd be back by five or so. We were going to walk up here, actually, for an early supper."

"So you left Edinburgh at . . . ?"

"About four. Perhaps just after."

"And you arrived at the farm?"

"Half past five. We were about half an hour later than we planned to be."

"And then?"

"We parked behind the other car and everything looked normal, but the lights weren't on. And I remember I said to Anthony, 'Perhaps they've walked up to the hotel?' I expected there'd be a note on the door or the kitchen table." She put her cup down carefully and stared out of the window for a moment. Then she looked back at Callum and began to speak again. "We went inside. Anthony went first and I came behind him. When we got into the kitchen, he turned on the light. I was looking for a note, you know, putting my handbag down, and he said, 'I'll just go upstairs,' and he stepped into the hall and he turned on the light and then he screamed." She looked up at Callum and blinked. "He screamed and screamed and I couldn't think what it was. He'd sort of collapsed against the door, and I went to him and at first I didn't even see because I was looking at him, trying to—and then I did see. I did see."

She closed her eyes and swallowed. Sergeant Trew

glanced at Callum, but he raised his hand and she stayed still. A moment later Angela Derringham opened her eyes and continued to speak.

"I got Anthony, I sort of dragged him to the table and I put him in a chair and I made him put his head between his knees. And then I—I knew I had to go down to the sitting room. I didn't know where the others were, if it was just Claudia or if—I thought . . . I thought if they were there, that one of them might still be alive, might need . . ." The room was utterly silent as she paused and then went on. Only Ross noticed the slight movement of a side door, saw the almost imperceptible turning of the knob. "I went down the hall," Angela said. "I tried not to look at her, just to look straight ahead. I stepped over her and I saw into the sitting room. I saw there was no one there who could be alive. I stood there and then I ran. I ran back to the kitchen and I grabbed Anthony and I pulled him with me. I pulled him outside and I made him sit in the car and I told him to stay there, and I ran down to the shepherd's cottage. I remember I banged and banged on the door and I was shouting and then I realized it was open. I thought someone was there, I was sure of it, and I shouted, but no one answered. And then I saw the telephone on a table in the sitting room and I picked it up and I dialed 999 and nothing happened. And then I realized that there was no noise coming out of it. Nothing. It was dead."

"What time was it then, Mrs. Derringham?"

"Quarter of six. I remember. There's a clock in the sitting room, in the shepherd's sitting room, on the mantel. I was staring at it. I was trying to remember when he usually came in. We'd watch for him. He'd bring in some ewes and lambs usually, and we'd gone down to see them. And he had the collie and the pup. The puppy had a broken leg. It was in a splint, and sometimes he'd carry it in a sort of frontwise papoose thing. You know, like you do a baby.

Anyway, he wasn't there. I went back outside and I looked down at the farmhouse and there were no lights there either. And then suddenly I just felt hopeless. And I started to cry and I walked back up the hill to the cottage and our car, and Anthony was crying too and he was shaking all over, and so was I and I didn't know what to do. I got in the car and we just sat there, and then, finally, we came here."

"And you called the police at what time?" Callum asked.

She shook her head. "Not me. Mr. Coley, the proprietor. We came in and we must have looked an utter fright. Anthony couldn't really talk at all and he was shaking again. Just shaking. Shock. And Mrs. Coley went to fetch him a brandy and said we ought to call a doctor. I think they thought we'd been in a car accident or something. And I told Mr. Coley. He kept saying to me, 'Sit down, sit down, you can tell me all about it in a minute.' He was trying to be kind. But finally I shouted at him. I said, 'No. No, you don't understand. They're all dead. At the farm, they're all dead.' Because, you see, I'd got it into my head that that's why I couldn't find the shepherd and why the lights were off in the farmhouse. I didn't even dare look there. I was too scared. I thought I'd find—"

She stopped talking, and Ross could hear the sound of footsteps on the front stairs, the crunch of gravel as a gardener wheeled a barrow down the outside path.

"So Mr. Coley called the police?" Callum said quietly.

Angela Derringham nodded.

"At what time?" He glanced at Detective Sergeant Trew. She flipped back a few pages on her notebook.

"The call was logged at Blairlochie at six-forty P.M., sir."

"I see," Callum said. He was about to ask another question when there was a discreet tap on the door. A detective Ross did not recognize entered. He whispered a few words to Callum, who nodded and then stood up.

"Mrs. Derringham," he said, "you've been a great help.

Thank you. We shall want to talk to you and your husband again, perhaps this afternoon. You should be free to leave by tomorrow morning."

Angela Derringham was staring at Callum as if she didn't quite understand what he was saying. The words seemed to have the same effect on Jane Trew.

Callum turned to Ross and smiled. "A word before you go, Superintendent?"

Ross got to his feet and followed Callum out onto the porch, where they were joined by the unknown detective. Callum turned to Ross. He was grinning.

"We've got him," he said. "The shepherd. Twenty minutes ago they found his shotgun stuffed down behind a feed bin in one of the outer sheds. Next bin down they found a bag full of stuff: cameras, jewelry, cash. And I'll guarantee you that in an hour or two, when she sees them, Mrs. Derringham will identify them as the Furnivals'. Those prints in the cottage are going to be his. Clearly he's been cleaning the place out, went off his head and shot the lot of them. Bloody good thing she didn't meet him to ask for help." He shook Ross's hand and turned away toward the Range Rover. "Thanks for your help, Superintendent. I'll be in touch."

Ross stood on the porch and watched as the two policemen walked away through the rain.

5

It was none of his business. In the two days since Ross had been to the cottage, the story of the Furnival murders had been edged out of the headlines by an IRA bombing in London and the discovery of a cache of semiautomatic weapons under a hedgerow outside of Stirling. Andrew Callum had stopped by Gleneagles to thank him for his cooperation and to inform him that the shepherd from the farm, Danny Blaine, was being questioned at Blairlochie prior to being charged with the murders of Claudia and Juliet Furnival, Tarquin Lassiter and Edward Hall. The shotgun believed to be the murder weapon was his, and his fingerprints had been found all over the cottage. It appeared that he had come to rob the cottage, possibly in the belief that it was empty, surprised the occupants, gone berserk and shot them all. Callum had showed him a list of the loot that had been found in the feed bin, identified as belonging to the occupants of the cottage. It came to little more than a video camera, a string of pearls, a couple of watches, and less than a hundred pounds in cash. Such was the price of life, Ross thought. He had listened to Callum mainly in silence, and the conversation weighed heavily upon him. Now, as he walked down toward the hotel shooting range, the shotgun tucked neatly into his elbow, he found himself thinking not of speckled flights of lifting grouse, but of that blood-smeared room and of the pale, aristocratic figure of Angela Derringham.

The gun was a .20 bore over and under, often called a "ladies gun" due to its light weight. It held two cartridges at a time and was identical to the alleged murder weapon. Ross positioned himself in one of the shooting booths, lifted the shotgun, fired twice, cracked it and reloaded. Six seconds. And that was with the shells laid out beside him on the bench. He had been playing this game for almost a half hour now. Once in twenty rounds it had taken him as long as five seconds; sometimes it took him seven.

A pile of spent cartridges littered the floor of the shooting booth. He emptied the gun and laid it across the bench before bending to collect the cartridges and putting them in the bin. At least he had gotten good at potting double clays. That was something. As for the other, well, he couldn't see that it made any sense at all.

"Good morning, sir."

Ross turned and saw Alan Campbell, the head instructor at the shooting school, standing behind him. He lowered his earphones as Campbell spoke.

"I would say the pheasants haven't got much of a look in," Campbell was saying as he helped Ross collect the last of the cartridges. "You should try the high traps," he went on. "I'll open them for you, if you like."

"Thanks," Ross said, "I'd enjoy that."

The new clay traps were built on elevator towers. They released clays individually or simultaneously from any level on the tower at a variety of speeds. The two men settled themselves into a shooting booth, and Campbell adjusted the trap two-thirds of the way up the tower. He loaded his gun, also a .20 bore, like the one Ross held, and released the safety catch.

"The gun is live," Campbell said, and then he nodded to Ross, who pushed the button releasing the clays. They flew up and out over the shooting range in a perfect arc. Campbell raised his rifle and took them both in rapid succession with dead-center hits. He cracked the gun and ejected the cartridges.

"Do me a favor," Ross said as Campbell stepped back from the shelf of the booth. "I'm curious about how fast you can shoot, reload, and shoot one of these. I can't get it much below six seconds."

Campbell raised his eyebrows and smiled. "Shoot, reload, and shoot again?"

"That's right," Ross said, "as fast as you can."

"Right you are."

Campbell loaded his gun, readjusted his headphones, and nodded to Ross. Again the clays flew, and again Campbell took them out. In almost the same motion he cracked the gun, slid two more cartridges into the barrel and raised it to hit the second set of clays that Ross sent flying overhead. It took between five and six seconds. Alan Campbell was an expert. It simply couldn't be done any faster.

The telephone was ringing as Ross opened the door to his room. Slightly breathless as he answered, for a moment he thought that it had been disconnected, as there seemed to be only dead silence on the other end. Then he heard the voice of Angela Derringham.

"Inspector," she said. "I'm so very glad I caught you.

41

You see, we're going back tomorrow, to London, and I . . . well, I wanted to thank you."

Ross was inclined to ask her for what. He had done nothing to be of assistance to her that he could recall. She seemed to feel otherwise.

"It was so good of you to come," she said, and he realized that she was under the impression that when she was questioned at the hotel, he had been there in the role of knight-errant rather than witness for the prosecution.

"Anthony and I thought that if you might be over in this direction you could perhaps join us for a drink or an early supper this evening. Our flight's not until tomorrow morning."

There was something in her voice that went beyond a mere desire to repay one good deed with another. To Ross's practiced ear, it sounded as if Angela Derringham very much wanted to see him.

"Of course, Mrs. Derringham." he said. "I should be delighted to join you for a drink."

"I'm glad," she replied. "Shall we say six?"

"Six it is," Ross said. After he put the receiver down, he stood for a moment staring at it, as if it might tell him what exactly was on Angela Derringham's mind.

A soft golden light diffused the sky, turning the heather that ran across the hillsides pink and gray, lighting the long stretch of water that was Loch Earn to copper and bronze. Even the darker, peatier strip of the Balnacoil water seemed to soften and ripple in this northern summer light. The rhododendrons that lined the driveway of the Rob Roy were no more to Ross's taste tonight than they had been two days before, but the sinister quality had left them. With the front door standing open and several cars parked in the forecourt, the hotel looked at least somewhat welcoming.

He was closing his car door when he looked up and saw

Angela Derringham coming toward him from around the side of the building. She was wearing a pink silk dress that accentuated both her height and her lingering quality of frailty. She was smiling, but as she took Ross's hand, he could see the gray undertinge of exhaustion just below the powder and lipstick of her face. She was putting up a very good front indeed, and he could not help wondering why.

"We're in the garden drinking Pimms," she said, releasing his hand.

"What a good idea," he said. And she smiled at him again as they started back across the forecourt.

"It's rather gruesome, don't you think?" she said. He was not altogether certain whether she was referring to the murders or the hotel. "But they're frightfully proud of it," she went on. "And I do suppose they've done a nice restoration job. Personally, the Victorians have always given me the creeps." They were apparently discussing architecture, not homicide.

"It's never been my favorite," he concurred. They stepped onto the graveled path that led through another rhododendron hedge and out to the back garden. Here a wide lawn opened and ran down to a small ornamental pond and the pine plantation beyond. There were tables and chairs set out on the graveled terrace at the back of the house, and a croquet lawn, recently rolled, was on the right. Somewhere, Ross thought, possibly beyond that cypress hedge, there would be the remains of a grass tennis court, its posts tilting slightly in the old turf, and at its edge a pavilion badly in need of painting.

Anthony Derringham sat at one of the ornamental iron tables. As they approached, he got to his feet and put out his hand. Ross was startled at the change in the man. He had certainly seen shock before, on numerous occasions, but Anthony Derringham actually appeared to fulfill the phrase "aged overnight." He appeared to have lost at least half a stone, and his hand trembled slightly as Ross took it.

"Superintendent," he said, "how good of you to come. Angela says you were a veritable pillar of strength." It was interesting, Ross thought, that Anthony Derringham had gotten his rank correct. He wondered who he had asked about it.

They made conversation in a general and desultory way, about fishing and the highlands and weather, until a girl in a black skirt brought Ross a Pimms, complete with a flourish of cucumber. When the waitress had gone and they were again alone in the garden, the effort to make small talk seemed to run out.

Angela Derringham turned to Ross and said, "Is it true that they've charged the shepherd?"

Ross nodded. "Yes," he said. He saw her face tighten.

She continued, "I went in, you know, to his cottage to try to use the phone. Do you think . . . I mean, was he upstairs the whole time, do you think?"

"I don't know," Ross said. "What do you think?"

She paused and shook her head. "No. I'm almost sure not. It felt, well, you know, empty. You know how you can sense someone else in a house, even if you can't see them?"

"The way Claudia did in the cottage?" Ross asked.

"Yes," Angela replied. "I suppose that was him, that he'd been creeping around in the cottage all that time."

"What's he like?" Ross asked.

"Normal." The reply came from Anthony Derringham. "He seemed like a normal sort of bloke. Bit quiet. Had a nice dog, a collie bitch and a puppy. But I suppose they do—don't they?—seem normal, I mean, most killers? I mean, they don't go around with a sign on their foreheads saying 'Watch out. I'm a homicidal maniac.'"

"Not as a rule, no," Ross said. "If they did, it would make our job an awful lot easier."

"Is it true," Angela asked suddenly, "that they found his fingerprints all over the cottage?"

"Apparently," Ross said. He wondered suddenly if she

was afraid, if that was what this was about. After all, how could she not be? She'd discovered the slaughtered bodies of her four closest friends.

"I mean they are sure that it was him?" she said.

"Yes, Mrs. Derringham," Ross replied. "The case against him is quite strong." He shifted in his chair to look at her. Was he betraying Callum's confidence? The details of the case would become common knowledge soon enough. "His fingerprints have been found in the cottage. The shotgun found was his, and you yourself identified the possessions as belonging to the Lassiters and the Halls as well as being your own."

"I'm sorry." She smiled at him quickly and shook her head. "It's just, well, one does want to know. It seemed so little to die for, some video stuff and barely a hundred pounds." She looked away across the garden, and Ross could feel something nagging at him. There was something wrong, something he had almost thought of and then forgotten that he wanted to ask her. Before he could settle on the thought, Anthony Derringham was asking him something.

"Does it happen often?" he asked. "People just going mad for the sake of nothing and blowing people to bits with shotguns?"

"As a matter of fact, it doesn't," Ross said. "Contrary to popular opinion, or popular fiction, most homicides occur for a pretty solid set of reasons."

"Which doesn't include homicidal mania?"

Ross shook his head and took a sip of his Pimms. It was cool and filled with the slightly sharp taste of crushed mint.

"Not in the sense of serial killers, or general lunatics. Most murder is quite well-planned and relatively rational, within its own parameters."

"Which," Anthony said, "thank God, most of us never enter."

"That's right," Ross said. Anthony Derringham seemed

to have recovered some of the color in his face. As he put his glass down, Ross noticed that his hand no longer shook. He wondered idly if it were the fact that they'd gotten used to his presence or if it was the effect of the Pimms.

"I suppose that we'll have to come back to testify at the trial?" Angela said. "Do you have any idea how long it will be before they try him?"

"Angie, how could he possibly know that?" her husband asked, smiling.

"Well, I don't," Ross said. "But I should imagine in a high profile case like this one they'll want to get it to trial as soon as possible."

"It shouldn't be too difficult after all," Anthony said. "It's pretty open and shut."

"Is it, Inspector?" Angela Derringham asked.

"It certainly looks to be," Ross replied. "Don't worry, Mrs. Derringham. I'm sure that it will all be very straightforward."

6

The Derringhams asked Ross to stay to supper, but he declined, saying he had a prior engagement. The invitation was offered with little enthusiasm, and it was easy for him to get out of it. Lying was something that he did fluidly, if not often, and the ease with which deception rolled off of his tongue sometimes gave him pause. Now, however, as he drove down the shadowed drive and away from the Gothic pile of the Rob Roy, he was glad that he was not one of those people who feel compelled to tell the truth at all times and occasionally against their will. He wanted very much to be on his own. The evening remained as light as a midwinter afternoon and was filled with the sort of stillness often accompanying the end of the day. Ross felt an odd sense of nostalgia. It seemed a particularly English time of day, the hour in which one expects to hear from across a close-clipped lawn the sound of cricket bat and ball, youthful laughter, perhaps a horse's hooves going up the lane, echoing back from some long forgotten valley. These were, he thought, the hours of Brooke and Houseman, a daily time travel back to the national memory of an England that no longer was. Perhaps it had never been.

The lane wound sharply to the left, and as Ross slowed for the bend he noticed a drive and a neat green Scottish Historic Trust plaque that read: ST. ANDREW'S BALNACOIL, ROB ROY BURIAL PLACE. He braked and turned into a drive winding tightly uphill. He parked his rental car in the neatly graveled forecourt and unwound himself from behind the steering wheel. What were men of six-foot-two to do in these days of Japanese invasion? So much for renting from Avis because they tried harder.

Two manicured cypress trees grew on either side of the lynch gate, which was furry with moss. A slate path led through a graveyard and up to the door of a squat gray church with a porch and single tower. It was a true highland kirk, perched on a hill above the loch, defying the centuries in the angry name of Scots Presbyterianism, as solid and immovable as John Knox himself.

It did not take Ross long to spot the Rob Roy burial place. In the midst of the simple granite headstones a tall granite obelisk protruded, looking as if Cleopatra had left it behind on her way to somewhere else. Walking toward it, Ross's shoes left dark prints on the already dewing slate. The obelisk was ringed by a simple chain, and as he bent to read the inscription, he smiled. It had indeed been left by a woman, or rather by many women. The inscription, overwrought and quoting "Scotland the Brave" at some length, informed him that the obelisk had been raised in 1952 in the memory of Roy by the good ladies of the genealogical society of Cleveland, Ohio, each of whom could prove beyond a shadow of a doubt that they were directly descended from Rob Roy. He wondered if they had any idea who, or rather what, Rob Roy actually was. Popular imagination had made quite a hero of the man who made such a name for himself stealing cattle. Ross wondered what the old bugger would think if he knew he was so fondly remembered in no less a place than Cleveland.

He straightened up and stepped through the grass to the side of the obelisk. The true graves were there, and along with Rob Roy rested two of his wives and a multitude of sons, daughters, and other loyal companions of the great robber baron. Roy's stone was granite, simple, stark, and adorned only with his motto, "MacGregor Despite Them." Ross stood beside the headstone and listened to the silence that ran down the glen. As his ear became accustomed, he picked out the slow and steady burble of a highland stream, a burn running its way down from the hills to the loch below. From where he stood he could see the roof of the Rob Roy Hotel across the loch. He followed the narrow, darkening strip of water with his eye as it went away into the hills and was lost behind an outcropping of rock capped with scrub oak. Somewhere, the lane wound down its edge and ended at the farm where Rob Roy had brought his family to barricade himself into the hills and fight out his life, the place where, not seventy-two hours ago, blood had been spilled again in a frenzy of rage and terror. Here, in the chosen place of a man who had lived and died by the sword, Ross strongly felt the presence of violence. It echoed back to him over centuries and again over days. Angela had said ghosts were a living memory, an echo, something some of us hear and others do not. Claudia Furnival had heard, and Claudia Furnival was dead.

He shook himself. Kendal had called this the fey side of his nature, joking that he had been drawn to police work because of his extraordinary empathy with the dead. Otherwise, she had said, he might just as well put a Marks & Sparks Kashmiri shawl over his head and buy a crystal ball. She had been teasing, but there was some truth to it.

A flight of swallows left the church tower and circled it, snatching dinner from the air before cutting down toward the water. It was a perfect night for trout, and if he were not mooching aimlessly around graveyards, he could be casting happily off the bank of a loch. The light was lowering, and his stomach informed him that by the time he had made the drive back to Gleneagles, he would be well ready for dinner. As he turned from the grave and back toward the path, he heard a sound that was quite definitely not the wind and had nothing to do with Rupert Brooke. It was the familiar buzz of a moped engine, or, in this case, two of them.

They waited for him as he came through the lynch gate, two of Hell's Cherubs, their mopeds parked and resting on kick stands, their helmets carefully placed on the shiny new black seats. Ross tried to look appropriately serious.

"Good evening," he said.

"Good evening," they said in unison, the boarding school accents not quite rubbing out the last traces of North London. They were both dark, and one was slightly taller than the other. The taller one stepped forward slightly.

"Um, excuse me," he said, "my name is Colin and this is my cousin David. We wondered if we could, well, have a word?"

"Of course," Ross said, extending his hand. "Ross, delighted to meet you."

"You're a policeman, aren't you?" It was Colin speaking again. He was clearly the designated talker of the two. "From London?"

"From Kent," corrected Ross.

"Are you with the CID?" David asked.

"I am."

"Detective Chief Inspector, then?"

"Detective Superintendent," he said.

This provoked a pause while David studied his feet.

"Go on, Dave," Colin said. "You've got to."

David looked up at Ross. "Colin says I got to tell you about the lady."

"Oh yes?" Ross said.

"The lady that's staying at the hotel, the one you came to see tonight and saw before, the one who called the police the night of the murders."

"Yes."

"Well," David said, "you see, I listened." Ross remembered the doorknob turning and the slight crack in the sitting room door as Angela Derringham gave her statement. "I didn't mean to," David continued. "I mean, well, I was just there, you know. And anyway, I listened and I have to tell you. That night, the night of the murders, well, we were down there."

"At the farm?"

"That's right," Colin said. "They'd gone to St. Andrews for the day, the people from the farm. They always do. And when they're away, well, they don't like us playing in the sheds, see. But when they're away, well, we do. We go see Danny sometimes, see."

"The shepherd," Dave supplied. "He lets us play with the puppy, and sometimes we stay for tea. He takes us up on the moor."

"That afternoon, about teatime, we went down to find him."

"And?" Ross asked.

"Well, he wasn't there, was he?" Dave replied. "We had a good look too. We went in his cottage an' all. Danny didn't mind."

"Did you go up to the other cottage?" Ross asked.

They both shook their heads.

"No. We never went near there," David said, "Not where the renters were. But we did, like, have a good look for Danny, and when we couldn't find him, well, we went in and had a sit down and a biscuit."

"We were hoping he might come back," Colin said. "But he didn't. At least not before it got late."

"How late?" Ross asked.

The two boys glanced at each other.

"Six," David said quietly. "We were in Danny's kitchen. He, well, he keeps magazines, you know, *Playboy* and stuff. We forgot what time it was, and then it was six. We're supposed to be back by six to help in the hotel. We were late and we got a right bollocking."

Ross spoke quietly, "At six, when you left, you're quite sure there was no one at the farm?"

David nodded. "Yes. I'm positive, sir. That's why we had to tell you. We went out the top drive. It's faster. There was no one on the place. No one but us."

"I see," Ross said. "And what time did you first arrive at Danny's?"

They looked at each other and shrugged.

"I think about four or half four," Colin said, "and the whole time, sir, we didn't see a soul. So the lady, when she said she got to the farm at half five, well, she was lying, wasn't she?"

Ross toyed with his salmon. After ordering, his enthusiasm for dinner had diminished considerably. He looked across the dining room. It was bright with candlelight and festivity. Couples and families filled the linen-covered tables. From the conservatory beyond he could hear the soft sound of harp music. He looked toward the conservatory door and could just make out the edge of the large table where they had sat; the Furnival twins with their

Modigliani necks, Edward Hall and Anthony Derringham, who had pretended to be friends and were not, The Right Honorable Tarquin Lassiter, who looked too much like Heathcliff, and Angela Derringham. Angela Derringham, who was kind, sophisticated, and as elegant and pale as blown glass. Angela Derringham, who was a liar.

7

There were two kinds of killers, Ross thought. There were those whom he thought of as ticking clocks, time bombs, the humans who lived on a knife edge of rage and insecurity that could, at any time, or perhaps never, be triggered into the kind of frenzy that ended in beating, stabbing, rape, or strangulation. These rarely dealt in malice aforethought. On the whole they were too unpredictable, too unconnected to the world around them to be able to plan and calculate, to deal in the mechanisms of deception and evasion. They were the ones who bragged about it in the pub, close psychological cousins to the husband who bludgeons his wife to death and then calls the ambulance. The other category was what Ross thought of as the killing machines. These were the planners, the meticulous dealers in death for whom murder is a game of cunning, of risk, of matching wits with the police. These play the board game in cold blood: planning, stalking, trapping. Whether for kicks, cash, or revenge, they always have a motive, always have a plan. They were neat, precise people and they did not commit random acts of violence.

On the whole, it was not an original insight, he thought as he turned the car out of the Gleneagles drive, but that did not make it less valid. Like many clichés, it was based on solid truths. At the moment these truths were bothering him quite a bit. The more he thought of it, the more the idea of Danny the Shepherd indulging in a random shotgun massacre disturbed him. That scenario, in so far as he could decipher it from the bits and pieces he had heard, would fit into his first category, a time bomb that had exploded without warning, detonated by the wrong mix of tension, fear, rage, time and place. The only problem was that the crime didn't fit. Someone had chosen a day when the Careys always spent the afternoon and evening in St. Andrews. Someone had cut the telephone line, effectively isolating the entire farm. Someone had made a plan. And then there were a few other problems, not the least among them the fact that Angela Derringham had lied.

That alone was enough to give Ross an excuse to contact Andrew Callum. It would, moreover, be grossly negligent if he did not report his conversation with the two boys to Callum. Of course, he could do it over the phone. It would be a perfectly adequate method of communication, and if he felt a compelling urge to relay the point to Callum in person, he could go to the incident room at the Blairlochie police station like any other normal human being. There was really no reason on earth why he should disturb Callum at home and invite himself over for a drink. No reason on earth to invade the man's privacy, except that Ross wanted to see him alone, to talk to him away from the confines of the police station, to look him in the eye and try to see if Andrew Callum shared his instinct that there was something very wrong indeed with the Balnacoil killings.

Callum's directions were excellent, and Ross found his way to Brae Farm without any trouble. He supposed that in some snobbish hidebound backwater of his mind he had assumed that Brae Farm would be what estate agents and newscasters refer to as "a fine, detached residence," something with three bedrooms and a silly name—Inverness Lodge, Whiteacre. Dunroamin'—perched on its own half acre along a well-lit street with a Safeway at the end. Well, that would teach him. The drive that he turned into had to be a good ten miles from the nearest news agent, let alone a Safeway. And from the length of it and the looks of the large stone house that he could now see ahead, he assumed Brae Farm sat on a good deal more than a half acre. As he got out of the car and shut the door, the assumption was validated. A warm manure smell rose into the summer air, and a barking collie appeared around the edge of the stables. This was a proper farm, all right. Ross put out his hand and spoke to the dog. She slithered onto her belly, grinning at him.

"Her name's Margaret and she's no end wicked." The voice came from the doorway of the farmhouse. Ross looked up and saw a woman standing on the step.

"Superintendent Ross," she stated, smiling. Ross left the dog and came up the front path to shake her hand. She introduced herself as Sheila Callum.

"Do come in," she said, stepping back into the hall. "Andrew's just putting our daughter Rosie to bed." She led him down the entrance hall and into the sitting room.

It was a pleasant room, wide and wood-paneled, the home of a gentleman farmer. A large and rather worn Turkish carpet covered most of the floor, and, despite the fact that it was August, a fire was burning in the hearth. A child's stuffed rabbit lay on the sofa, and two Madeleine books were stuffed down between the arm and the cushion. Sheila Callum waved him toward one of the two winged chairs pulled up to the fire.

"We light it anyway, most nights," she said as he sat down. "These old stone places get a chill on them when the sun goes." She stood by a bureau in the corner of the room. "What can I offer you?" she asked. "We've gin and vodka and the usual lot. Or there's a single malt that's local?"

"That sounds lovely," Ross replied. She was right, the fire was comforting, and he stretched his legs toward it. As she poured the drinks, he had a chance to look at her. She was a young woman, perhaps in her early thirties. She nearly looked the part of a conventional English rose but for the fact she was larger and stronger and undeniably Scots. She wore an old pair of men's canvas trousers and a cashmere pullover with a hole in the back that had been inexpertly darned with mismatching wool. Her long blond hair was braided like a schoolgirl's and flecked with red. When she handed him his drink, he saw that her hands were broad and blunt-fingered and that her eyes were a clear, crystalline blue.

She sat in the opposite wing chair and raised her glass to him. "Your health," she said.

The malt was soft and peaty, and as he rolled it across the back of his tongue, she watched him.

"It's from the Balnacoil distillery," she said, "just down the road from the murders."

"I've never heard of it before," Ross said.

"No." She shook her head and sipped again. "We get it in this area and a bit goes to England, but most of it goes to the States or to Ireland. Did you know how much of our whiskey the Irish drink? And all the time claiming to love only their own."

Ross smiled and took another sip. He held the glass up to the firelight. It was a heavy cut crystal and it felt reassuring in his hand. He wondered how many generations of farmers had sat before this fire, sipping this same stuff while talking of lambing and milk yields and winter wheat.

"Stuart?" he asked her, nodding to the glass.

"That's right," she said. "They were my grandfather's. A wedding present from his wife. I'm the fifth generation of my family on this farm," she added.

"And do you farm it yourself?"

"That's right." She smiled. "Imagine my father's horror, and me an only ewe lamb. Thought he'd make a farmer of Andrew, but no hope. So I see to the farm and Andrew catches the villains." She cocked her head and Ross heard the sound of a footstep in the upstairs hall. "That'll be him now," she said, getting up. Ross started to rise and she waved him back down into his chair. "No, no, Superintendent," she said. "You stay put. I'm not stopping. I've got the books to do tonight, as it's my night off from reading Babar."

Andrew Callum poured himself a drink and settled into the chair his wife had vacated. He stretched his stockinged feet toward the fireplace, and Ross noticed that the holes in his socks had been darned with the same mismatching wool and same inefficiency as his wife's. He wondered suddenly how many acres they had at Brae Farm and how much of a strain it was on a DCI's salary.

"I'm sorry," Callum said, smiling into the fireplace, "I'm still reacclimatising. It's been one of those days. Those bloody guns over at Stirling, which means I've got IRA on my patch again. And then there's some sod that's violated his parole and done a bunk."

"Surely you're not involved in that sort of thing?" Ross asked. In his experience it happened every four and a half minutes and was generally the realm of unfortunate detective sergeants or, just possibly, detective inspectors.

"Normally no," Callum was saying. "But in this case I'm afraid that everyone in the Glasgow area and beyond, which means most of Scotland, is involved. Do you remember Kenny MacDonald?" Ross shook his head. "Well, no reason for you to, really," Callum said. "He's the older of a pair of brothers from Glasgow, Scotland's answer to the Kray twins. Protection, small organized crime, bigger organized crime. Enterprising lads, the MacDonalds. We finally got him put away on a minor charge, and now he's done his five years and he's out again. I don't suppose we should be surprised that he doesn't love his parole officer, but he's the sort of chap that you want to know where he is, if you know what I mean." He drained his glass and stood up, reaching out for Ross's tumbler as well. Callum poured them each another drink. "But I don't suppose the woes of this policeman's day are what you came here to talk about."

"No," Ross said, accepting the glass and watching Callum as he sat down, "Well, not exactly. I saw the Derringhams yesterday. Mrs. Derringham rang and asked me to come 'round to the hotel for a drink. They were concerned about the arrest of the shepherd."

"Danny Blaine."

"Has he confessed, by the way?"

"No." Callum looked into his glass for a moment, swirling the whiskey against the edges. Ross waited. "It's strange, that. In cases like this, where the evidence is so heavily weighed against them, they usually do. A lot of the time it's just a relief, I think, to tell the police. Like going to confessional. But this boy hasn't said a thing. It's driving the solicitor barmy. Can't get him to say a bloody word. He just sits there. Like Job."

Ross was silent for a moment before he said, "You are certain that he did it?"

The words seemed to have no immediate effect. Callum stared into the fire and said quietly, "The circumstantial evidence against him is overwhelming. His fingerprints are all over the cottage. He knew the layout. The cartridge shells found in the cottage were the same make and brand as his. I take it, Superintendent, that you don't agree."

"I'm afraid not." The two men stared at each other for a moment before Ross continued. "I don't think the profile of this crime fits anything spontaneous. I think it was carefully planned, by someone who knew, for instance, that the farmer and his wife, the Careys, would be in St. Andrews all afternoon and evening. By someone who cut the phone line to the farm, probably in advance. By someone who knew that the Lassiters and the Halls would be in that cottage." He leaned forward and rested his elbows on his knees, fixing his gaze on Callum's. "It doesn't make sense otherwise," he said. "If this Danny Blaine wanted to make a few quid by robbing the cottage, why not do it when they were gone? He'd had ample opportunity. My God, the very day before, they were away for half the day, according to the Derringhams. The night before, they were at Gleneagles the whole evening. Why not do it then, under cover of dark? Unless, of course, you really believe that he simply went berserk and killed them."

"Apparently he did," Callum said.

Ross looked at him for a moment. "I don't think he could have," he said.

"What do you mean?"

"I mean," Ross said slowly, "that a twenty bore over and under only carries two shells. There were four people, two of them men, in that very small room. It takes a minimum of six seconds to fire, reload, and fire a twenty bore, and that's if you've got the shells laid out in front of you and are practiced, not if you've got the blood and gore of a quadruple killing going on and are rummaging for the shells in your Barbour pocket. You saw that room, you showed it to me. Edward Hall was dropped where he was standing, Tarquin Lassiter barely had time to take a step. Juliet Furnival never even got to her feet."

"What are you saying?"

"I'm saying that one man couldn't have done that with a twenty-bore shotgun."

Callum looked away into the fireplace and then gave himself a little shake. "Nonsense," he said. "Of course he could. Those people were paralyzed by fear, sheer terror. And as for the phone line, he cut it afterward, after he realized what he'd done and that the Derringhams weren't there. So they couldn't phone for help. To give himself time."

"For what?" Ross asked. "Give himself time to do what? Rob the cottage? Hide the stuff? Run? But he didn't run. He was sitting there when your men arrived."

"He went somewhere," Callum said. "Unless he was hiding under the bed when Angela Derringham tried to use his phone."

"That's another thing," Ross said. "Has anyone really checked the Derringhams' story?"

"Why?" Callum asked.

Then Ross told him about his visit to the church, about Colin and Dave and their excursion to the farm at the end of Balnacoil Glen.

Callum looked at him blankly. "Children often get things confused," he said.

"What's Blaine's motive?" Ross asked.

Callum got to his feet and leaned against the mantelpiece, looking into the flames, which had withered and were beginning to die along the charred remains of the apple log.

"Why does anyone kill anyone, Superintendent? I'm buggered if I know. So if he's bloody innocent, why doesn't he say so?" Ross had to admit he had no particular answer to that question. "I don't know why those bloody people were in that wretched cottage to start with. I don't know why Danny Blaine decided to kill them, but I'll tell you something, I've got enough on my plate. The government doesn't like this one damned bit. It doesn't do a lot for the tourist trade, if you know what I mean. And I've got a case that will stick, and that's good enough for me."

The evening was at an end. Ross put his glass on the side table and got to his feet.

"I'm sorry, Superintendent," Callum said, "but there's the beginning and the end of it. I do appreciate your concern."

"Thank you for letting me take up your time," Ross replied. The two men shook hands before he stepped over the threshold and heard the front door of the Brae farmhouse close quietly behind him.

The night air was soothing, and Ross stood for a moment on the path, breathing it in before he walked to the car. He was less angry than disappointed. He liked Callum, but he was unable to shake the growing certainty that Danny Blaine, if he had acted at all, had not acted alone. He was just opening the car door when he heard a noise behind him. He turned to see Sheila Callum coming across the farmyard. At first he thought she was simply coming to say good-bye, but then he heard the urgency and furtive quality in her voice.

"Superintendent?" she said. "You came to talk to him about Balnacoil, didn't you?" He nodded, and before he could speak, she touched his arm. "He doesn't believe it either. He doesn't think it's right. It's keeping him up nights. But there's a lot of pressure on him, an awful lot to see this case solved. Help him. Please." And then she turned and quickly walked back to the house, leaving Ross in the dark looking after her, hearing the gentle rising of the wind as it gathered and moved across the moor.

8

Owen Davies was a Welshman, which, given his name, would come as no surprise to anyone. He was also a detective inspector in the Kent County CID. Davies had been assigned to Ross shortly after he transferred from the Met down to Kent. From the first moment Ross had set eyes on the short, stocky man with his black Welsh hair and equally black Celtic eyes, he had the sneaking suspicion that he was in the presence of a changeling, a reincarnation of Llewellyn or John of Gaunt, come back in the guise of a policeman. Now, almost three years later, though his impression was unchanged, he had considerably added to his sum of knowledge concerning D.I. Davies. Owen was a sneak, a flirt, and an incorrigible runaway. He was intelligent, fiercely loyal, and—like himself, Ross thought—not above lying if it suited his purpose. In short he had all the makings of a truly spectacular detective, if he didn't get fired for insubordination first. Not that insubordination bothered Ross mightily. It was an odd quirk of human nature that the tall rather patrician superintendent and his terrierlike sidekick shared a healthy disregard for the rules and regulations so beloved to the police bureaucracy.

Now, as Ross folded himself into his rental car and backed it carefully out of its parking slot in the Gleneagles car park, he went over the talk he had had with Owen on the telephone a few hours before. Ross had called Owen at home early that morning. After a brief conversation with his wife Miranda, an unexpectedly lovely creature who ran a highly successful interior design business in Tunbridge Wells, Ross had gotten Owen on the phone and given him a rundown of the events surrounding the murders at Balnacoil.

After a pause, Ross had felt Owen smile as he said, "I see, master, and I take it, then, that you're ringing me in the comfort of my own home because this is a strictly private conversation, not infringing in any way on the business of the police."

"Perceptive of you," Ross replied.

"And I don't suppose further, master, that there's anything that I could do to help you? Unless, of course, I happened to be lingering near a Holmes terminal with some spare time on my hands?" Holmes was the new centralized information system, the pride and joy of Great Britain's police. There were those who claimed that, had it been in operation earlier, the Yorkshire Ripper and several other unpleasant characters would have been apprehended a good deal sooner than they were, if not overnight. While Ross considered newfangled gadgets all very well in their place, he would never cede the superiority of the human mind. After all, Holmes could only give the right answer if asked the right question.

"Well," he said to Owen, "it did occur to me that if you happened to be standing idly beside your terminal, you might ask it to give you the goods on the following names. Have you got a pen?"

"Go on," Owen said.

Ross gave him the names of Danny Blaine, Claudia and Tarquin Lassiter, Juliet and Edward Hall, and Angela and Anthony Derringham.

"Right ho," Owen said, "I'll leave you a message at Gleneagles, shall I?"

"Yes," Ross said. "Ring me from home this evening." On the other end of the telephone he could hear Owen laugh.

"Good thing they've just made you a super, master," he said, "or they might be tempted to think that you were meddling in police business outside of your jurisdiction."

The wind ruffled the water across the body of Loch Earn, making it look like a small gray ocean. The day was warm and overcast, holding the promise of rain. As Ross drove toward Balnacoil he listened idly to Radio Four and wondered if it were somehow immoral to be sick of Mozart. The news came and went. The killings were no longer even mentioned. Not a week later they had been pushed aside, their horror supplanted by the new horrors of a hijacking out of Athens, renewed unrest in the Golan Heights, a spate of bombings and counterkillings in Belfast.

Ross turned in to the lane that ran along the edge of the loch and slowed as he passed the entrance to the church, giving a small mental salute to Rob Roy. He half expected to hear the sound of mopeds, but they were not in evidence today. As he left civilization behind and entered the peculiar closed world of the glen, he could not help wondering what on earth it was that brought the Furnival twins and their husbands here. Perhaps it was his imagination, but he could not help feeling their presence had been attributable to something more concrete than chance.

About a half mile before the end of the lane, he stopped his car and got out. As he stood staring up at the telephone pole, he could see the shiny new circuit box where the wires had been repaired only a few days before. This was where they had been cut on the day of the murders. Sometime before or after the killings, someone had come deliberately and carefully up to this telephone pole and cut the communication to the whole of the farm that lay below. Whether done before or after, Ross found it hard to square the action with the present theory of a petty robbery gone wrong. He looked at the wires for a few moments longer, as if they might tell him something. He then turned, got back into his car, and proceeded down the lane to the farm.

The main gate was open and the track that led to the main farmyard was muddy and rutted from the traffic of ambulances and police vehicles. As Ross pulled into the farmyard, he noticed a maroon Ford Capri parked in one of the sheds. He parked his own car and walked across to the Capri. There was a thick layer of dust across the hood, and the front tires were flat. It hadn't been moved in a long time. As he bent to inspect the state of the front tires, Ross was overcome with the sudden and distinct feeling that he was not alone. He stood up and turned to find himself face-to-face with a tall, broad Scotsman whose head was crowned with a mane of white hair. The man was over six feet, as tall as Ross himself. He wore a Barbour jacket that had seen better days and carried a large walking stick. A border collie sat at his feet. As Ross came forward to shake the man's hand, he noticed that his eyes were a startling, clear blue.

"Superintendent Ross, CID," Ross said. His hand was taken in a grip that had the potential to be frighteningly powerful.

"Angus Carey," the man said. Ross presumed that he

66

was the owner of the farm. In a split second he decided that, while he did not intend to lie, he would let Mr. Carey assume what he liked about his presence on the farm and the questions he wanted to ask.

"I'm looking into the murder of the Lassiters and the Halls," Ross said carefully. "I wonder if you might have a few moments to spare? I'm interested in talking to someone about Danny Blaine."

Angus Carey looked at him for a moment before he nodded and said, "Perhaps you'd best come in. I was going to have a cup of tea."

The farmhouse was relatively new. Ross guessed it was just postwar, part of the stucco, steel, and central-heating revolution that had hit the U.K. in the first flush of rebuilding. It was a solid, well-proportioned house lacking the age and charm of the Callums'.

"Have you been here long?" Ross asked. He watched Angus Carey wipe his sturdy boots on the rush matting that lined the vestibule. Carey glanced at him and waved the collie to a basket beside the Aga stove.

"My wife's family has lived in this glen for generations," he said. "I come from Aberdeen myself, but that was a long time ago. Elizabeth and I bought this farm just after the war. Wasn't much but a ruin then and land was going cheap." He paused, watching Ross. "They do say that it once belonged to Rob Roy, that the cave where he hid his treasures is on this very land, though I have never found it in near to fifty years. Do you take tea?"

"Thank you, I will." Ross watched as Carey filled the kettle and set it on the Aga.

"Elizabeth," Carey called through the kitchen door. "We've a visitor." He took his Barbour off and hung it on a peg in the vestibule. "We're that upset about these killings," he said, coming back into the room. "And if that weren't enough, the idea that it was Danny."

"Are you sure it was?" Ross asked. Carey looked at him

for a moment and then turned to take a set of mugs from one of the kitchen shelves.

"The police are sure," he said.

"I don't think that's what the gentleman was asking." The woman who stood in the kitchen doorway looked like Mrs. Santa Claus, small and round and bright, with powdery white curls and a newly ironed apron.

"Elizabeth," Angus Carey said, "this gentleman is a policeman, and would like to talk to us about Danny."

"Superintendent Ross," Ross said, standing up and taking her hand.

"Well, it's about time someone came to talk to us about Danny," she said, taking the chair across from Ross.

"No one has?"

She shook her head. "Angus, there's a packet of those nice biscuits in the cupboard, and if the superintendent wouldn't like one, I certainly would." She turned back to Ross. "They came, of course, asked us questions, but the case appeared to be open and shut, as they say."

"And what do you think?" Ross asked, accepting a biscuit from the packet Carey offered.

"That boy never hurt a fly in his life," Angus Carey said. "And I'll tell you something for nothing." He placed three mugs of tea on the table and stared hard at Ross. "He never shot those dogs. There's not a chance of it."

"Dogs?" Ross asked. Silence hung in the room.

Elizabeth Carey rose slowly and fetched a sugar bowl from the counter. She placed it carefully on the table, watching her husband. "Aye," she said softly. "You see, that's what they're saying. When they came that next day to take him away like, the dogs were missing. He had a border collie bitch and a pup. They're saying he killed them, took them up on the moor and shot them after killing those children in the cottage." It took Ross a second to realize that the "children" she meant were the Lassiters and the Halls. Just as Danny Blaine would be a child to her.

"So the dogs have disappeared?" Ross asked.

"They were here when we left that morning," Elizabeth said. "We spoke with Danny on our way out and he had the bitch, Cass, and the puppy with him, didn't he, Angus?"

"That's right," her husband said. "Standing right there in the yard, we were."

"And how did he seem that morning?" Ross asked.

"Fine," she answered. "Mind, he was a quiet lad. Always had been, ever since he came to us. Kept himself to himself. And we didn't speak to him long that morning as we were a bit late, weren't we, Angus? We go to St. Andrews every Wednesday afternoon," she added, "to see my sister Laura. She's in a home there now, poor thing, since her husband died. And she's got no one but us, so we go once a week like and take her out for the afternoon and then to supper or the pictures."

"I see," Ross said slowly. "So Danny would have known that you'd be gone most of the day and into the evening on Wednesday?"

"Oh yes," Elizabeth said.

"Danny and everyone else," Angus Carey added. "It's been like that for the last two years now. Since Danny came to us. Before it was difficult to be so regular about it, and I suppose that it will be again until we find another shepherd."

"Was he a good shepherd?" Ross asked.

"The best," Angus Carey said, leaning over to toss a biscuit to the collie. "He had a rare talent with the dogs, that boy. You can't teach that. Though mind you, he'd been trained well."

"He came to us from Jane Trewhitt," Elizabeth said. "She raises some of the best dogs in Scotland. The bitch that he had was one of hers, and so was the puppy. He'd started doing some trials with Cass last summer and had had a bit of success. We were lucky to get him, really, it happening the way it did."

"And how was that?" Ross asked.

"It was odd, really, like Mary Poppins," Elizabeth said, smiling and taking a sip of her tea. "Our last shepherd was married, and his wife was going to have a baby and they wanted to move back south, closer to her family. We'd not really even started to look for someone else when Danny just turned up one day. Drove into the yard in that wretched old car of his with the dog and said he'd heard we needed the help. Mind you, there's a sort of bush telegraph that works like that, I suppose."

"What about family?" Ross asked. "Did he have relatives, a girlfriend?"

"Not that we knew of, did he, Angus?"

Angus Carey shook his head. "Occasionally he'd come down to the pub with me, but no, there was no one that I knew of. Like we said, he kept himself to himself."

"You might ask Mrs. Trewhitt," Elizabeth said, getting to her feet. "He was with her for a few years, I think, and he was younger then. I've her address upstairs somewhere, I think. She wrote us a recommendation letter for him, just after he came."

As Elizabeth Carey went upstairs, her husband got up from the table and took the tea things to the sink. Ross joined him, lining the mugs up along the draining board.

"I don't understand it," Angus Carey said suddenly. "It's not right, this business."

Ross looked at him, then looked away. He agreed.

A moment later Elizabeth Carey returned and handed him a slip of paper with an address and telephone number on it.

"Perhaps that will be of help," she said.

"Thank you," Ross replied. "I hope so."

Angus Carey was lacing up his boots and reaching for his stick. The collie got out of her basket and sat by the door, watching him.

"Please let us know if there's anything at all that we can do," Elizabeth said, "or that Danny needs."

"I will, Mrs. Carey," Ross replied. "And thank you again for your help."

When the two men stood outside in the yard, Ross turned to Angus Carey and asked about the maroon car with the flat tires. Carey smiled and nodded.

"Aye," he said, "Danny's. Don't think it's run in the better part of six months. Always saying he was going to fix it, the boy was. He was brilliant with dogs, but not much good as a mechanic."

"I wonder if you'd mind if I had a look 'round his cottage?"

"No, I don't mind. I'm not sure what's left there. But feel free. The door's open. I'll be in the back barn if I can be of help." With that he set off across the farmyard, the collie trotting at his side.

Ross picked his way across the overgrown front garden to the cottage door. It gave after a sharp push. In less than a week the damp had swollen the sills and made it stiff through lack of use.

The layout of the shepherd's cottage appeared to be identical to the one that the Halls and Lassiters had rented. Once again Ross found himself standing in a narrow entrance hall. He looked through the streaky glass of the hall door into the kitchen beyond. The door swung open easily. The kitchen had the same linoleum counters and iron-framed windows as the farmhouse. A brown teapot sat on the cheap melamine table, identical to the one just used in the Careys' kitchen. He wondered if they bought them in bulk or if it was merely the only kind stocked in the local shops.

Uncertain of what exactly it was that he was looking for, Ross opened the cupboards, giving them a cursory going over. There were the usual kitchen implements, a couple of pots and pans, a frying pan, the requisite cheap china plates in a flowered pattern, four more ugly pottery mugs, and a set of six Luminarc glasses. The search was pointless. Forensics would have been over the whole place. Anything of any conceivable interest would be long gone. He closed the cupboard doors and wandered into the hallway.

Empty less than a week, the cottage felt deserted, the aura of human presence long gone. The stairs led up on his left, and ahead of him the hallway stretched on in the same narrow passage as the other cottage. There was one difference, however: at the end of the hallway there was a door. He came along the passage, his footsteps echoing on the linoleum tiles, and opened the door. It led straight outside, into a set of dog runs that joined the back wall of the cottage to four substantial stone kennels. The fencing on the runs was high quality mesh wire and had been recently replaced. The kennel doors were wooden, their panels painted a deep, glossy green. Ross smiled to himself and thought that the old cliché about England and Scotland really was true: the dogs fared better than the humans.

Back inside the cottage the sitting room opened up to his left. There was a large, lumpy sofa covered in a cheap plaid that faced a gas-fired grate. The television sat on a set of shelves built into the wall. Two equally lumpy armchairs, covered in the same unattractive material, sat on either side of the sofa. A pair of oak laminate side tables and an oak laminate coffee table made up the rest of the furniture in the room. Muddy brown carpeting covered the floor. A large picture window filled the far side of the room. The curtains had been removed, and Ross had a clear view of the hills that rose above the farm. There was no tree, bush, or hedge to obscure the perfect view of the cottage the Furnivals had rented. As he started to turn away from the window, he noticed the phone jack. It was set low in the wall, to the left of the window and beside one of the armchair tables. The phone itself would have been bagged and printed, removed to the forensics warehouse. But on the evening of the killings it would have sat here. It was here that Angela Derringham must have come to try to use it, all the way through the kitchen and along the passage. He doubted that she would have known about the kennel door.

As he went upstairs, Ross wondered where Danny Blaine had spent his salary. Not that there would be much of it, of course. But there would have been something, and it certainly wasn't spent on his cottage or his car. Perhaps he had a savings account stashed away, a secret fund for dreams and ambitions of a better time.

The upstairs was identical to the holiday cottage, with the exception that one of the bedrooms had been made into a small office. There was nothing of note in any of the rooms. It occurred to Ross that even the old issues of *Playboy* that Colin and David had come to look at seemed to have disappeared, removed by the police with Danny Blaine himself and the rest of his life.

He was about to shut the drawers of the empty desk and head back to Gleneagles when he heard the noise. It was so soft he first wondered if he had sensed it rather than heard it. It came again: the light pad of a footstep in the passage below, a click, the opening of a door.

Ross wheeled and ran down the narrow stairs into the passageway. As he got there he saw the shaft of daylight at the end. The kennel door was swinging open. He reached it in a few steps and saw the gate to the kennel blowing to and fro in the early breeze. A small black figure was scrambling up the hillside beyond.

As he stood watching her move steadily farther up the hill, he realized his hand was trembling as it rested on the kennel gate. Angus Carey's voice made him jump.

"I see you've met Finn," Carey said as he came to stand beside Ross.

"Not exactly met," Ross replied. "Who is she?"

Carey shook his head as they stood watching the black figure grow smaller, running from them across the ridge of the moor.

"Finn's been here as long as I can remember," he said. "She must be a hundred if she's a day. Lives in a croft out on the moor." He looked at Ross and smiled. "There's folks 'round here who say that she's the great-great-granddaughter of Rob Roy." Carey turned and walked back across the yard toward the barns.

Ross slowly went back into the cottage, closing the kennel door behind him. He wasn't certain what it was that he had hoped to find, but if he had been looking for traces of Danny Blaine, he was out of luck. The forensics unit had been here before him and had been thorough.

He was about to leave, walk through the kitchen and close the door behind him, when he noticed it. It lay on the melamine table, beside the brown teapot. He was absolutely certain it had not been there before. Carefully, he reached down and picked it up. The photograph had been well-handled and the edges were slightly worn. He turned it over and felt a small throb of excitement. There was a developing date on the back. It had been taken nearly a year ago. He turned it over again and held it up to the light.

They were standing beside some kind of monument or statue, perhaps in a park. The girl looked to be almost a child, with long blond hair parted in the middle, blue jeans and a patterned sweater. The little boy who stood beside her holding her hand must have been four or five. He too wore jeans and running shoes. The rest of him was encased in a bright red windbreaker. He smiled into the camera, his brown hair ruffling in the wind. Beside him, sitting obediently, was a collie.

* * *

He came today to look, to search for something that he will not find because they have taken everything. But they will not find anything either and they will not know. I know. I have seen them and seen her too, and I know. I left the tall man a gift. And when he comes to me, I will tell him.

9

Berwick-on-Tweed is a border town that sits on a series of gentle slopes above the river Tweed. Ross's car topped the first hill and the town was laid out below him, its soft gray stone inviting in the summer sun. Beyond the far ridge of the land he could just make out the blue flash of the sea. He let the clutch out and rolled the car slowly into the verge of the road to a rest area, empty save for a neatly kept picnic table and a bright red phone booth. He checked his watch. It was just after one o'clock. It had taken him just two hours to get here from Balnacoil. The photograph was locked in the glove compartment of his car. In the moments after he found it, he had been tempted to follow his first instinct, to run up the hill after the woman called Finn, to catch her and then try to cajole or threaten her into telling him what she knew. But common sense had prevailed. If she had wanted to speak to him, she would have stayed, and if she did not want to speak to him, he doubted that there was any way on God's earth that he could force her. He also strongly suspected that whatever it was that she had to tell him was meant for him alone.

The next day was Wednesday. As the killer had just a week before, tomorrow he too would take advantage of the Careys' weekly visit to St. Andrews. He would wait until they were gone and then seek Finn out. In the meantime he had decided he would try to find the woman Elizabeth Carey had told him about: Mrs. Trewhitt. The farm address was Berwick-on-Tweed, and according to the ordnance survey map that he had purchased on his way through Blairlochie, it sat a few miles to the west of Berwick on the banks of the Tweed. He had decided against calling in advance, hoping to use the element of surprise in his favor, but looking at his watch, he decided to take ten minutes to call Owen, just in case there was anything about Danny Blaine that he should know. He went to the phone booth.

"Hello, master," Owen said, answering his private line on the first ring. "Eating a lot of haggis, are you?"

"Pounds of it," Ross replied. "Can't get enough."

"I'm not partial to haggis myself, but Miranda's mad on the stuff. But then, Miranda's mad in general."

"How is Miranda?" Ross asked, thinking of the tiny blond china doll and of what a very unlikely pair she and Owen made.

"Miranda is as potty as ever. Mad as a blinking hatter. Makes a lot of money, though, so that's a good thing, especially since you keep me chasing my tail on silly jobs like this and not getting any work done."

"You've got the goods then, have you?" Ross asked.

"Such as they are," Owen said. "And just on this Danny Blaine, mind. I've not got 'round to the others. It couldn't be simpler. There's not a damn thing. Not even a whisper. I've run Blaine through every computer that God ever made, from traffic tickets to fare dodging on the tube. Not a whisper. The geezer's clean."

"Ah," Ross said.

"You knew that, didn't you?"

"I thought I did. Needed to be certain."

"I see," Owen said. "Well, now that you're bloody certain and I've wasted half a day on this, I don't suppose that you'd like to tell me what you're up to?"

Ross smiled. "I'm looking for a couple of missing dogs. Keep on the others, will you? I'll ring you at home this evening." Before Owen could protest, he hung up.

White Lodge Farm was spread out across the side of a hill so steep that Ross wondered if his rental car would make it into the farmyard without the benefit of four-wheel drive. When he finally parked, he made certain he did so across the hill and with the hand brake engaged. As much as he'd come to dislike the little car, he didn't particularly want to return to see it jumping the series of stone walls dividing the fields below.

As Ross made his way across the cobbled yard, he couldn't help noticing the obvious prosperity of White Lodge Farm. The buildings were painted white with a neat navy trim. The fencing looked solid and had recently been creosoted. Two Land Rovers and a Range Rover were parked in one of the sheds. It could not have been more different from the Careys'. He wondered if what he was seeing was the hereditary difference between the highlands and the lowlands, between those who traditionally refused to be tamed, even by Rome, and those who had invested in toeing the line. He found his heart going out to the Careys, to the bumpy loch roads, the hills, and the harsh reminders of hard times.

As he stood staring at the shed that housed the Land Rovers and contemplating this lesson in the sociology of Scotland, he heard a voice behind him.

"Is there something I can do for you?" she asked.

She was tall, thin, and dressed in moleskin trousers and a blue shirt. Her dark hair was cut short and tinged with silver. The voice was not Scots, but English. He would have guessed that she was in her mid-fifties. A silver-gray collie rested at her heel.

"Mrs. Trewhitt?" he asked, extending his hand. "My name is Superintendent Ross. I'm with the CID." It was not a lie, exactly. "I wondered," he went on, "if you might be good enough to spare me a few moments?"

Her handshake was firm and dry. She looked at him, considered asking to see his identification and changed her mind. Clearly he fitted whatever idea she might have had of the appearance of senior police officers.

"Of course, Superintendent," she said. "Perhaps you'd care to step into the office?" She reminded him powerfully of the head hockey mistress at his niece's boardingschool; not an altogether pleasant association.

The office contained a large desk, several filing cabinets, and a row of bookshelves. There was a computer and a printer on a side table. Rosettes and photographs of sheep and collies were mounted on the wall. Ross settled into the visitor's chair as Mrs. Trewhitt seated herself behind the desk.

She looked at him for a moment and then said, "I can think of only one possible reason that you should be here, Superintendent, and I thought that that business had been taken care of."

"In a manner of speaking," Ross replied. "As I am sure you're aware, Danny Blaine has been charged with the murder of four people in the killings at Balnacoil last week." He paused, watching her face. There was no tremor of regret, or emotion of any kind, at the mention of Balnacoil. She waited patiently for him to go on. "We're interested in Mr. Blaine's background," he said carefully.

She smiled slightly. "I see. Well, it's no secret Danny

Blaine was with us for just over two years. When he came here, he was as green as they come. When he left, he had all the makings of an absolutely first-rate shepherd. I taught him most everything that he knew. Not that it was difficult."

"He was talented?" Ross asked.

She nodded. "Oh, yes. One gets a student like that once, maybe twice in a lifetime. He had the knack. The dogs would do anything for him. He could have been first-rate at trials, if that was what he wanted. I let him buy one of my own puppies, a bitch, just before he left. He took Cass with him, and when he bred her a year later, I bought two of that litter back from him. Jen's one of them." She nodded at the silver collie, who had looked up from her basket at the mention of her name.

"The dogs are missing," Ross said. "There's a suspicion that he might have killed them after the shootings. Perhaps to prevent them from going to someone else?"

She looked down at her lap for a moment, and when she looked up again, she shook her head decisively. "That's not possible," she said. "It's utter nonsense. He would have left them with Angus Carey or with me. I would be glad to have them, and so would a dozen other farms I could name. I don't know, Superintendent, what it is that causes people to kill one another, but I can tell you absolutely that Danny Blaine would sooner die himself than lay a finger on either Cass or the puppy. They were, after all, all that he had in the world."

"No friends here. Girlfriend?"

She shook her head.

"Are you certain, Mrs. Trewhitt?"

"I'm quite sure of it," she replied. "He lived in the flat above the stables, here on the farm. I knew every time that Danny Blaine stirred from this place, and it was very rare. Occasionally he might have gone down to the pub, but on the whole he was a loner, a gentle, very shy boy who was exceptionally good with animals."

"How did he spend his salary?"

"Superintendent, I assure you, I have no idea. The flat was furnished. He didn't have a car, and it could hardly have all gone for food. Eventually he did buy a wretched old Ford Capri, but that couldn't have cost much. When he did drive it, which was almost never, he wasn't gone long. He did ask me once about shepherding in New Zealand, and I believe I even gave him the names of some farms that he might contact. Perhaps he was saving up for that. We paid him well, especially considering he had no experience."

"How did he come to you, Mrs. Trewhitt?" Ross asked.

Her face softened and she smiled. "Out of the blue," she said. "I don't know if you're aware, Superintendent, but my husband and I have something of a reputation when it comes to border collies and sheep. I get quite a few young people who turn up here wanting to learn. I usually give them a few minutes and send them on their way."

"But not Danny Blaine?"

"No," she said. "When I first saw him, I thought he was just another one. He turned up here in the yard one day. Rather like you," she added. "Except he took the bus and then walked. He said he wanted to be a shepherd, to learn how to work dogs. Well, I didn't need anyone. But I did have to go up to one of the upper fields to have a look at some ewes, and there was something about him. I felt sorry for him, I suppose. So I let him come along. At the end of the afternoon I told him that he could stay in the stable flat and work his way for six months. As I said, he was with us for something over two years. When he left to go to the Careys, I was sorry to lose him."

"Any idea why he left?" Ross asked.

"No," she said. "Perhaps it was just time to move on. We

would have been happy to have him stay. We told him so, but he seemed set on leaving. He was a young man. Perhaps he wanted a change of scene."

"What about references when he came to you?"

"He had none. He was quite honest about that. He said that he had come from Aberdeen and that he'd been out of work a long time and that he had no experience at all. That was a lie, of course," she added, smiling, "but it didn't seem necessary to embarrass him by mentioning it."

"It was a lie that he had no experience?"

"Oh no. That was quite true. And very obvious. No, he lied about where he came from, about Aberdeen. He was Glaswegian. My husband's rather good at that sort of thing, he comes from Glasgow himself. Danny Blaine came from the Gorbals. Really no question about it." She looked at Ross and smiled. "We didn't feel it necessary to mention it," she added. "I'm sure he had his reasons for wanting his privacy."

Ross felt a flush of embarrassment. It was the same humbling little interior kick to the stomach that he always felt when he had underestimated the hearts of others. He half wished that he could apologize to this woman for his assumptions, but he knew that it wouldn't do. From the way she was looking at him, he also felt that it was unnecessary. He got to his feet and stretched out his hand.

"Thank you, Mrs. Trewhitt," he said. "You've been generous with your time."

She gave him her firm schoolgirl's handshake and then walked him to his car.

"There is one more thing," he said as they stood beside the rental car, which was, thank God, still where he had left it. "I wondered if you'd mind looking at this for me." He reached into the glove compartment, retrieved the photograph and handed it to her. She took it and stood staring at it for a moment without speaking. When she handed it back to him, her face was puzzled.

"The dog is Cass," she said.

"Are you certain?"

"Absolutely. She was one of mine; you know them like children. Besides, she's a blue merle, like these." She nodded at Jen. "The color and the markings are highly distinctive. I'm one of the few people who breed them. Superintendent, that is very definitely Cass. And I would have to say that this child is Danny Blaine's. Unless, of course, it's his younger brother."

"The boy looks like Blaine?"

"Very much. How extraordinary." She looked away across the fields for a moment and then back at Ross. "I never would have guessed," she said. "Not in a million years. People are extraordinary, aren't they?" She sighed and suddenly looked older. "I suppose he's in the most awful trouble now. I never even suspected, though perhaps that explains where his salary was going. I wonder why he was hiding them. Or what he was protecting them from."

"I don't know," Ross said.

She reached down, patted the collie's head, then straightened and looked at him again. "You don't think he killed those people, do you?" she asked.

"No," he replied.

"Well, Superintendent," she said, "I hope you find what you're looking for."

He took his time, driving slowly from the borders across the lowlands toward the rising hills of the Scottish highlands. As he drove, the weather changed, and his mood with it. In Berwick a bright sunshine cheekily appeared between the fast-moving clouds. As he drove north, the clouds closed in and a drizzle began. The prosperous farms and shooting estates gave way to craggy countryside on the far side of Stirling. Stone walls and hedges banked the back lanes that he had chosen to follow. Though nothing could be seen beyond them, he could sense the isolation of the farmhouses and crofts that sat there, some for centuries. Its wildness was as undeniable as its beauty. In the rain this countryside felt timeless. The effect was dreamlike. Ross felt that he could be in any century, that he might come across a ravaged Roman legion, a Jacobite regiment, or an old man and a fool wandering across the moor.

It was after seven when he got back to Gleneagles.

It glowed with white electric light, unmistakably twentieth century. As Ross pushed through the huge revolving doors with their polished brass rails and thick wavy glass, he thought of a hot bath, a drink, and perhaps a call to Owen. He was collecting his keys from the front desk when the receptionist handed him a note. It said, "Please may I speak with you? I'm waiting in the bar." It was signed, "Andrew Callum."

❧ ❧ 10

Andrew Callum sat in a wing chair beside one of the tall sash windows that looked out onto the Gleneagles forecourt. He rose as Ross approached. "I hope I'm not disturbing you, Superintendent," he said as the two men shook hands.

"Not at all." Ross sat in the empty chair opposite him. "Let me get you the other half of that." He nodded toward Callum's empty glass, which sat on one of the patterned coasters beside a half full bowl of nuts.

When both nuts and drink had been replenished, Callum leaned forward and said, "I owe you an apology. About Balnacoil."

"Not at all," Ross said again. He took a sip of his whiskey and soda and waited for the younger man to continue. Callum looked tired. He leaned forward and rested his elbows on his knees. Ross noticed the first tinges of gray streaked into the blond-red hair above his temples.

"There are things you have to understand," Callum said slowly. "Off the record." He glanced up at Ross and smiled at the use of the cliché.

"Of course," Ross agreed.

"This part of Scotland's in one hell of a mess economically," Callum said. "The EEC's not done us much good here; the fishing quotas, farming subsidies, the lot. It's hard to underestimate how important tourism is, crucial really. That and whiskey. A young actress comes up here with her sister and their husbands. They rent a holiday cottage on a farm in a program promoted by the Scottish tourist board. Claudia Furnival won a SWET award last year for her work with the RSC. She's on her way to making her first big film. She's young and beautiful. They're all young and beautiful for that matter. They're on summer holiday, and someone walks into their sitting room and kills them all in an apparently motiveless murder. Do you understand?"

He stared at Ross for a moment, breathing hard, as if he had just run a fast mile. Finally, he sat back in his chair, took a sip of his drink and began to speak again. This time his voice was measured, tired, as if this was something he had struggled with.

"All of the evidence points to Blaine: fingerprints everywhere, the gun, the cash, the stuff lifted. And Blaine won't offer any defense, not a word. The barrister's going mad. He'd like to plead diminished responsibility, but he can't even manage that. Unless Danny Blaine speaks up, he's going down for four consecutive life sentences. He's going down very fast, and there are quite a few people who will be very relieved to see that happen."

"Are you one of them?"

"No."

"Why?"

"Because I don't believe he did it," Callum said. He took a long sip of his drink and closed his eyes. The relief this statement gave appeared to be enormous. Ross wondered again at the great peculiarity of the human race. The catharsis of the spoken word never ceased to amaze him. After a moment Callum opened his eyes.

"Officially this case is all but closed. It's been handed over to the Crown Prosecutor already. I have nothing further to do with it. Christ, I'm up to my neck in these bloody guns we've turned up. Danny Blaine, you see, is no longer my concern."

Ross picked a cashew out of the bowl and examined it carefully before biting off half.

"If someone asked you," Callum said, "just for the sake of the thing, what you thought, what would you say?"

Ross ate the cashew's other half and looked straight at Andrew Callum. "I would say," he said quietly, "that Danny Blaine had been set up. I would say that he was working hard to go along with it. As for the killings, I would say that this was a professional hit."

"Why?" Callum asked.

"For a start, I'll lay even money that there was more than one shooter. This was made to look like a shotgun killing, but that's not all it was. I don't think one man could have killed four people with Danny Blaine's shotgun in that cottage and have the bodies fall the way they did. It just isn't possible to load and reload that fast. Juliet and Edward Hall never even had a chance to move. This happened fast and it was neat. The phone line to the entire farm was cut a good half mile back up the loch road. It was the day the Careys always go to St. Andrews. And there was no way Blaine could have thought they were out if they weren't. There's a clear view of the rental cottage from his own, and their car would have been clearly visible. It was there, wasn't it, by the way?"

Callum nodded. "So all that's true," he said. "But what about Blaine?"

"I don't know," Ross said. "I'm certain that he was set up. It's simply too neat. If he was going to rob them, why do it when they were all home? And why carry a shotgun?"

"His fingerprints are all over the cottage."

"Yes," Ross said, "there's every indication that he was there. It's possible he was even one of the shooters, but if he was, I'm certain he didn't act alone." He reached into the inner pocket of his jacket and retrieved the photograph. He laid it on the table.

"Who's that?" Callum asked.

"I'm not sure," Ross said. "But I believe it may be Danny Blaine's wife, or girlfriend, and his son. I'm almost certain that's his dog."

"I don't suppose I can ask where you got it?"

"Not just yet. Let's just say it was a gift."

"But we've found no trace of a wife or son," Callum said. "None whatsoever."

"I'm beginning to think that's the idea," Ross replied.

"Go on."

"His dogs are missing. I don't believe he killed them. I think he gave them to someone. I think that's where he was during the afternoon last Wednesday."

"When the boys were there?"

"That's right."

"So he knew it was going to happen?"

"I think so, yes. Or he knew that once it had happened, he'd be taking the fall for it. Do we know, incidentally, about the time of death?"

"We're estimating sometime around noon. It's difficult in the summer, and the gas fire'd been left on in the sitting room."

"The gas fire?" Ross asked. As far as he could remember,

the day had been warm. It might not have been sultry and hot, but he was quite certain it was too warm for a gas fire. "I didn't know that," he said.

"Are you assuming he's protecting them?" Callum waved toward the picture.

"Perhaps," Ross said. "If that is the case, I'd like to know who he's protecting them from: us or them?"

"All of this means, of course," Callum said, "that there was a motive. If this is what it looks like, then someone went to quite a lot of trouble to kill the Halls and the Lassiters."

"Yes."

"Add to that the fact that it appears that Angela Derringham could be lying, if the kids are right." He let the thought dwindle, and the two men sat for a moment, contemplating their now empty glasses. A waiter appeared, padding silently across the thick carpeting, and asked if he could get them each another drink. They agreed, and he left as quietly as he had come, replenishing their silver bowl of nuts. Around them the contented sound of before-dinner drinkers rose and fell in a tide of conversation concerned with golf and shooting and the day's play of croquet.

Finally Callum said, "And what should I do?"

Ross swirled the ice against the edge of his glass. "Nothing for the moment. Give me a couple of days. This is purely supposition. You're going to need something rather more concrete. Reopening this isn't going to be popular, especially if Blaine won't help you." He said suddenly, "I wish to God I knew what was in that young man's head!"

"You could always ask him," Callum said. The two men looked at each other for a moment. "They do have visiting days at Glenleven."

"When?" Ross asked.

"Fridays, in the afternoon. I could let you know. Strictly as a member of the public, of course."

"Of course," Ross said. "Tell me something else: how thoroughly did you check the Derringhams' alibi?"

"Routinely. We certainly didn't go to any length to try to tear it apart. There didn't seem to be any reason to until now."

"Could I see a copy of her statement," Ross asked, "if it happened to be lying about?"

Callum smiled. "If it happens to be lying about."

"And there's one other thing," Ross said. The mood was such that it felt worthwhile to try to push his luck. "Can I get into the evidence warehouse? I'd like to look at the furniture that was in the cottage sitting room."

"That shouldn't be terribly difficult. I'll see what I can arrange." Callum stood up, and Ross rose with him. "I can reach you here?"

"Yes."

"Thank you." Callum reached out and shook his hand. "For the drink," he added, smiling.

"Of course," Ross replied.

When Detective Chief Inspector Callum turned and walked from the bar, Ross could not help thinking he looked like a man who'd had a great weight taken off his shoulders. And even as he was relieved on Callum's behalf, Ross wondered exactly how much of that great weight had been transferred to his own broad back.

At midnight there was no wind. In the stillness, Ross could hear the church clock in Auchterarder some two miles away as it struck. He sat at the desk in his room and stared out the window. The electric lights of the hotel made even the midsummer darkness beyond seem blank and total. He couldn't see the shadow of Glendevon before him or the outline of the hills beyond. Still he sat, staring into the darkness. A legal pad of yellow paper lay at his elbow, and across it he had placed his old fountain pen. The paper was empty. By the time the Auchterarder clock struck in the new day, he had already been sitting at the desk for over two hours.

As Ross stared at the windowpanes, he saw not the reflection of the lights glinting off the conservatory below, nor was he looking for the outline of the massive hills that formed the first ridges of the mountains rising to the east of Gleneagles. Instead he saw a room cluttered with cheap furniture. A gas fire burned in the grate. On the coffee table a teapot was overturned and broken. Pottery mugs had tipped onto their sides and fallen onto the melamine tray. Two bodies sprawled on the floor, a third was slumped in an armchair. On the walls and on the ceiling and on the rug there was blood.

For two hours Ross held this picture in his mind's eye. Now, at last, he bowed his head and massaged his forehead. He heard again the urgency in Sheila Callum's voice, saw the mist sitting in a fine film on her fair skin. He remembered the look of distress in Elizabeth Carey's eyes as she talked about the dogs; the way Angus Carey turned his head away at the mention of the killings. And he remembered Andrew Callum. He looked down at the fire flickering gently across the coals in the elegant little gas grate under the mantel on the room's far side. Kendal and he had had a fire like this in their London house. He could still hear her voice clearly, but her face now came to him only in dreams.

If he was going to back out, he should do it now. The time was rapidly approaching when it would be too late. It was still possible to pretend his visit to Mrs. Trewhitt and his conversation with Callum had never happened. He wondered at the wisdom of it, thought perhaps it better to let sleeping dogs lie, and knew even as he thought it that it was not possible.

From his desk the girl in the picture looked up at him. There was nothing that he could do now for Kendal. Nothing he could do for Claudia Furnival. But for Danny Blaine and for this girl whose name and voice he did not know, perhaps it was not too late.

11

The moor opened before him in a series of ridges, each seemingly the last and each giving way to the one beyond. The gorse and heather turned from purple to blue to gray, fading into the horizon. The ground was peaty, and rockier than it appeared from a distance. It was hard going. Ross was glad he'd had the good sense to wear his heavy walking boots. The sun was breaking through the thin layer of cloud cover, and he stopped to take off his Barbour jacket. He took the ordnance survey map from his pocket and checked it again.

The Carey farm, where he had left his car, was outlined in a neat series of rectangles and squares. The map showed just one footpath leading from the farm, running northwest across the moors. Ross had yet to locate the path. He was glad he had thought to bring a compass. The little square he was seeking lay some two and a half miles along the footpath from the Carey farm. He'd been climbing for approximately a half hour, and doubted that he'd covered a mile. He returned the map to his pocket, swung his coat over his shoulder and went on.

Nearly forty-five minutes later he came to the top of another ridge, paused and let out a sigh of relief. Below him, half tucked under the shelter of a stone bluff, was the croft. Its deep, weathered-gray walls mingled into the mauve of the heather and the slate of the sky. From this distance the roof looked to be stone tile. Smoke came from the chimney. The map indicated a burn running behind the croft, bringing snow melt down from the foothills of the Trossachs. He supposed that was where she got her water. Or perhaps she had a well. He had a sudden and bizarre sensation of being transported in time. He gave himself a smart shake and made his way down the ridge.

Apart from the smoke, there was no sign of life. As he approached from the side of the tiny house, he saw a well stand and pump set out behind. There were two small windows in each of the walls. Ross circled the croft. There was no sound or motion apart from the vague whistling of the wind blowing down the moor and around the rock. Finally there was nothing to do but look inside.

He had to bend considerably to get in under the low-hanging door lintel. The door stood open. He noticed it had recently been painted the same dark, glossy green as the kennels behind Danny Blaine's cottage. Halfway through the doorway, his shadow blocked out most of the outside light. It took his eyes a moment to adjust before he realized that he was looking at the single room that made up the interior of the croft. There was a bed alongside the far wall, and beside it an old dresser. A table stood in the back of the room under the window. She sat in a chair by the fire. Beside her, something that looked like a dog was curled in a wicker basket. Ross wondered if he had found

Danny Blaine's collies. She watched him, staring intently at his face.

Finally, she nodded and said, "I've been waiting for you."

Ross stepped fully into the room. "Hello, Finn," he said.

She wore a shapeless black dress with a thick black shawl wrapped around her shoulders. Her pure white hair was brushed and pinned up behind her head. He thought the eyes that peered up at him were blue, but he couldn't be sure in the dimly lit room. A peat fire smoldered on the hearth. He reached into his Barbour pocket and produced a box of tea and a packet of sweet biscuits.

"I've brought you these," he said.

She reached out for them in a quick, scrabbling motion, and he saw that her hands were bent and twisted with arthritis. She examined the presents for a moment and then gave him an appraising look.

"I don't like tea," she said. Ross felt himself smiling.

He reached into the other Barbour pocket and drew out a fifth of whiskey. She nodded and took it from his hands, carefully placing it on the floor beside her chair. The creature in the basket moved, uncurling itself and looking up at her. Ross had been mistaken. It was not a dog but a fox, a small red fox with a luxuriant brush. It regarded Finn quizzically for a moment and then settled again in its basket.

"Fox," Finn said, leaning down to stroke its head.

Ross looked around the room, wondering if perhaps there was a raven. He reached for the other chair and brought it over to the fire, sitting across from her with the hearth between them. "Finn, my name is Ross. I want to thank you for the present you gave me."

She glanced at him, suddenly shy, and continued stroking the fox's head, muttering to it in a language of her own.

"I wanted to talk to you about Danny Blaine," Ross said.

"Aye." She stopped stroking the fox and solemnly looked into the fire. "That boy, he were my friend. Did door for me." She looked toward the still-open door. For a moment the two of them sat in silence watching the new paint glisten in the sunlight. It threw a mellow patch of light onto the swept flag floor. "Did door and pump when it broke," Finn said. She looked at Ross, smiling. "I did things for him too," she said. "We were friends." She looked into the fire. "They took him. After all the lights."

"Did he come here to visit you that night, Finn? The night when there were all the lights?"

She shook her head, still watching the flames. "Not here," she said.

Ross paused for a moment. He was so sure that he'd been right, that this was where Blaine had been during the evening when the boys had found him missing from the farm. If he wasn't here, where the hell was he? Ross tried again. "Finn, that night, the night with the lights, did you go to the farm?"

She gave him her quick sidelong glance. "Go to the farm most nights. Not fox."

"That night. The night they took Danny Blaine away?"

"Before," she said. "Before. With the guns."

Ross felt himself stiffen. He tried not to let the eagerness creep into his voice. "The guns?"

"Aye. That came to kill the women with one face. To hunt them."

"Who was hunting them, Finn?" He held his breath.

"Men," she said.

"Danny Blaine?" he asked.

She shook her head, still staring at the fire. "Not him," she said, exasperated by Ross's stupidity. "Men."

"How many men?"

"Two men. They walked with guns."

Ross felt the excitement almost lift him from his chair. That would make sense. They would have parked down the loch road, cut the phone wires, and walked in so as not to risk the noise of a car.

"Did you know them, Finn?" he asked. "Were they friends?" She shook her head. He asked the next question very carefully, the implications making the hair on his neck rise. "Did they see you, Finn?"

She laughed. "No," she said. And then she looked straight at him. "Sometimes no one sees Finn." They stared at each other for a moment, and then she looked away from him again, stroking the bright paper of the biscuit packet.

Ross wished he'd thought to bring another. He wasn't sure how much longer he could hold her attention. "Finn," he said as quietly as he could, "where was Danny when the men came hunting? Was he there?"

She looked at him, studying his face carefully, then she shook her head.

He leaned forward. "Finn, it's very important. Do you know where Danny was when the men came?"

"He took dogs onto moor."

"Where are the dogs now, Finn?" he asked. "Did he leave them with the girl in the picture you gave me?"

"Julie," she said, looking at him. "She's a secret. Not meant to tell about Julie." She smiled her half-sly smile and nodded again. "I've seen Julie," she said. "He doesn't know, but I've seen Julie."

"Did Julie come here?" he asked. "Did he meet Julie here?"

She shook her head. "At the special place. At the road. I took things there for him." She turned back to the fire, reaching out and stirring the half-burned peat blocks with a fire iron that leaned against the side of her chair. In its basket the fox stirred and stretched. "Danny was my friend," she said.

She was slipping back into whatever quiet world it was that she inhabited. Ross realized it was time to leave. He had no idea how old she was, but thought it likely this meeting was more intense human contact than she usually experienced in the space of months at a time. He stood up, instinctively ducking to avoid banging his head on the smoke-blackened rafters.

"Thank you, Finn," he said. "May I come back and see you again?"

She nodded without looking up, and he turned and walked toward the open door.

Ross felt light-headed as he emerged into the sunshine. He paused, then began the climb back up the ridge toward Balnacoil.

The girl's name was Julie. Danny Blaine had met with her a week ago on the afternoon of the killings. Possibly he met with her every Wednesday, or perhaps he had summoned her specially. Probably he had given her his dogs. Perhaps it was coincidence, though Ross was no great believer in coincidence. He thought it more likely that he had given her the dogs because he knew he was not going to be able to take care of them, knew that something was going to happen that would take him away from his job and his life at the Careys'. Yet, if he knew about the killings, knew he was going to be arrested, why go back? And since he had been arrested, why not use his alibi? If Julie were his alibi, and he was refusing to bring her into this, it must be her he's protecting. He stopped at the crest of the ridge, but what he saw before him was not the blue sky filled with puffy broken cloud, the hawk circling aimlessly against the noontime sun. What he saw were the bloodstrewn walls of the Balnacoil cottage. Despite the heat, a shiver ran through him, chilling him to the bone.

The small car was stuffy. Ross threw his Barbour jacket into the backseat. He sat in the driver's seat with his legs stretched out the door, shoving a rock back and forth with the toe of his boot, making a little trough in the packed clay of the farm track. A special place that was by the road, somewhere Finn had taken things for him. He reached into the back of the car and once again pulled the ordnance survey map from his jacket pocket.

The Carey farm sat at the end of the Balnacoil road. Directly to the north of it a steep series of crags rose above the loch and then gave way to the equally forbidding Trossach Mountains. The woods bordered the area to the south and to the east, and the moor stretched west and northwest behind the farm. Finn's croft, marked on the map by a small square, sat about two miles into the moor. Beyond the croft the map showed the moor running for close to five miles before it gave way to another road. Two rectangles marked what might be a farm beside the road, which then ran off the map, following a printed arrow that simply read "To Balnacairn."

Ross studied this for a moment before he reached into the side pocket of the passenger door and pulled out the Avis map of Scotland. Balnacairn was marked by a small red dot. The roads that led away from it were marked in yellow, with a green line running alongside them. The yellow meant they were single lanes, the green designated them as being of scenic interest. As far as Ross could tell, the road to Balnacairn that threaded its way south, bounding the far side of the moor, eventually met up with the larger road from Blairlochie. If Danny Blaine had set off across the moors with his dogs, and if he had not been heading for Finn's cottage, then as far as Ross could see, he could only have had one other destination in mind. Ross swung his legs back into the car, shut the door, and turned the key in the ignition.

12

It took Ross nearly forty minutes to reach Blairlochie. He drove slowly through the old market town, and on the other side turned northwest, passing the newly built police station where Andrew Callum sat in the CID offices, where the 999 call had been routed one week ago on the night of the murders.

Eventually he turned right onto a single-lane road that was signposted to Balnacairn. The road ran up the side of the moors, dropping away suddenly into a valley. Stone walls had once bordered it, but these had now fallen away, crumbling back into the rock and heather they had been taken from. As he came down into the valley, Ross saw a waterfall tumbling off a crag, pouring itself into a burn that ran under a small humped-back bridge at the bottom of the hill. He crossed the bridge and pulled the car onto the verge. As far as he could tell from the ordnance survey map, this was the stretch of road that bounded the moor some five miles beyond Finn's croft. He got out of the car and walked back to the bridge.

The burn ran underneath in a swift, clear torrent of mountain spring water. The melt was in full flood and the little stream was swollen and rushing. The sound of the water rose and fell, and beyond it Ross could hear only bird song. The pavement on the lane was showing the wear and tear of hard winters. There were frost heaves, and the edges of the road were crumbling into the grass and heather. Looking back, Ross could see the waterfall where the hill crested and the road ran out of sight. Looking the other way, the road ran uphill to the opposite crest of the valley. Just before it disappeared over the far hill, there were two blotches of red. Ross walked uphill toward them.

The telephone booth was a satisfying red rectangle with a proper door and little square panes of glass, the sort of thing Dr. Who would get into without a backward glance. Infinitely superior, Ross thought, to the unpleasant yellow and gray molded plastic that Telecom was now strewing about the countryside. The post office pillar box was also one of the old-fashioned kind. It was made of cast iron and embossed with King George's coat of arms. Under the coat of arms there was a glass-fronted slot in which rested a notice giving the collection times. Monday, Wednesday, Friday, Saturday, and Sunday were blank. The mail was collected from this box only twice a week, on Tuesdays and Thursdays at four P.M. Ross considered this for a moment. There was nothing else on this road for as far as he could see in either direction. He had a hunch, and today he was feeling lucky. He returned to his car and began the drive toward Balnacairn.

The map had shown two rectangles, designating farm buildings, about a mile farther up the road. Ross crossed two more small hills and saw the buildings below him in the next valley. He slowed as he approached them. They were barns but nothing had lived in them for a very long time; perhaps a family of rabbits. The roofs had fallen away completely and ivy had grown up the old stone walls, winding itself through the mortar and door joists, eating at the wood and stone. Ross slowly drove on. If his instincts were correct, the fact that the barns were ruined and not in use was going to make his job much easier. For the first time in several days he felt a lift in his mood. A small surge of excitement ran through him.

The village of Balnacairn was strung out along the road, no more than a succession of houses. He could not even see a kirk, but there must be one, unless the parishioners had walked the seven miles to Balnacoil for their Sunday service, which was not altogether impossible. In the middle of the row of cottages, Ross spotted it. The village shop had an old-fashioned bowed window and a bright blue door. Over it hung the insignia of the Royal Mail. He checked his watch. It was just after two. They ought to be open.

Stepping into the Balnacairn village shop, Ross again had the eerie feeling he was time traveling; he was firmly in 1935. A long counter ran along one side of the shop, and behind it packets and tins were displayed on fitted walnut shelves that ran up to the ceilings and bore carefully hand-printed labels giving the price and name of the item. Ross half expected the prices to be in shillings and pence instead of the newfangled decimal system. The wall space behind him was crowded with hardware; household buckets, scrubbing brushes, and balls of string hung from hooks and pegs. Beside them were row upon row of glass jars filled with sweets. There were sherbert balls, jelly snakes, pink marshmallow shrimp, and airplanes made of licorice, all of the things that he had craved and saved for as a child, eking out his weekly pocket money on sherbert tubes and fruit pastilles.

He was contemplating a jar of rather violently colored jellies when he heard a noise. A tiny woman—who also bore a disturbing resemblance to Mrs. Santa Claus—had come through the inner door and now stood behind the mesh wire that topped the post office counter. She looked so very much like Elizabeth Carey that Ross was certain they must be twins, or at least sisters.

She smiled and nodded to him. "May I help you?" she asked.

"I'm not certain," Ross replied. "I'm looking for the postmistress."

She beamed. "That'd be me. And the baker and candlestick maker as well."

"Ah," he said. "Well, Elizabeth Carey from Balnacoil suggested that I speak with you." The lie rolled off of his tongue without hesitation. "My name is Ross."

"Lizzie sent you, did she? We're cousins," she added. "I don't suppose you'd be Lizzie's fancy policeman, the one's been asking questions about that poor boy?" She shook her head and clicked her tongue. "Horrible business, that."

"Yes, that's right," Ross said. "I'm afraid so. Actually—"

"Mrs. Kennedy," she said, beaming at him again. "Mrs. Donald Kennedy."

"Well, Mrs. Kennedy, as a matter of fact, it was Finn I wanted to ask you about."

"Finn." She shook her head and clucked again. "Oh, that Finn. What a one. Wild as a hare."

"Does she ever come down to Balnacairn?"

Mrs. Kennedy reached for a box of Bic pens and began sorting them by color, placing the blue, the black, and the red ones into three different cups that had "Twenty-five pence each" written on the front. He thought for a moment that she wasn't going to answer him, and then she said, "Only if she has a letter."

"A letter?" Ross felt his skin prickle.

"That's right," Mrs. Kennedy was saying as she sorted the pens. "Though why any soul would bother to write to her, I've no idea."

"Perhaps it's the social services or the council?"

Mrs. Kennedy glanced up at him. "Perhaps," she said. "If they came in brown envelopes, which they don't. Not that it would make any difference if they did. It would all be the same to her, wouldn't it?"

"Why would that be?" Ross asked.

"Well, she can't read, can she? Can't even sign her name. And I know for sure because Lizzie told me so. Lizzie and Angus look after her, like."

"She can't read or write?"

Mrs. Kennedy shook her head. "Not a single blessed word. So, whoever sends her those letters isn't doing much good. Of course, she could take them to Lizzie to read, but she doesn't."

Ross didn't need to know how she knew. "These letters, how often do they come?"

"Once a week," Mrs. Kennedy said. "Mind you, there hasn't been one this week, and she hasn't been here either." She cocked her head and looked at him with her bright little eyes. "She always seems to know when those letters are coming. They never sit here more than a day before she's in. Queer, isn't it?"

Ross nodded, aware that he had to be very careful as to how he phrased the next questions. "Perhaps she has relatives? They're on stationery, are they?"

"That's right, like that, there." She indicated a shelf that held Basildon Bond tablets and envelopes. "Cream-colored," she said. "No return address."

"I see," Ross said, repressing the urge to grin.

"Never had them before," Mrs. Kennedy said. "And I can't imagine where Finn would have met a new friend in the last two years."

"The last two years?"

"That's right. Been coming regular as rain for near two years now. Until this week, that is."

"Do you collect the mail from down by the bridge? Or does it go to Blairlochie?"

"Oh no." Mrs. Kennedy went back to sorting her pens. "Donald collects that. Tuesdays and Thursdays, and then he holds it for the Blairlochie post van. They come 'round on Friday mornings."

Ross moved over to the jars of sweets and began studying the marshmallow shrimps. They were a startling shade of bright pink. He decided on the licorice airplanes instead. "Could I have a quarter of these?" he asked. He reached for the jar and handed it to her as she came around behind the service counter.

He stood watching as she shook the little airplanes onto an old-fashioned scale.

"I don't suppose there's much mail in that box," he said. "The one down by the bridge, I mean."

She didn't look up. "Not much," she said, putting the jar down and screwing the lid back on. "There didn't used to be any at all, mind. Not for years. Oh, the odd postcard, now and then." She poured the airplanes carefully into a white paper bag.

Ross reached for the jar of fruit jellies. "And a quarter of these, please."

She began shaking the fruit jellies out onto the scales as he replaced the airplanes.

A jar of jelly snakes caught his eye. He had always been fond of those, but at this rate he was endangering every tooth in his head.

"Mind you," she went on, "I can't think who there is who would be putting letters in that box to go to Glasgow."

Ross studied the snakes intently. "Glasgow?" he heard himself ask.

"That's it. Fifty-four Stevenson Road, Glasgow. Same every time. To a J. Taylor. Odd, isn't it?"

Ross turned around and, as casually as he could manage, reached for the jar of fruit jellies to put it back on the shelf for her. "Hmm," he said. "Were there many letters to Glasgow?"

She was twirling the white paper bag of jellies over on itself to twist it closed. "Once a month," she said. "Regular as rain. Anything else then for you, dear?"

"No, thank you, Mrs. Kennedy," he said.

She smiled. "Then that will be fifty-four pence. Twenty-seven a quarter."

Ross sat in his car, chewing on a licorice airplane. The neon digital clock in the dashboard told him it was half past two. He pulled the Avis map from the driver's door pocket and contemplated it, leaving a smudge of pink sugar syrup on Auchterarder as he ate the last of a raspberry fruit jelly. A few minutes later he consigned his bags of sweets to the glove compartment, where they would undoubtably be forgotten and turn into a squidgy melted mess. He turned the car in a neat U to head back toward Blairlochie and pick up the road that led to Glasgow.

13

Much had been made of the fact that Glasgow was named European City of Culture for 1990 by the EEC, and, Ross thought, the restoration work was impressive. From the pictures he had seen, it appeared that there were now a series of spectacular museums, a chain of pristinely kept parks, a suitable complement of tastefully renovated pedestrian districts and attractive residential areas. But if that was one side of Glasgow, Stevenson Road, where Ross now found himself, was the other.

This was a district of Glasgow common to every large city. It was an area that housed the poor, the out of work, the displaced, the dishonest, and the unlucky. The police spend an unfortunately high proportion of their time on such neighborhoods' inevitably narrow streets, where generations are born, live, and die sleeping many to a room, heating water on the stove, and wondering how they're going to manage the next week. Romantic writers often find these areas "teeming with life." Ross could remember being at cocktail parties where those who had never experienced them spoke of districts such as this with ethnic nostalgia. In Ross's experience, those he'd met who lived there merely wanted to get out. Once out, they wanted only to forget. For those that live it, he thought as he parked his car, the romance of poverty is elusive.

Stevenson Road looked like most other roads in the area. He'd seen quite a few since he'd gotten thoroughly lost searching for it. It was straight, and barely wide enough for two cars to pass, which would be unnecessary in any case, since it was one-way. Semidetached row houses that had been built by Glasgow's now-defunct shipping industry lined either side of the road. Each house had a small concrete patch of front yard bounded by a low brick wall and a gate. Each house had a front door with four glass panes and a window to the left of it. And even though he could not see them, Ross knew that each house would have a thin rectangular strip of "garden" in the back. It might be filled by a clothesline, washbasins, and a child's bike. Equally likely, it would be a repository for bits of wrecked cars, stray cats, and litter tossed over the back wall from the inevitable narrow alley running between the backs of the houses.

The cars parked along the street were old. Some would never run again, their tires and hubcaps already removed. There were several motorcycles in one of the front yards, and from somewhere up the street Ross could hear the inane rhythm of a mediocre rock 'n' roll station. The shop and news agent was on the corner, just ahead of him. He followed the street numbers past it.

Number 54 Stevenson Road was on the right-hand side, two doors after the shop. The gate and front door were once red, but the paint had since chipped and faded. Several old flowerpots sat in the concrete yard. Beside them lay a rusted bicycle wheel. Ross could see no evidence of dogs or little boys. Instinctively he looked up at the windows, but no curtains twitched, no blinds moved, betraying anyone behind. Already his policeman's instinct was telling him that Julie Taylor was not here. He was not surprised when he reached the front door and saw that the name slots beside the bells read PATEL on one and nothing on the other. Of course, that did not mean she wasn't there. He put his finger on the bell beside the empty slot and heard it ring in the flat above. No one answered. He waited a moment and then tried again. Perhaps she was at work or collecting the child from school. He pushed the bell three more times. Perhaps she was out grocery shopping. He tried the Patels.

The Indian woman who opened the door was in her thirties. She wore a sari. A small child stood behind her, shyly looking at Ross from behind his mother's skirts. Mrs. Patel smiled.

"Good afternoon," Ross said, as gently as he could. The woman's manner suggested she might shy easily. "I'm looking for someone, and I wonder if you might be able to help me."

She smiled at him uncertainly. At least she wasn't closing the door in his face, he thought.

He showed the snapshot to her. "Do you know these people?"

She looked at the photo for a moment, creasing her brow in concentration, and then she looked up at Ross again. "Who are you?" she asked carefully.

He reached into his jacket and brought out his identity card. "I'm a policeman," he said.

She looked at him for a moment and then looked back at the photo. He was certain that she was going to say no and close the door. Instead she said, "You should talk to my husband." She gestured up the road with her hand. "In the shop. Talk to my husband." And then she smiled at him again and gently closed the door, leaving him standing on the step.

The shop had a small green sign above the door that read, PATEL, NEWS AGENT, GROCER, ICE CREAM. On the window was a seal that announced "Propane Fuel Sold Here." Ross pushed open the door and entered.

Mr. Patel was behind the cash register. He was a small, balding Indian man wearing a short-sleeved Marks & Spencer white nylon shirt and a pair of black trousers held up by a shiny brown plastic belt. He was ringing up groceries for a woman who stood beside the register, his hands methodically tallying Rice Krispies, Smash, Nescafé, milk, and Angel Delight Chocolate Dessert mix. The woman was fat and wore a brown tweed coat. A child stood beside her, mindlessly batting her thigh as she stuffed the boxes of cereal and milk cartons into a string bag.

"Angie!" she said to the child, who took no notice.

"That's six quid forty-two, love," Mr. Patel said in an Indian accent that sat peculiarly with the vernacular. The woman paid up and started out the door, the string bag in one hand and Angie in the other. A younger woman wheeling a stroller occupied by a child that appeared to be at least five years old came through the door. It crossed Ross's mind that the stroller might be as much a method of restraint as transport. The two women stopped inside the door, leaning on the ice cream freezer, and began to chat. The shop's proprietor looked at Ross.

"Mr. Patel?" he said. "I've just spoken to your wife and she suggested that you might be able to help me. I'm looking for someone."

The women by the door didn't seem to take any notice.

Ross went on. "I think that they used to live at number fifty-four. The name was Taylor."

Mr. Patel smiled obligingly. "I don't know the name," he said. "They never put one over the bell. A girl called Julie lives there with her little boy. Or at least she did. Came near a year ago. Before that there was the MacDurries, but they moved on. So did she."

"When did she move?" Ross asked.

"Just last week," Mr. Patel said. "Suddenlike. One minute she's there, the next she's gone. Perhaps now we'll be able to buy it. I'd like to have the whole house. It would be nice for my wife."

"You rent, do you?" Ross fingered a packet of Typhoo tea stacked along the counter beside the register.

"We all do 'round here," Mr. Patel was saying. "At least the most of us. And it's not cheap, I'll tell you. Like throwing money away, rent is, if you want my opinion."

"Do you remember when she left last week?" Ross asked.

Mr. Patel nodded. "Of course I do. It was Wednesday night. She packed some suitcases, some boxes, said her mother was ill and that she had to go take care of her. I helped her put it all in the car and off she went. Said she'd be back for the rest of the stuff." Ross didn't even need to ask the next question before he had the answer. "'Course she hasn't. A fellow did come 'round the other day, had a key. I didn't see him, but my wife said he was inside a little while before he left. My wife didn't like it. That sort of thing makes her nervous. Not that you'd need a key to get in," he added, smiling.

"Oh?"

"Kid always came and went without one, didn't he?"

"Did he?" Ross asked.

Mr. Patel laughed. "You know kids, clever little buggers they are. He went right up onto the coal shed and through the kitchen window. Taken the vent out, he had. I used to watch him stick his arm through, unlatch the window, go on in and then put it all back so his mum never knew." Mr. Patel chuckled in appreciation. "There's nothing like a kid for a bit of breaking and entering. The Artful Dodger an' all. Dickens had that one right."

Ross put the photograph on the counter. "Is that the girl who used to live in the upstairs flat—Julie?"

Mr. Patel looked at it for a moment. "Never knew her name was Taylor," he said. "Never knew her name at all. Hoy." He gestured to the women in the doorway. "D'you know her name was Taylor?"

They stopped talking and crowded around the cash register, looking at the photo. "Taylor?" the fat one said. "Well, could 'ave been, I never knew. Quiet she was. But that's the little boy all right. That's the bairn, David."

"David?" Ross asked.

The other woman said, "Used to play in the street sometime, had a blue bike."

"A new one," the fat woman said, staring at the photo.

"That's right. Brand new. Wondered where she got the money for it, being on dole."

"She wasn't on dole!" the fat woman said. "I know she wasn't. She didn't collect, I can tell you that much. God knows I know every face from this street that's down there Thursday afternoon, and that's too many. Seven bloody years since my man worked."

"Did you ever see her husband?" Ross asked, steering the conversation away from the inevitable topic of the shipyard closures. Both of the women shook their heads.

"Naw, no husband there, love. No one, not even a boyfriend, and she so young."

"What about the dog?"

"Dog?" The thinner woman laughed. "No, love," she said. "Most of us in this street are trying to feed these mouths." She waved toward the stroller. "Not enough to go 'round for a bleedin' dog."

"Mrs. Burrows 'ad a dog," the fat woman said. "Nasty, ratty little thing. Made a mess in the street it did. Disgusting."

Ross looked at Mr. Patel, who had been watching this exchange with an impassive, slightly amused expression. "What about you, Mr. Patel?" he asked. "Did you ever see anyone with her?"

He shook his head. "No," he said. "She didn't have visitors. Wouldn't even send the little boy to school. She kept herself to herself."

Ross was standing by his car fiddling with his keys when he saw Mrs. Patel come out of the house. She wore a beige-colored raincoat over her sari and she clutched the little boy by the hand. She paused for a moment at the end of the walk, looking either way before she stepped out onto the pavement and made her way up the road, away from Ross toward the bus stop. She had timed it perfectly. Within thirty seconds the bus swung around the corner below Ross, trundled past him and drew up to the bus stop. Mrs. Patel and the child climbed on board, the doors whooshed shut, and the bus lumbered away up Stevenson Road.

It was only then that the thought truly came into Ross's head. He glanced each way. The street was empty, quiet in the late afternoon lull. It would be an hour before it became busy with people returning from work, children coming home from school. Carpe diem, he thought, while you still have diems to carpe. He pocketed the keys and turned back along the pavement toward the bottom of Stevenson Road.

The narrow alley ran between the rows of houses, just the width of a coal barrow. Its dirt surface was packed and hard, dusty in the summer afternoon, littered with bits of paper and a few beer cans. The walls on either side were high, blocking off any view of the row houses' back gardens. Doors were set into the walls, their paint peeling, hinges cracked and rusted now that electricity and gas had taken preference over coal. Some of them still had their black iron numbers. As Ross picked his way down the path, he could not help wondering how many neighborhood romances had been born, flourished, and died within the confines of these narrow walls.

He counted the doorways in order to find the Patels', which ought to be the sixth on his left. In the end he needn't have bothered; theirs was one of the numbers that was still intact. The door was in better repair than most, and as Ross stood in front of it, he felt a momentary twinge of anxiety. Surely someone as neat and orderly as Mr. Patel would have secured his garden door, protected his domain against the sinister and unnerving forces of the outside world? He pushed the door gently and felt it move, giving slightly against the wooden jamb. Mr. Patel had indeed secured his door, and done so neatly and efficiently with a relatively simple household Yale lock. It took Ross under thirty seconds to open it with the edge of his Barclay card.

It occurred to him, as he stepped into the Patels' garden, that he was well and truly on the lam. He'd started out by sticking his nose into an investigation that was absolutely none of his business, and was now carrying on by meddling with police business and breaking and entering. As he surveyed the back of the house, the coal shed and the kitchen window with the telltale vent above it, he realized that he was thoroughly enjoying himself. Ross the Lone Ranger, the solo guardian of justice.

He took off his Barbour and carefully folded it, leaving it on the ground beside the Patels' door. In his corduroys and sweater he hardly looked like the gas man, but at least he looked less like a photo from *Country Life*. On second thought, he took off the sweater too. It had been a long time since he'd climbed in a window, and it would be undignified to get caught up on the latch and have to wait for Mr. Patel to come home and rescue him. It was easy to see how David had got onto the coal shed roof. The blue bike was still propped against the wall, new and shiny, its finish glinting in the afternoon sun. She must have left in a hell of a hurry to have left behind her child's treasure, he thought. Had she promised him they'd be back for it, or simply that she'd buy him another, a bigger and better bike with more gears and a bell? What was she driving? he wondered. He ought to have asked Mr. Patel. Perhaps he could persuade Callum to put out an APB on the car, or get Owen to run it through the computer.

He felt badly leaving such a large and ugly footprint on the bike's new seat, but there was really nothing else for it. He hoisted himself up onto the coal shed roof, stepping gingerly along the wooden tiling. When this was built, things had been made to last, but even so, he was aware that he was a good deal heavier than a small boy. Falling through the shed ceiling and breaking his ankle would be worse than undignified: it would hinder his getaway. David had done a neat job with the fan vent. Ross wiggled it a few times and it popped obligingly into his hands, leaving a neat round rubber-ringed hole in the kitchen window. The fit was snug, and he was glad he'd thought to remove his sweater, but he was able to reach straight through and undo the window lock.

Even as he swung the window open and began to climb

through onto the counter, he could see that someone else had been there before him. Every drawer and cupboard was open, their contents strewn across the little room. Plates were smashed on the floor. Pots and pans lay amongst the bits of broken china where they'd been thrown from under the sink. A mess of caster sugar, flour, and broken packets of spaghetti, macaroni, and cereal covered one half of the counter. Bottles of spices and tomato ketchup had rolled under the small linoleum-topped table. Ross stepped gingerly through the mess and into the hallway, wishing suddenly he'd thought to wear gloves.

In the hall there was less to destroy. A small telephone stand had been tipped over. The potted plant that had sat on it now lay withered on the carpet, earth spilled out around it, the pot neatly whacked in two. The telephone had been yanked from the wall. He hunkered down to peer beneath the little table without touching it, but he could see no trace of an answering machine. The chaos was repeated in the tiny sitting room in the flat's left-front corner. A knife had been run through the back of the sofa, its cushions ripped open, gutted, their pale Styrofoam innards exposed through the rips of bright floral nylon. The built-in shelf had been emptied of its few books. Some other house plants had received the same treatment as the one in the hallway. The back of the television set had been taken off. Across the hall, a child's tiny bedroom looked much as he would have expected: the ruination was total and methodical. But it was in the larger bedroom in the right front corner that the rage was most palpable. Ross did not even need to enter the room to feel it. From where he stood in the doorway—observing the overturned mattress, the ripped sheets, and tipped-up dressing table, its mirror cracked from side to side—he could feel the frustration, the anger, the pure fury that had driven this force through the flat like a hurricane. He felt a crawling along his scalp, and without waiting to see more, he returned to the kitchen and was out of the window the way he had come.

He wanted to escape Stevenson Road. Suddenly the sight of the Gorbals, of the row upon row of sameness, made him feel choked and exhausted. The picture was forming in his mind, filling itself in little by little, like a water color whose form seeped in from the edges. It would need time to gel, but he could feel it. He started toward the motorway that would take him west, and then pulled the car into a "scenic turnout" beside the river. He switched off the ignition and stared at the lights of the bridge, the city beyond, and the water.

"The long dark river of the dead," that was what the poet Alexander Smith had called the Clyde. Staring at it through the windshield, Ross could almost feel the chill of those deep, gray waters. It was as much the chill of despair, of hopelessness, of lives ground down by poverty and defeat, as it was the chill of temperature. Danny Blaine made a run for it and had been defeated farther on down the road. What about Julie? Had she taken her child and got clean away? Had she made it? Or was she still here, bounded, trapped by the smokestacks and tenements of Glasgow, by these dark waters that flowed endlessly down to the Firth of Clyde and the sea?

He had gone straight to his room upon returning, straight to a hot bath and then clean clothes, as if he could change his mood along with his shirt. The attempt was unsuccessful enough that he contemplated a room service supper and television, but he knew himself well enough to know that that would only make him gloomier. What he wanted around him was light, the false security of money, conversation made by people who had nothing better to think about than which beat of the river they would fish tomorrow. In this company he could be alone and yet surrounded, which was on the whole how he had become accustomed to living. So he was more than slightly taken aback when, on arriving at the dining room, the maitre d' smiled at him and said, "Good evening, Mr. Ross, your table is ready, and I took the liberty of seating your guests a few moments ago."

14

He saw her first, the shining blond cap of curls, the long neck and tiny, elegant shoulders that from behind made her look like one of James Barrie's lost boys, a Tinkerbell without wings. His step faltered, arrested by a vague mixture of surprise, dismay, and pleasure. Before he could further contemplate the state of his feelings, Owen was on his feet and holding a chair for him.

"Master," he said, his face solemn while his eyes lit on Ross with the cheeky grin of a naughty child who knows it's done right. "We were beginning to be afraid you'd become lost in the bonny hills and glens."

Ross bent to kiss Miranda's cheek before he sat. "And to what do I owe this unexpected pleasure?"

Owen sat and grinned at him. He turned to his wife. "I think, Nanda, that's the posh way of saying, 'What the bloody hell are you doing here?'"

"Actually, it was my idea," Miranda said.

"There's some sort of la-di-da decorator's show going on in Edinburgh," Owen said, "and Nanda suddenly fancied she'd better be there or else she'd be behind on the latest curtain swags. We decided we'd stay out here rather than in town."

"Fascinating." Ross took the menu the maitre d' handed him. "I assume that you plan to play golf?"

"Croquet, actually," Owen replied.

Ross brought the menu to his face in time to hide the large grin of pleasure that was spreading across it. He looked to the hovering waiter. "I think I shall have the consommé, followed by the pheasant, and I should think you'd better bring us along another bottle of whatever it is these people are drinking."

Miranda immediately excused herself after dinner.

"There honestly is a conference I intend to go to," she said as she stood on tiptoe to give Ross a quick kiss. "And it really does start very early tomorrow morning in Edinburgh, so I am going to retire and leave you two to your own devices." With that, she flitted away, weaving a path on small gold slippers between the now empty tables. It only made Ross think of Tinkerbell again, and how very unlikely it was that she should be married to the short, Welsh detective inspector seated beside him.

The dining room was nearly empty as Ross and Owen made their way across it to the hotel bar. When they had found a corner in which to hide themselves and had ordered a brandy each, Ross stretched his long legs across the carpet and looked at Owen. "This could get ugly, you know."

Owen nodded. "That's why I'm here."

"Are you quite sure you want to be?"

"You mean you won't be able to protect my career if all

hell breaks loose and someone decides we're meddling in police business?"

"That's right."

"So why are you here?" the Welshman asked.

"Because I don't think that boy killed them. But someone did, and that someone is still out there."

Owen looked at him and smiled. "Tomorrow's my birthday," he said. "I've taken some leave. A long overdue holiday. I rarely get to spend any time with my wife."

Ross smiled. He leaned back in his chair and closed his eyes for a moment. Then he opened them and leaned forward, resting his elbows on his knees, and told Owen what he knew about the killings that had taken place at Balnacoil. When he had finished, he sat back in his chair and stared at Owen.

"So," Owen said, "the girl's disappeared and the flat's been tossed since she went? By the same people who did Balnacoil?"

"I assume so," Ross said.

"It's quite a little tea party, isn't it?" asked Owen. "I've been having a bit of a look at some of the others."

"The Derringhams?"

"Hmm. She works at the National Theatre, P.R. He's something or other in banking. They'd like to move to New York."

"New York?"

"Uh-huh. She's been offered a rather big job at Lincoln Center, or so I hear. They're having trouble selling their house. Islington. The property market's gone a bit dead. Not very interesting on the whole. Except for the fact that their alibi is weak, pretty breakable, from what you've said. The Halls, on the other hand, are a bit more interesting. At least he is."

"Go on."

"I'm not certain really. Just a feeling."

Ross smiled. "Policeman's instinct?"

Owen laughed. Instinct was something he frequently accused Ross of. "Perhaps," he said. "Hall's a solicitor. Rather, he was. Not actually doing very well. I've had to tread a bit carefully here, but from what I hear, he wasn't overly popular in the firm. Bit of a lad about town, our friend Edward. Fond of a knees up, perennially short of cash, which is odd since they've just bought a rather large house on Kensington Church Street."

Ross frowned. The street Owen had just named ran behind Kensington Palace and was one of the more desirable residential areas in central London. No matter how dead the property market was or how in need of loving care the residence, a house there wouldn't have come cheap.

"Inherited money?" he asked.

"Not that I've got wind of," Owen replied. "Hall comes from a relatively well-to-do family, but nothing like that. Went to one of the rather better public schools, didn't make Oxford but got a place at Bristol."

"So what's unusual?"

"I'm not altogether certain," Owen said. "His first job, before he married Juliet Furnival, was as a solicitor for a firm that specialized in maritime law. Shipping, cargo, that sort of thing. He was with them for about six years, was on the verge of making partner when he left rather suddenly. Relocated, as a matter of fact."

"Relocated?"

Owen nodded. "Upped sticks and moved to London. Found himself a new job, married Juliet Furnival. Quite a change for him at that point in his career. Perhaps he just wanted a change. People often do. I just thought that while I was having a look at the Derringhams' alibis, and keeping my wife company, of course, I might have a spot of lunch with a pal of mine in the CID up here. You see, the job Hall left so abruptly? It happened to be in Glasgow."

Ross looked at him for a moment. "That's a bit close to home," he said quietly.

"On the other hand," Owen said, "it could just be coincidence." He knew what Ross's answer would be even before he heard it.

"I don't believe in coincidence."

If Ross had anything further to say on the subject, Owen was not destined to hear it, for in the next moment Ross was on his feet and smiling as a large fair-haired man in a Barbour jacket and corduroys came striding across the room toward them.

"I'm glad I found you," he said, shaking hands with Ross. "I was afraid you might have gone to your bed, but I thought I'd take the risk and stop in on my way home." He clearly had something else to say, but at this juncture he stopped and looked at Owen, who suddenly felt that he was in the company of giants.

"Andrew, this is Detective Inspector Owen Davies of the Kent County CID. He and his wife are taking a few days holiday here at Gleneagles to play croquet. Owen, this is Chief Inspector Andrew Callum. He is, or I suppose was, the chief investigating officer in the Balnacoil killings."

Owen took Callum's hand and looked into the wide-set blue eyes. "I've heard a good deal about you," he said.

"I see," Callum replied.

"Will you join us for a moment?" Ross asked.

Callum hesitated before he said. "Yes, all right. Sheila will have given up on me by now in any case." He smiled as he unzipped his Barbour and hung it over the back of the chair. "She has to be up early to do the milking."

"Owen has worked with me for some time," Ross said as Callum sat down. "I've discussed the Balnacoil case with him, off the record of course, and he's been good enough to look into some background in London for me."

"I see," Callum said. Ross thought for a moment that he

was about to object, but instead he changed his mind and smiled. "And has he found anything?"

"Nothing concrete," Owen said. "Only one thing of interest really. Edward Hall's first job as a solicitor was here in Scotland, in Glasgow, in a firm that specialized in maritime law. I thought perhaps it was worth looking into." He wondered if Chief Inspector Callum believed in coincidence.

"Actually," Ross said, "it's fortunate that you stopped in. I was going to ring you tomorrow. I was in Glasgow myself today. I've put a name to our young lady."

"The girl in the snap?"

Ross nodded. "She lived in the Gorbals until last week. It appears she left in a hurry."

"Don't tell me," Callum said. "On Wednesday?"

"Wednesday evening," Ross said. "Sometime shortly after that, within the next few days, the place was ransacked. According to the neighbors, a fellow appeared with a key, let himself in, stayed for a bit and left. From the looks of it, I'd say he didn't find what he was looking for and it made him bloody annoyed."

"Oh Christ," Callum said, staring at him. "I won't even ask how you happen to know all this." Ross smiled. "I take it," Callum went on, "that you're making the assumption that the Balnacoil killings, this girl disappearing, and the flat being tossed are all related."

"Unless, of course," Owen said, "it's coincidence."

"Quite," Ross said. "It might be interesting if you were to fingerprint the flat. Not, of course, that I think you'd find anything."

"No," Callum said, "and beyond that we can't legally get into it. According to you, no burglary has been committed, and we can't exactly race to the scene of the crime on a warrant for bad housekeeping. Beyond that, this case is closed, in case you don't remember."

"Assuming that we don't believe in coincidence," Owen

said, "isn't it safe to guess that whoever did Balnacoil knew Danny Blaine, knew this girl, in fact had a key to her flat? Doesn't it begin to look like Blaine met her sometime on Wednesday afternoon or evening and gave her something, as well as the dogs, and told her to run?"

"In that case," Callum said, "we can assume that whatever it was, it was highly incriminating."

"And," Owen said, "if it was the same thing that they came to the holiday cottage to find, then this girl could be in a lot of trouble."

Ross closed his eyes for a moment and saw the rose-patterned wallpaper, the crooked picture, the smearing stain where Claudia Furnival had fallen onto the stone floor of the hallway. He saw the shattered window, the upturned tables, the tea mug that had rolled across the carpet, the blasted, torn remnants of the cheap armchair with its lurid nylon print where Juliet Furnival had sat when she died, shot so suddenly that she had not even had time to get to her feet. He opened his eyes. Fool, he thought, when it was right there in front of you all this time. He turned to Callum.

"Tell me," he said, "if we could prove that there was a second shooter, that even if it was Blaine, he didn't work alone, if we could prove that, then you could reopen this case, couldn't you?"

"I'd have no choice," Callum replied.

"I shall need to get into your evidence warehouse," Ross said.

"I shouldn't think that's any real problem," Callum said slowly. "I've a few hours spare tomorrow morning. I can take you myself. It's better that way, then officially you're never there. Unfortunately, the more people there are—" He looked quickly at Owen.

"Oh, don't worry about him." Ross waved his hand in Owen's direction. "He's having a tour of the metropolises of Scotland tomorrow, as a special birthday treat. He's going to Glasgow in the morning to check up on Edward Hall's past employment history, and then he's going to spend the rest of the day in Edinburgh waiting for his wife to finish talking about curtain swags. And while she's doing that he might, of course, have a few moments to look more closely into the Derringhams' alibi."

"Well, in that case," Callum said, "you're going to have a busy few days, because the day after tomorrow I've arranged for you to meet with Danny Blaine. He has visitors' hours beginning at nine A.M." He got to his feet and picked up his Barbour. "Since the witching hour is almost upon us, I must be gone. I'll meet you here at seven," he said, nodding at Ross.

15

The warehouse storing material evidence was on a flat and anonymous industrial estate on the outskirts of Edinburgh. White concrete roads led through a series of long, shedlike buildings that looked as if they had been erected and could be removed in a matter of hours. Even the high wire fencing and security gates that surrounded the area somehow looked temporary, as if it had been bought by the mile and placed there by some transient civilization that had sprung up and might just as easily dismantle itself and move on.

Ross felt a small push of sourness as he followed Callum's Range Rover down the cement road toward Unit 52. Europe was no more, he thought. Given time, the EEC would turn it into one vast characterless piece of prefabrication, an homage to efficiency, free trade barriers, and homogenization of culture. He pulled over and parked in one of the marked spaces and thought, Oh dear, I'm beginning to sound like an old bat from a gentleman's club. Fifty years ago he would have been drooling into his port and lamenting the loss of the empire, and now he was driving a Ford Fiesta through nowhere and griping about the decline of culture. As he got out of the car and locked the door, he realized that he was in a very bad temper indeed.

Callum had been right on time, arriving at Gleneagles at precisely seven A.M. He'd informed Ross that he'd come up with one or two things that he wanted to check on at the evidence warehouse himself and that he had to go straight back to Blairlochie after. Ross volunteered to follow in his own car. He wanted to pay a visit to the Careys afterward, and he wasn't willing to let Callum or Owen in on all of his wanderings. A sense of urgency nagged at him, like a child pulling on his sleeve, but he could not quite put the story together yet satisfactorily: too many things were missing. This visit to the warehouse would hopefully supply at least one of them.

He had thought at first that Callum was simply being tactful in making up his own reasons to visit the evidence stacks, but after Callum had signed in and led Ross past the front desk and into the bowels of the warehouse, he handed him the key with the Balnacoil case number on it and said, "Down there on the left, I think. I shall be up here in the office. There's a couple of files I need to check. How long do you think you'll need?"

"Fifteen, perhaps twenty minutes," Ross replied, taking the key.

"Right ho," Callum said. "If you don't reappear, I shall come looking for you." He smiled his broad outdoorsman grin and turned toward the office door.

The warehouse consisted of long corridors lined with large wire cages. Each cage housed the material evidence from a police investigation, catalogued and secure, until it was to be given as evidence in court or a case was closed or dismissed. The cage housing the evidence from the Balnacoil killings was about halfway down the second corridor on the left. Ross fitted the key into a shiny new padlock and pushed the wire door open before him.

The furniture was stacked more or less in an orderly fashion at the back of the cage. Cardboard boxes arranged numerically were stacked along the sides of the cage. They contained all of the bits and pieces that had been taken out of the Furnivals' holiday cottage and Danny Blaine's home. In a fit of morbid curiosity Ross wondered if one of them contained four ugly brown pottery mugs. He was tempted to check the catalogue and see, but his more adult instincts brought him up short. Forty-eight hours ago he would have stood here under this strip lighting looking at these macabre remnants and wondering what on earth it was that he might be searching for. Now he thought he knew. As far as he was concerned, every murderer left a trail; all you had to do was find it. Sometimes you did so through dumb luck, sometimes through common sense. Other times you never found it, but not because it wasn't there. Then there were the investigations that resembled bird-watching: you sat in the right place without moving and you looked and looked, and then suddenly you saw something. The trick might be finding the right point of observation, or simply knowing what to look for. Most often, Ross thought, it was neither. It was a matter of recognizing what it was that you were looking at, understanding what sat before your very eyes.

It took him a few minutes to locate the two armchairs that had been in the cottage's sitting room. They were at the back of the cage. In order to get to them, Ross had to pull a variety of cheap side tables and a footstool or two off the sofas. He had to tip a cheap leatherette recliner off of the back sofa and pull over a hutch that had presumably housed one of the televisions. He wondered if the recliner was the one Danny Blaine had been sitting in when the police came for him. What had he been watching on television: *Wheel of Fortune?* Old replays of *The East Enders? The Guns of Navarone?* By the time he had pulled the last sofa aside and revealed the armchairs, he was covered in dust and felt as if he was poaching to a slow death in his jacket. He wiped his eyes, took the jacket off, and extracted from its pocket a pair of surgical rubber gloves and a Swiss army knife.

Both of the armchairs were covered in a cheap nylon chintz. The roses were an overblown red with a background of green leaf. Lurid pink rosebuds shimmered under the close light of the flashlight Ross had pulled from his other pocket. There was no question about which of the two chairs he was looking for. The seat, arms, and chair back were a deep, flaking brown. The nylon was encrusted, stained forever with the lifeblood of Juliet Furnival.

Ross looked at the chair and took a deep breath. He could not even pretend that after more than a week there was any stench left to the dried blood, but nonetheless the sight of it slightly unhinged him. It never ceased to amaze him that even the smallest human body could hold so much of the stuff. The back of the chair was ragged, the cheap foam cushioning shot away, blown to pieces by the shotgun blast that had also torn her chest out. Ross remembered the police pictures from the site. He must have been standing just above her. Did he speak? Ross wondered. Did she even have time to scream or whimper? Or was she numb, unable to move while death approached? He took another deep breath and opened the blade to his penknife.

For nearly ten minutes he dug through the back of the chair. The foam cushioning was old and crumbled in his hand as he dug it out. He would dig for perhaps a square inch and then reach in and remove the foam, crumbling it carefully in his hand before dropping it to the floor. Bits of crumbling foam clung to the legs of his trousers and the arms of his sweater like fake snow from a downmarket nativity scene.

He reached the back of the cushion and felt the frame of the chair. It was slatted. Pushing his hand in farther, he ran his fingers along the wooden slat. He stopped suddenly, pricked by something sharp. The slat was broken, splintered about halfway down. He paused for a moment, said a small prayer to anyone who might be listening, and dug farther into the foam. His fingers met something solid. He groped for it but only managed to push it farther down and away from his hand.

He went behind the chair and slit the fabric open in one long, easy motion. The ripping sound was loud in the cavernous quiet of the warehouse. He could see the splintered slat of the frame now. He reached in and grabbed the handful of foam cushioning that rested between the slats. He didn't even have to spread it out on the floor before his fingers found it. Holding his flashlight in his teeth, he crouched on the floor and spread the foam with both hands.

The bullet that had killed Juliet Furnival lay there neat, shiny, and intact. The tip hadn't even been blunted. This bullet had ripped straight through her, and then another gun, the shotgun, was used to cover the presence of a second killer, to make it appear that only one person had been in the cottage.

In the weird flat light of the fluorescent strip that filled the wire cage, Ross crouched and looked at the bullet on the floor before him. The armchair that Juliet Furnival had died in was ripped to pieces, its covering split in two, hanging like the wings of a dead thing from its back. There was no sound. In the utter silence he stared at the bullet and felt something within him turn cold. The bullet still carried with it the horror of its purpose. It was a small metal cylinder, a fetish of death and terror.

He had not quite reached the door of the cage when he spun around to find Andrew Callum standing there. Already Callum's eyes were fixed beyond Ross at the small metal object lying on the floor amidst a mess of crumbled foam. He nodded without looking at Ross and stepped forward, drawing a plastic evidence envelope out of his pocket.

"You came prepared," Ross heard himself say.

Callum nodded as he crouched down and pushed the bullet into the envelope. "Given you were so certain, I thought I'd better. I'd have put money on the fact you'd find something, though I'll admit a part of me wishes you hadn't."

"What will you do?"

Callum straightened up and shrugged slightly. "I suppose I'll say I found it myself, on a hunch. It will go to the Crown Prosecution and to the defense, through the discovery rules. The case will be reopened, I should think." He looked at Ross and smiled slightly. "I suppose I should thank you," he said.

Angus Carey was bent over the tractor engine. The dog lay in the sun outside the shed door. She thumped her tail halfheartedly when she saw Ross coming across the yard.

"Gladys has had a turn," Angus said, straightening up as Ross approached. "It's her oil filter." He patted the tractor and began to wipe his hands on a rag. "That will mean a trip to Blairlochie, but I don't suppose you came here to talk about tractor innards, now did you, Mr. Ross?" As he spoke, he folded the rag carefully and placed it back on top of the toolbox.

"I wish I had," Ross said. "In fact I wanted to ask you if you'd show me exactly where it was that the telephone line was cut last week."

"Oh aye?" Angus looked at him and nodded. "I can do

that. You can follow me out if you like, since Gladys here is sending me to Blairlochie."

"Thanks," Ross said quickly. "But there was something else if you've got a minute." Angus leaned back against the body of the old tractor, reached into his pocket for his pipe, and filled it with tobacco. Ross took this to be a sign of cooperation. If they were in a cowboy movie, Angus would have looked at him, crossed his arms over his chest, and said, "Shoot." Instead he took a very old lighter from his pocket and puffed furiously at the pipe until a thin stream of blue-gray smoke rose into the summer afternoon's still-warm air.

"I was wondering about the cottage," Ross said, "about how you go about renting it. Do you put an ad in one of the tourist magazines?"

Angus shook his head and looked out toward the moor. For a moment Ross thought he wasn't going to answer and wondered why. Then Angus said, "We list it with an agency that the Tourist Board runs. Put out a catalogue they do, you know with a picture and all, bit of a description, price. Elizabeth deals with that," he added. "She's not in," he said, in reply to Ross's unasked question. "Gone to Pitlochry with a cousin."

"I see," Ross said. "And the agency contacts you when they've booked the cottage?"

"That's right," Angus said. "Tell us when the people are coming and when they're leaving and such. Even pay us, after they take their booking fee, of course. The money comes in handy." He looked up toward the holiday cottage on the hill above them; the remnants of the neon police tape still fluttered in the tiny breeze that moved off the hill. "Don't suppose many folk'll want to come and stay there now though, will they?"

"I'm sorry," Ross said.

Angus nodded and looked back at him. "Agency's in

Stirling," he said, again answering the question before Ross had time to ask. Ross wondered if he was becoming quite so transparent or if Angus Carey was simply very intuitive. He had a swift mental image of a conversation with Carey that consisted of him saying nothing at all and Carey replying. "Listed under the Scottish tourist authority," Carey now said. Ross nodded and handed the farmer a copy of the photograph of Julie Taylor. He didn't see the point of saying anything.

Carey held the photo carefully by the edge. His brow furrowed slightly as he looked at it. After a moment he said, "Is the bairn Danny's?"

"I think so," Ross said. "Do you recognize the dog?"

Angus nodded. "That's Cass. The bitch."

"Have you ever seen the girl or the child? Perhaps in a local pub? In the village?"

"No," Angus said after a moment. He handed the photo back to Ross. "She's not from 'round here. You can come back and ask my wife, if you like, but I'm that certain. Where is she, then?" he asked.

"I don't know," Ross said. "I'd like to find her. If you think of anything at all that might be of help . . ." Ross hesitated, uncertain how to phrase what he had to say next. He didn't want to frighten them any more than they'd already been frightened; his policeman's instinct was telling him to tread carefully. He needn't have worried.

Angus Carey smiled slightly and took his pipe out of his mouth. "We shan't mention it to anyone, Mr. Ross," he said. "Danny was a good boy. If he kept them a secret, he had a good reason for it. We'll just go on keeping it for now."

"Thank you," Ross said.

"I suppose Finn gave you that, did she?" Angus Carey motioned to the photo.

"That's right," Ross said.

"She's a terrible thief, that Finn." Carey smiled as he

relit his pipe. "Nothing big, mind you," he added between puffs. "She's not interested in money. It's bits and pieces, like a magpie. Gets into anything, she does. No point in locking doors 'round here." He nodded toward the ridge. "She'll be up there now, or in the copse, you mark. She's watching us as we stand here." He shook his head and turned toward the old Land Rover parked next to the shed. "You follow me, Mr. Ross," he said. "I'll show you where that line was."

Ross followed him for the better part of a half mile when Angus Carey pulled his Land Rover into a passing spot on the loch road and got out. Ross pulled in behind him and cut the ignition.

"It's just here," Carey said as they walked up the loch road. He pointed to one of the telephone poles on the woodland side of the road. "That's it there."

The single telephone wire looped from pole to pole. Ross could see the bright white porcelain of the new fuse joints.

"It wasn't a tree down?" he asked. "A branch? The wind?"

"No," Carey said. "I walked up here and looked at it myself. Neat as a pin, right at the fuse. I can't make it out," he went on. "If Danny cut it, why come all the way up here to do it?"

Ross shook his head. Why indeed?

"I must be getting on, Mr. Ross," Angus Carey said. "We'll be seeing you again?"

"Indeed you will," Ross said. "And thank you."

The two men shook hands and then Carey walked back to the Land Rover and started down the loch road toward the kirk and Blairlochie and Gladys's new oil filter.

Ross stood in the narrow road listening to the sound of the Land Rover's diesel engine as it faded down toward Balnacoil. He looked up at the phone line. There were no other houses for a good mile up the loch road. This phone line served only the three houses on the Carey farm. He looked behind him. The loch road twisted just before the passing spot, and he couldn't see the farm or the cottages or the long line of the ridge. He was closed in by the scrub oak and the hillside and loch. The line was cut here because it was the last pole on the road before the farm came into sight and this was the last passing place where they could leave a car without it being seen from the farm. They didn't want to give anyone notice that they were on their way. They came in the daylight to avoid using headlights. They came on the one day that they knew the Careys would be in St. Andrews. They drove down the loch road and they parked in this lay-by. Then they cut the only line of communication out. And then death walked down the loch road on two feet, and it carried a gun.

16

He thought about motive, why people killed each other and why they didn't. He could not, for the life of him, think of a reason for killing Juliet, Claudia, Edward, and Tarquin. And yet someone had carefully planned their deaths. There had been a reason far more significant than the theft of one hundred pounds in cash, some not-very-impressive jewelry, and a video camera.

"The problem is, I don't know a bloody thing about them," he said aloud to himself. At that moment he looked up and noticed the entrance sign for the Balnacoil distillery.

Its parking lot was nearly full. It looked to be a popular destination for tour groups. A sign announced that tours would begin every hour on the hour and that tickets were available for purchase in the shop. The buildings were arranged on three sides of a courtyard, and the shop was on the far side. Ross found a fortuitous parking spot at its entrance, parked the car and entered the shop. It was new and large and dedicated not only to the sale of single malt whiskey produced at Balnacoil, but also to various other souvenirs of the highlands. These ranged from Edinburgh Thistle whiskey glasses, on the tasteful end of the scale, to tartan tam o'shanters with pompoms and six-inch plastic highland cattle with tags hung around their necks that said "Yoo hoo Mucklecoo" on the not-so-tasteful end. Ross could not resist purchasing one of the latter for Owen's birthday, although he was nearly too embarrassed to take it to the cash register. In order to make himself look a little less ridiculous, he also purchased a bottle of the best aged Balnacoil single malt. It came in a very nice presentation box that included a booklet on the history of the distillery and the making of malt in general. The girl behind the register obligingly put a ribbon around the box for him, and he felt that he had fulfilled his obligations in the gift-giving department. He wanted to ask her to put a ribbon around the Mucklecoo as well, but he didn't quite dare.

"Oh, it is lovely," Miranda said, taking the Mucklecoo from Owen and looking it in the eye.

"I think so," Owen agreed. "In fact there's a strong family resemblance. It looks like your mother."

"I shall ignore that remark," Miranda said, placing the Mucklecoo on the table of the lounge, where they waited to go in to dinner.

"I shouldn't think you'll ignore this," Owen said, holding up the box with the bottle of single malt in it.

"I should say not!" Miranda exclaimed, relieving Owen of the box.

"I say, master," Owen said, smiling, "you were feeling

generous. I should hope that means you had a better day than I did."

"I'm not sure," Ross replied.

Miranda opened the booklet that had come with the whiskey. "Did you know that Balnacoil malt is shipped to over fifty countries worldwide," she said, "and to twenty-six cities in the U.K. alone? Including Chester?"

"Never," Owen replied.

"Absolutely," Miranda said. "Or so the good Andrew P. Dalkeith, general manager, informs us, and he does not look to be a man who would tell a lie." She held up the booklet, displaying a picture of the aforementioned Andrew P. Dalkeith standing beside a smartly painted black delivery truck that had "Balnacoil, Pride of the North" lettered in gold along its side.

"I must say he looks the soul of integrity," Owen said. "I wish I could say the same for the late and not very lamented Edward Hall."

"Oh?" Miranda and Ross said at the same time.

"Snap," she added, putting the box and the pamphlet down on the table beside the Mucklecoo.

"What have you got?" Ross asked.

"I wish it was more than just instinct."

"But it isn't?"

"I went to Glasgow, as you know. Hall had his first real job there, in a general litigation firm. Not especially stellar for an Oxford graduate, but perfectly respectable. I should think he wanted the experience a smaller firm could give him, or some such thing. In any case, he left before he made partner, the reason given that he wanted to go to London."

"And the real reason?" Miranda reached forward and picked up the Mucklecoo.

"Everyone at the firm was being very circumspect, went all tasteful on me," Owen replied.

"Oh dear," Ross said.

"I suspect a major fuss of some type, possibly over money? I don't know. But I'd bet that it was a sort of 'you leave quietly and we'll be quiet and everyone will be relieved' sort of arrangement."

"Hmmm," Ross said. "Perhaps we might be able to find someone who worked with him at the time who might be a bit more forthcoming?"

"He did share an office with someone called Dilworth, if you can believe it," Owen said. "Dilworth happens to be living in London at the moment. Works for a firm called Tobin Parker Doyle and lives in Shepherd's Bush. I didn't do an awful lot better in Edinburgh, I'm afraid."

Miranda gazed at the Mucklecoo. "We went to lunch in the same Italian restaurant where the Derringhams supposedly dined. It was perfect."

"What do you mean?" Ross asked. She tore her gaze away from the Mucklecoo and treated him to her best smile.

"I mean," she said, "that if I were going to fabricate an alibi that would be very difficult to verify, it's exactly the sort of place I'd choose. It's huge, lots and lots of rooms hung in red and gold gilt and filled with tourists. Three hundred harassed staff, a menu as long and as unmemorable as my arm, and a maitre d' who's too busy shouting at the waiters to notice anything else."

"So no one will remember them, and they could say they'd eaten anything from spaghetti to moose al dente and the odds are that it was being served last Wednesday?"

"That's right," Owen said. "Then you pay in cash and there's no record that you were ever there. Or weren't, as the case may be."

"All in all, a good choice, Angela. Just like Waterstone's and the high-rise car park. Trillman's, however, was a bit unlucky."

"Isn't that the small hotel down the road from the Caledonian?" Ross asked.

Miranda smiled and nodded, her blue eyes cheeky and full of her secret. Ross thought how true it was that married couples come to resemble each other, to be almost convincing as brother and sister in some cases. Miranda and Owen could almost be twins instead of husband and wife.

"Go on, Nanda, tell him. Don't be unkind," her husband said. "He's dying to know, but he's far too posh to come out and hop up and down over it like he'd like to."

Miranda said, "We decided we'd go for tea at Trillman's. The Caledonian's so big and barny, and we were both getting a bit fed up with the heat. So in we went, and while Owen was ordering, or trying to at any rate, I excused myself and went to the powder room. It's one of the old-fashioned ones, you know, or perhaps you don't: huge, with a sofa and dressing tables and a little lady who hands you linen hand towels and collects fifty p. coins in an ashtray. In any case, I was the only one in there, and the little lady was feeling a bit chatty, so while I was brushing my hair she asked me where I was from and I told her London. And then I suddenly got this flash of inspiration, rather like when you're playing a game and you just know what the other person's got in their hand. So I said I was here with my husband and we'd never been to Scotland before and weren't we just finding it super, and in fact we were going to go to tea at the Caledonian but we'd come to Trillman's instead because my sister had been here just the week before and had enjoyed it so much."

"And did your sister happen to be tall and blond?"

"Amazing, isn't it?"

"And I take it," Ross said, "that your sister had been in Trillman's?"

"As a matter of fact, she had," Miranda said. "And as a

matter of fact, the little lady in the powder room remembered her quite clearly on account of the fact that she'd come in several times."

"Several times?"

"Yes," Miranda said. "But you see, that's not really so strange, since she was there for almost three hours. And in a bit of a temper she was too, but who wouldn't be? You see, her husband was supposed to meet her at three P.M. And the last time the powder lady saw her, it was just after five and my sister was really getting livid that he hadn't appeared. Especially since he had the car."

"I think," Ross said, "that perhaps it's time I had a chat with your sister."

It was the third story on the eleven P.M news. Ross had returned to his room to find the message light on his phone flashing. The message was from Andrew Callum, and it simply said, "Watch the news."

Now he sat in his armchair, aimed directly at the cabinet in which the television screen was so tastefully hidden. He saw the familiar early footage of the Balnacoil cottage come into picture. The news announcer dutifully announced that a statement had been released from the Royal Scottish Constabulary to the effect that the investigation into the killings that had taken place at Balnacoil barely a week ago had been officially reopened as of two P.M. this afternoon. The police had apparently uncovered new evidence which, while it did not exonerate the suspect already being held, led them to believe that a second gunman had been present at the scene of the crime. The picture switched away to a brief press statement given by a visibly strained Detective Chief Inspector Andrew Callum. He stood on the steps of the Blairlochie police station in his Barbour jacket, looking like a cross between a recruiting poster for the police and an advertisement for the highlands. No, Callum was saying, he was not prepared to release the details of the new evidence to the press at this time, though it had, as of this afternoon, been made available to the legal counsel for the accused, Danny Blaine. This did not rule out Blaine as a suspect. The police would make another statement in a few days. And he was not prepared to comment on the cache of arms found outside of Stirling. The picture switched to the weather map, and Ross's telephone rang.

It was Callum. "Did you happen to catch the news?"

"Your mother will be proud," Ross replied.

"So's the milkman. Danny Blaine's counsel wants to speak to you tomorrow morning. Before you see Danny."

"I should like to speak to him too, if you don't mind."

"Oh, I don't mind. The more the merrier. And it looks like it's about to get very merry. We got a warrant and got into that flat today. We're trying to put out an APB on the girl, but it's not easy. As you said, the place'd been tossed right and proper. And there's not a bloody thing in it to give us so much as a whisper about who she is or where she'd gone to. A right thorough job, that. Whoever got in there didn't leave us so much as the gas bill."

"Perhaps she did it," Ross said.

"What? Oh, yes, I see. Well, then she did a good job. No one's going to trace her from anything left there. The Indian neighbor can't remember a thing about the license plate on her car. Nor can anyone else. Not the swiftest lot around there, I must say. Still, it won't matter much since I reckon that she won't be driving the car in any case."

"No, I shouldn't think so," Ross said. "She'll have taken it to a bus or a train and dropped it. If you do find it, there won't be anything in it."

"Well, thanks for that thought. We're running the prints found in the flat now. I'll let you know what we find. I don't suppose you've any other helpful hints for me?"

"Well, I would like to ask for a favor," Ross replied.

"Oh Lord," Callum said. "I suppose you want me to dig up the entire back garden at the cottage or have the loch dragged?"

"Not yet. I was wondering if you were planning to talk to Angela and Anthony Derringham again?"

"I suppose I shall probably have to have them up here again, shan't I?"

"I should think so," Ross said. "I was just wondering if you might be able to wait twenty-four hours. Until, say, Saturday evening?"

"Do you mind telling me why?"

"I'd like to have the chance to ask her why she's lied, that's all," Ross said. "I also thought I might suggest you check the mileage on the rental car the Derringhams had while they were up here."

"The mileage?"

"I think you'll find that it was serviced at a garage somewhere very close to Balnacoil. They'll have made a note of the odometer. It might be interesting to have a look at that and then check the reading that the agency took when the car was returned."

"How much of a gap am I looking for?"

"Well, of course you'll have to get a detailed statement from them of everything that they did with the car between the time they picked it up from the service and the time they returned it, but offhand I'd say you were looking for about a hundred and fifty miles. Enough, say, to get from Edinburgh to Balnacoil and back again."

There was a brief silence before Callum said, "I see. And am I allowed to ask what you're doing?"

"Yes," Ross replied. "I'm off to London for the night tomorrow. I should be back by Saturday evening. I'll leave as soon as I've talked to Danny Blaine. Oh, by the way, what's the fellow's name?"

"Name?"

"The defense counsel for Blaine. What's his name and where do I find him?"

"You don't find him. She finds you. I told her you usually have breakfast at about half seven. She's going to collect you and take you up to the prison. Her name's Eileen Kennedy."

17

Ross was halfway through his second kipper when he looked up and saw a short, rather stout person who bore a startling resemblance to the Queen coming across the dining room toward him. He got to his feet, and she presented her hand.

"Superintendent Ross? I am Eileen Kennedy, Crown appointed counsel for the defense of Danny Blaine."

"Will you please join me?" Ross said. "Or do we need to leave immediately?" He looked longingly at the second half of his kipper. Her bright eyes followed his gaze.

"There now," she said, seating herself and accepting a cup of coffee from the waiter, "I've disturbed you in the middle of your kipper, and that's a dreadful thing to do to a man."

"Not at all," Ross heard himself say, and dutifully tried to return his attention to the fish. He was finding it a difficult job. This very proper middle-aged lady in sensible shoes and tweed suit was not exactly what he'd expected. She watched him, smiling her cheerful Ladies' Auxiliary smile. It reminded him of World War II posters exhorting the women of Britain to knit socks and mix glycerin with their butter.

"I take it I'm not quite what you expected?" she asked.

Ross felt himself blush. "No," he admitted, "not quite."

"What did you expect, Superintendent? A young firebrand in a Morris Minor with a Scottish Independence Party sticker on the back?" Ross was far too embarrassed to admit that that was exactly what he had expected. "Oh dear, oh dear," she said. "Don't tell me you're one of those Englishmen who expects us all to rush about eating haggis and shouting 'auch the noon' the whole time as well?"

"I don't think so," Ross said. "I shall certainly try not to be."

"Don't you worry about it, Superintendent." She put her coffee cup down and reached into her handbag for her glasses. "We're going to get along grand. I'm a firebrand too, just a little bit older, that's all." Before Ross could gather himself to say he had no doubt of the fact, she went on. "Andrew Callum says you're a good chap. He also says you think my boy's innocent."

"I do."

"Why?"

"Because it doesn't make any sense. I don't believe that this was a spur of the moment crime, I believe it was planned, and I don't see why Danny Blaine would have planned to rob a cottage with four people in it when he could have waited until it was empty. I don't see why he would have killed them. And if he did rob them and kill them, which I don't for a moment believe he did, then I don't see why he'd dump the loot in a feed bin and sit around waiting for the police to arrive."

"Panic. Shock. Terrible remorse."

"I don't buy it. If he was that panicked, that shocked, he wouldn't have hidden the stuff, you'd have found it sitting on the kitchen table. Or he'd have run off across the moor and been picked up in Balnacairn wandering up the road. Terrible remorse? He'd have walked back to the cottage and rung the police himself. They often do in cases like this."

"He couldn't, he'd cut the phone lines."

"Exactly. Why?"

"So no one could call for help."

"Who was there to call for help? If he did it afterward, he knew they were all dead. If he did it before, it was premeditated, which goes back to my previous concern, and in any case someone did go for help and he made no move to stop them."

"Why not?"

"Because he either didn't care or he wasn't there."

"Or he didn't know."

"No," Ross said slowly. "I don't believe that. I think he did know. He knew something anyways. He either knew that something was about to happen or that something had happened; that's why he got rid of the dogs."

"Took them up on the moor and shot them, you mean?"

"I think he gave them to someone he trusted. What I'm very much afraid of is that he may have given them something else as well."

"Any idea what?"

Ross shook his head.

"And what else?" she asked.

"The second bullet discovered yesterday. Someone else was in that cottage."

"Danny could have been carrying two guns?"

"It's awkward. In fact very difficult, especially if one's an ordinary shotgun. And where's the second one? Why let the police find the shotgun and not the second weapon, unless you didn't want them to know that two guns had been used?"

"Go on."

"I think they'll find another bullet, unless the killers took it away with them, which they might have. It's certainly not lodged in the bodies or the autopsies would have turned it up. If they were shot at close range with something powerful enough, the bullets could have passed straight through the bodies. In fact that's exactly what happened with Juliet Furnival. They didn't get that bullet; perhaps they thought it had lodged in her, or perhaps they just didn't think of it, although I doubt that. I'd put money on the fact that either Hall or Lassiter was also shot with something other than a shotgun, at least initially."

"And then blasted again with a shotgun to make that look like the primary, in fact the only, injury?"

"I think so. I'm fairly certain that it would be almost impossible to detect in an autopsy."

"Violent."

"Rather."

She readjusted her glasses and looked away for a moment, as if they were both listening to the echo of gunshots as they traveled back over the nine days that had elapsed. When she looked back at him, she said, "Danny Blaine's fingerprints were all over that cottage."

"So were a lot of unidentified latents."

"Why were Danny Blaine's upstairs, in the bathroom, in the bedrooms?"

"Because he was looking for something," Ross replied. "And I have the idea he might have found it."

Eileen Kennedy accelerated quietly while maneuvering her car out of the Gleneagles parking lot, then said, "What you're telling me is that you think the people in the cottage, the Furnival twins and their husbands and these

Derringhams, had something. And someone wanted that something badly enough to kill them for it. You think that they came looking for it, that they did indeed kill for it, but they didn't find whatever it was. They didn't find it because Danny Blaine had already found it. He'd removed it before the killing. He gave it to Julie. And, whoever these horrible people are, they've now put two and two together and are after her. Perhaps she's even his alibi, but he won't talk about her because he's afraid of what will happen if she gets found." She let out a long breath and looked at him from the corner of her eye.

"Essentially, that is what I think," Ross said. He looked out of the window. Eileen Kennedy's car was not a Morris Minor, it was a rather old and very dignified Rover. She drove it at some considerable speed down the fast lane of the motorway that would lead them to the outskirts of Glasgow, where Danny Blaine was currently residing in Her Majesty's prison for maximum security offenders, Glenleven.

"So given what we now believe went on in that cottage," she continued, "this girl and that child are in some considerable danger."

Ross looked at her. "I'm very much afraid that may be true."

"I don't suppose you have any idea what it might be that Blaine gave her."

"I haven't even the vaguest idea. I was rather hoping I might be able to persuade him to tell me."

She glanced over at him and raised her eyebrows. "Well, mate," she said, "in that case you'd be doing an awful lot better than the rest of us because so far the little bugger hasn't said a single word to anyone. As you might guess, that's making my defense a wee bit difficult."

The prison sat about halfway between Glasgow and Edinburgh, firmly in the middle of nowhere. It had been built in 1979 as a working model for the new theories on prison reform and architecture. Even so, barbed wire remains barbed wire and walls are walls. In time, quite a short time actually, Glenleven faced the same problems of overcrowding, personnel shortages, and general wear and tear that every other prison in the country faced. There had been strikes and riots. A warden was held hostage and killed. Afterwards, the borders of the exercise yards were left unmowed, the modular furniture in the television room smashed, the two-person cells modified to take three and, in some cases, four inmates. All of the architectural design in the world couldn't stop it from becoming what it was: a place where men who had beaten, raped, and murdered were sent to live out the rest of their days in claustrophobic isolation.

Ross hated the look of prisons, and the feel of them, and the despair that hung over them in a near visible pall. Still, he could not help feeling a twinge of excitement. The interview room where Eileen Kennedy was to meet her client was in the administration wing of Glenleven, far from the maze of cells and cafeterias and exercise yards. The room was bare except for a table and a few chairs. The one window's panes were run through with wire. The lights were recessed into the ceiling and operated from the other side of the half glass door. A prisoner could conceivably do damage only if ambitious enough to attempt to beat his interviewer over the head with one of the chairs. The table was bolted to the floor.

Eileen Kennedy placed her briefcase on the table and motioned to Ross to take a seat. "Danny should be here directly," she said. "This is only the third time I've seen him. Perhaps he'll be more talkative today, but I frankly doubt it. He's made up his mind not to utter a peep. Or someone else has told him to keep quiet." She glanced at Ross and then back at the papers she was spreading across the table. "I'm trying to arrange a psychiatric evaluation, perhaps sometime next week."

"An insanity defense?"

"I may have to resort to that," she said. "My choices are hardly plentiful, Superintendent. In fact, I'll take what I can get." There was a click at the door. "Here we go."

A moment later a guard escorted Danny Blaine into the room.

Ross hadn't known what to expect, but he was at once startled and saddened by the sight before him. What struck him first was Blaine's youth. He knew that Danny Blaine was twenty-six years old, but the face of the man who stood before him belonged to a boy who looked scarcely older than a child. Danny Blaine had fine, sensitive features. A frown had fixed itself permanently between his dark, slightly almond-shaped eyes. His black hair fell across his forehead. He reminded Ross of the more romantic pictures of World War I soldiers. He had that same slender sadness, a poetic, doomed quality that fairly echoed of no man's land and the fair fields of France. His hands were cuffed in front of him. He did not even glance at Ross, but simply stood in utter passivity, betraying no interest at all in what was going on around him.

"Do you think you could take those off, please?" Eileen Kennedy asked the guard as she nodded toward the handcuffs.

"It's not advisable, ma'am," he said, smiling.

She studied him over the rim of her glasses and smiled back. "Make an exception."

The guard opened his mouth to argue, but then looked at her and thought better of it. He removed the handcuffs.

"Thank you," Eileen said, returning to the study of her papers. "You can wait outside. If we need you, I'll certainly let you know."

The guard left, closing the door behind him with a positive click. Ross could see his wide, pale blue back through the glass panel. He thought it was probably sound-proof.

Eileen muttered something that sounded vaguely un-printable under her breath and then she looked up at Danny Blaine and smiled, this time with genuine warmth. "How are you, Danny? Have a pew."

Danny looked at the remaining chair as if it might blow up, and then lowered himself cautiously into it. He moved as if his body were very fragile, each motion potentially painful. Ross wondered if he'd been beaten up. He felt the same thought go through Eileen's head.

"How's life treating you, Danny?" she asked.

Danny moved his head in a way that might have indicated a nod, and then turned to look out the window. Eileen watched him. Ross could almost feel the long sigh she was dying to exhale. She refrained and tapped the top of her pile of papers with her pen.

"We've had some good news, Danny," she said. Either he didn't hear her—unlikely, given the dimensions of the room—or chose to ignore her. Eileen glanced at Ross. "The police have found a bullet in the cottage, Danny. Do you understand what that means? They know there was another shooter." In the seconds that she spoke, Ross thought he saw the muscles across Danny Blaine's shoulders tighten. There'd been a stiffening of that thin body, a tensing like an animal that pauses, recognizing danger in the moment before flight. But then nothing more: just the three of them sitting in the tiny, airless room with a guard lingering outside the door.

Eileen said, "This means that for the first time they may be willing to believe that you didn't do this. Do you understand? Is there nothing that you can tell me that will help?"

Danny Blaine didn't move. Eileen watched him for a moment before removing her glasses, placing them on the pile of papers and leaning back in her chair. She threw

Ross a quick glance. He could see the rising tide of irritation. It must be difficult, he thought, to be a firebrand in the face of a stone wall. He wondered if they had actually checked to ascertain that Danny Blaine was not, in fact, a deaf-mute.

"Danny," Elaine said, "this is Superintendent Ross. He's a policeman. He knew the people killed at the cottage. He's not officially on the case, and he believes you're innocent. He wanted to meet you and tell you that himself."

Ross leaned forward in his chair and looked at the side of Danny Blaine's face as Danny continued to gaze absently out the window.

"I've spoken to Angus and Elizabeth Carey," he said. "Elizabeth wanted to know if there was anything you needed." He paused for a moment, acknowledging the by-now expected lack of response. "I've also seen Jane Trewhitt. She's worried about Cass and the puppy. And I've had a word with Finn."

Danny Blaine's head turned slowly. He looked at Ross. It was ridiculous, Ross thought, that such a tiny human reaction could bring such a wave of triumph rushing through him. He forged on, bloated by success.

"I don't think that you did this, Danny," he said, "but I do think you know who did. And you know why. You knew they were coming that afternoon. I think you may have had something they wanted very badly. And you left the farm that afternoon, possibly with whatever it was."

Ross paused, giving Danny the opportunity to agree with him wholeheartedly and spew forth the entire story in a frantic rush. It was not forthcoming. Blaine was, however, still looking at him, more than he'd bothered to do for Eileen Kennedy. Still, the boy was reminding him altogether too much of his teenage nephew, Hugh, at his most unattractive. Ross reached into his jacket pocket and brought out the envelope containing the snapshot.

"You went to meet someone, didn't you? You gave her the evidence and the dogs. Did you tell her to run or was that her own idea? Bloody good thing you did because they've tossed her flat right and proper. And unless you help me find Julie, Danny, they're going to find her first." With that, Ross slapped the snapshot down onto the table.

Three things happened at once. Eileen Kennedy leaned forward to look at the picture, Danny Blaine leapt up and made a grab for it, and Ross snatched it back. A second later the guard was through the door and wrestling Danny Blaine into handcuffs. Eileen was on her feet, staring dumbly at Blaine, who was in turn trying to watch Ross and struggle with the guard at the same time.

"I can help them," Ross said, "if you let me know where they are. I can get to them first. I can protect them!"

And then Danny Blaine spoke his only words of the entire interview. He stopped struggling with the guard, went suddenly limp, as if the air had been knocked out of him. Looking directly at Ross, he said, "Leave them alone, for God's sake. Please leave them alone."

And then Danny Blaine was gone, hustled out the door by the guard, leaving Ross and Eileen Kennedy standing in the interview room staring after him.

18

London City Airport, a brainchild of Thatcherism, was built to accommodate the incoming flood of very important executives and investors who were confidently expected to arrive in London in the aftermath of the "Big Boom." Now, in the wake of "Black Monday," it joined the Docklands development and the Isle of Dogs restructuring as a poignant reminder that prosperity cannot be counted on, despite strict orders from above. The economy had proved itself peculiarly resistant to Conservative Party manifestos and tantrums. Ross shook his head in quiet disgust and then remembered, with a childish twinge of pleasure, that the nasty lady, at least, was no longer. Britain had inherited a kinder and gentler Conservative Party, and the tyranny of the chemist's daughter had come to an end at last, though not before she managed to inflict upon the nation the Channel tunnel.

One of the problems with City Airport and the other developments along this end of the Thames was that no one had thought about how all of the people who were going to come flooding into them were going to get in and out of the city center. The road system had not been updated to match the swelling monoliths of concrete and tinted glass. The high-speed railroad broke down with alarming frequency. Ross had once read a study that estimated if London's Docklands development was occupied to its full capacity, it would take everyone living and working there eight hours to get to and from their jobs in the city every day. As it was, almost no one lived there and it still took almost forty minutes to get to Westminster. The taxi that now carried Ross rapidly toward his rarely used London service flat turned left toward the river, diving down into a crazed complex of lanes and one-way alleys that wound through the old Chinese section of Limehouse. The cab continued on into the docks and warehouses of Wapping.

Ross had always liked this part of London, and was glad someone hadn't yet decided to flatten it and put in a sixteen-lane freeway or a fast-breeder reactor. He settled back in the seat and watched the crumbling facades of the warehouses that had so far escaped being made into luxury flats. Occasionally, between them, he could see the sluggish gray waters of the Thames. The sight aroused in him, as always, a slight physical pang of emotion. The river is said to affect many Londoners that way, and Ross, though he had not been born or bred within the sound of the Bells of Bow, was no exception. As they rounded the Tower and sped into the city and down toward the Strand, he felt an absurd groundswell of pride. Royal barges had plied these waters, pirates had been hung at the docks of Wapping, and the guns of the Tower were fired only for royalty on the occasion of a birth, wedding, funeral, or beheading. The river bore the history of London, swelling and ebbing in an endless obstinate heartbeat. Ross found any overt symptom of too much emotion acutely embarrassing. He turned away from the river and watched the evening crowd climbing the steps to Charing Cross Station.

Stephen Dilworth lived at 54 Catherton Street in Shepherd's Bush, in what he had referred to on the telephone as the "garden flat." Ross knew from past experience that this was estate agent lingo for "basement." When he had rung Mr. Dilworth at work the previous day Dilworth had at first seemed somewhat cagey; but as soon as he realized that Ross was not interested in him personally, he became a good deal friendlier.

Ross paid off the taxi and walked up Catherton Street. His policeman's mind could not help wondering what, in Mr. Dilworth's past, caused him to behave that way. Contrary to popular fiction, people were generally quite cooperative with the police. Well, it was really none of his business, Ross thought, if Mr. Dilworth had had a little contretemps with the tax man, or had been a shade unwilling to pay his ex-wife's last installment of child support. Ross was merely thankful Stephen Dilworth found it a titillating idea to be part of a homicide investigation. He had seemed quite willing to spill the beans on Edward Hall, presuming, of course, there were any beans to be spilled.

The garden flat's door was opened to Ross by a slightly aging Hoorah Henry clad in the obligatory striped shirt, cuff links, dark trousers, and bow tie. He shook Ross's hand heartily, pumping it up and down as he bellowed. "Dilworth, Stephen Dilworth. Frightfully good to meet you. Hope I can be of some help. Bloody awful business, this. Couldn't believe it. Read it in the *Times*. Couldn't believe it. Teddy Hall gone and murdered. A shock, I'll tell you that much. Will you have a gin and tonic?" The last part of the monologue was delivered to Ross over Stephen

Dilworth's shoulder as he made his way down the passageway that seemed to run the length of the flat.

"Thank you," Ross replied, "that would be very nice." They emerged into a large kitchen-cum-dining room. Ross was embarrassed to find himself thinking it was a good deal more tastefully done than he would have predicted. The cabinets and counters were of a soft blond oak, the range was a sleek Danish design, and the floor was terra-cotta tile.

"Bought it whole from 'Rods, I'm afraid," Stephen Dilworth shouted as he reached into the refrigerator for a lemon. "Not much good at the decorating sort of thing myself, but thought I could trust 'Rods. I mean if a fellow can't trust 'Rods and Peter Jones, what's old England coming to?" He laughed jovially at this piece of wit as he handed Ross his glass. Only then did Ross realize Stephen Dilworth had been referring to Harrods.

"Come on." Dilworth waved his arm and bounded up three steps, out through a french window into what Ross presumed to be the garden. "Far too nice an evening to spend sitting inside!" Ross followed Dilworth outside to a neat square of lawn, into which was laid a small patio. A table with an umbrella and several wrought-iron garden chairs were casually arranged. The patio's borders were filled with a riot of color. It was all so tasteful that Ross suddenly wondered if there was a Mrs. Dilworth.

"I do so like my garden!" Dilworth announced, plunking himself down in the closest chair. He gestured to Ross to sit. "A service from the Chelsea Garden Center comes in twice a week and does the whole thing. Can't do that sort of thing myself, but a chap's got to have a garden." Ross wondered if the Chelsea Garden Center could be put on the same list as 'Rods and Peter Jones as one of the few eternally trustworthy institutions, a kind of divine triumvirate of domesticity into whose care could be placed the living standards of the British gentry.

He was spared having to think too long and hard about it by Stephen Dilworth, who said, "Well then, you're looking into the death of poor old Teddy Hall, are you?"

Ross smiled and put his drink down on the table. He did not bother to enlighten Mr. Dilworth to the effect that his role was strictly unofficial.

"Dreadful thing, just dreadful," Dilworth said. "Shot to death in some awful holiday cottage. Good Lord. And how can I help you, Superintendent?"

"Actually, I'm trying to fill in the background on the victims. You see, we don't really know very much about them."

"I see," Dilworth said. "Looking for motive, are you? Thinking that if you can uncover a little blackmailing or perversion along the way, bang-oh, there's your motive and Bob's your uncle, there's the killer."

"I'm not sure it's that dramatic," Ross replied, "but something along those lines, yes. I don't suppose that Edward Hall was involved in blackmail or any other, ah, perversions, that you know of?"

Dilworth looked genuinely sorry not to be able to oblige Ross, and shook his head. "I'm afraid not that I'm aware of, though he was an odd sort of a chap, if you know what I mean."

"Not really," Ross said. "Perhaps you could explain?"

"Oh well, I don't know," Dilworth said, fishing the lemon slice from his drink. "Ambitious. That was Teddy Hall. Wanted a lot, if you know what I mean." Ross nodded encouragingly. Being ambitious and wanting a lot were two ideas that he could follow. "I mean really," Dilworth said. "That's all it was up in Glasgow. Teddy just got ambitious, that's all. Now a chap like me, I'm happy with my kitchen and my garden and—"

"Perhaps you could tell me a bit about Glasgow, from the time you worked together. That's where you met, wasn't it?"

"Yes, that's where we met all right. Shared an office at first. We were both clerking there, you see, and then joined full-time. At first I thought Teddy a dreadful snob, and then I discovered he'd only been to Bristol after all that. I mean, I thought he was Oxford, with the nickname Teddy Hall and all, don't you know? But no, there he was, Bristol all along. Perhaps that's why he went into maritime law after all, when he got down to London. In any case, we got along all right. He was charming, funny. A good chap. A good game of tennis. Sad to think of him being dead. Liked a good knees up and had big plans for himself."

"Oh?" Ross asked.

Dilworth nodded. "Teddy Hall was always talking about money. His family didn't have it, you see, and he wanted it. Talked about the house he'd have in London, his own law firm, the lot. Suppose he got quite a lot of it in the end. Not that I saw him all that often in the last few years. Can't say we moved in the same circles. Teddy'd gone a bit arty, from what I hear. Probably the wife. That sort of thing happens when there's an actress in the family. I'm more a cricket bloke myself." Dilworth held his glass up and regarded the slowly melting ice cubes as if they might contain the secrets of the universe. "You play cricket?" he asked.

"I used to," Ross replied. "Tell me about Glasgow."

"Do you mean all that about them asking Teddy to leave?"

No, you silly ass, Ross thought, I mean about the street plan. "If you would," he said, trying to smile.

Dilworth's eyes grew larger and he regarded Ross over the rim of his glass like something out of *Alice in Wonderland.* "You don't think that might have anything to do with it? Clues buried deep in his past, that sort of thing?"

"Difficult to know, until you tell me what happened."

"Right ho," Dilworth said. "It was money, of course. Teddy wanted a raise, a substantial one I think. And they simply wouldn't give it to him, which was surprising, given how hard he'd worked on the McCavert thing. Broke himself in two over that, thought it would be his ticket to a partnership. So when he asked for a raise a bit after, well, I thought they'd let him have it. But no. And after that, Teddy got somewhat bitter about the firm. Started snarking at people, picking fights, that sort of thing. And then there was a trust fund he administered with a couple of thousand quid that couldn't quite be relocated. You know how these things are, Superintendent. Nothing could ever be proved really, but pretty much everybody knew where the money had gone, or they thought they did. A firm like that doesn't want the police in, especially over a couple of thousand quid, so they just agreed it was time Teddy moved along, if you see what I mean."

"I think I understand," Ross said. He had to admit that he felt terribly let down. He had been expecting blackmail and perversion after all. Instead there was a simple matter of a sordid little theft from some spoiled child's trust fund. He felt suddenly tired and hot, and filled with the desire to be sitting in his own garden contemplating the bees in the lavender hedge, perhaps considering a walk down to the pub for supper. Instead he was stuck in London drinking gin, which he didn't even particularly like, with a shouting, overgrown schoolboy in a Billy Bunter outfit. Tomorrow he could look forward to chasing his tail around the National Theatre looking for clues probably as nonexistent as this one. In the meantime, he had his expensive, half-furnished, empty little service flat to look forward to. The prospect annoyed and depressed him. He said his thank-yous and his good-byes to Mr. Dilworth, turned down the offer of "the other half" of the gin, and took himself into the dusk in search of a taxi.

19

It was raining. Not a benevolent summer mist, but a proper, old-fashioned downpour. It fell in sheets, blowing across the Thames and pouring in streams down the plate-glass panes of the administrative offices of the National Theatre.

The office in which Ross sat was perfectly square. The far side of it was made entirely of glass, and from his visitor's chair he could see the river and the embankment and Cleopatra's Needle. While it was not a fashionable position to hold, Ross had always been rather fond of the architecture of the National Theatre complex. It was concrete and glass, a poignant reminder of the late fifties when the government and the nation still cared about the arts. He shifted in his chair and stretched out his legs. Kendal would have laughed at him and told him that he was getting grumpy in his old age. She would have been right.

His ruminations on the state of his temper were interrupted when the door opened and Marion Ploughman stepped into the office. She might have been anywhere between thirty and fifty, was of average height with average brown hair cut in an average, fashionable shoulder-length cut. She wore camel-colored trousers, a red cashmere sweater, and pearls. She might have been purchased whole at Jaeger. When Ross got to his feet to shake her hand, he towered over her.

"I'm so very sorry to have kept you waiting, Superintendent," she said, smiling. Ross stared at her in astonishment. If the rest of her was average, her voice was extraordinary, deep with an undertone that could only be described as melodious. It was one of the sexiest voices he had ever heard.

"Please sit down," she said, going around to her desk chair. As she settled herself at her desk, she removed her glasses and looked straight at him. The shrewdness in her brown eyes matched the exceptional quality of her voice. So much for average.

"I'm having coffee brought in," she said. "I assume that you'd like some?"

"That would be most welcome," he said. "Thank you, Mrs. Ploughman, for taking the time to see me on the weekend. I know how busy you must be, and I'm sorry to intrude like this."

"Not at all," she replied. "I was planning to come in to the office today in any case. I often do on the weekends. It's about the only time I can actually get anything done. As Director of Personnel here, my job is a cross between psychiatrist and riot officer, so I don't get much time at my desk. In addition to that, my husband is on his way to Tokyo, and that is always something of a production, pardon the pun. So, this is a welcome break."

The penny dropped. Now Ross realized why the name had been so familiar to him.

"Of course," he said. "Christopher Ploughman."

She smiled. Ross's reaction was one she was used to. Christopher Ploughman had recently been appointed director of the English National Opera. In newspaper photographs he appeared as tall, blond, artistic, and very handsome. Perhaps the cashmere didn't come from Jaeger after all. Ross wondered if he was losing his touch.

The coffee was poured. Cream and sugar were measured out and the secretary departed, taking with him Ross's dripping raincoat.

Marion Ploughman leaned back in her chair and said in her glorious voice, "Now, Superintendent, which one of my little lambs is it? Or do I know already?"

"Mrs. Ploughman," Ross said, leaning forward in his chair, "I'm not here to speak to you in an official capacity."

"Yet," she said, smiling.

"Possibly," he agreed. "You are aware that the investigation into the murders of the Furnival twins and their husbands has been reopened?"

She looked at him for a moment. "I see," she said very slowly. She swiveled her chair around and looked out of the window. Across the river the lights of the Savoy made yellow pinpricks in the heavy blanket of rain. When she turned back to him, her face had changed. The humor had gone from it; in its place was a kind of fatigue.

"The shepherd didn't do it?" she asked.

Ross shook his head.

"Look, Superintendent," she said, "I'll do anything I can to help you. But as far as I am concerned, this conversation is confidential. We were all fond of Claudia Furnival. How can I help?"

"Do you know what Claudia Furnival was doing up there in that cottage? What was her husband like? Her sister? Could she have been in some kind of trouble? Tell me anything at all that you can think of, no matter how trivial it seems."

She nodded. "Claudia was extremely talented. She was nervous, highly strung, I suppose you'd say, sensitive, intelligent. Some people found her difficult. But she wasn't a prima donna, she was extremely professional. The parents are dead, you know. Juliet and Claudia's parents, I mean. Have been for some time. There's a much older brother, I believe. He emigrated to Australia a long time ago. So the girls were very dependent on each other. Every cliché that you've ever heard about identical twins was true where they were concerned. It could be disturbing at times. I felt, as a matter of fact, that Juliet had much to answer for."

"How so?" Ross asked.

"Of the two of them, Juliet was the adult, the little mother. Claudia was never really able to separate her identity from Juliet, and Juliet wasn't interested in having her try too terribly hard. It wasn't just that Claudia was a shooting star—she was Juliet's shooting star."

"And Tarquin Lassiter?"

"Tarquin was lovely, utterly devoted to Claudia. He understood her, and I think he wanted to take care of her."

"Was there friction between Juliet and Lassiter?"

She shook her head. "Tarquin was too clever for that. He went with Claudia when she was reading for the part in the film in the States. They were planning to spend a couple of years in California. Tarquin would never have taken Juliet on full force. It would have been stupid and too painful for Claudia. Instead I think that, in time, he simply would have increased the distance between them to make the relationship, how shall I say, less claustrophobic? No," she said, shaking her head, "Claudia and Tarquin would have been fine. Juliet, however, well—that, as they say, is a different story. I suppose you want to hear it?"

"I'm afraid that I do."

"I don't know that it's actually all that interesting. Juliet, as I said, was the controller. Even though they were twins, Claudia was very much the 'little sister.' Juliet was here all the time when Claudia was working, so we knew her fairly well. She too could be very charming, and she was very bright. But there was a rather obvious ruthless streak in her, a very hard edge. Her husband, Edward Hall, was not a pleasant person. He was affluent, handsome, a very smooth dealer. And I do mean dealer."

"Cocaine?" Ross asked.

"That's right," she said. "As far as I know, Claudia never used it. I don't think Juliet used it either. But I am very sad to say that there were others who did."

"I see," Ross said. "And the Lassiters and the Halls spent a good deal of time together?"

"Oh yes," she replied. "Of course, if the Lassiters had made it to California, all that would have changed. Or at least come into perspective. So one would have hoped, anyway."

"And the cottage in Scotland? Do you have any idea why they went there?"

"I really think, Chief Inspector, that it was holiday, pure and simple. I know that Claudia had got rather worn down in the last year. It was a big time for her. She and Tarquin were short of money, I also know that. It's not uncommon. Contrary to popular opinion, there are only a small percentage of actors who get paid in the millions. She would have been one, had she lived. But she wasn't there yet. They'd just bought a house and they were strapped for cash. I think they wanted to get away somewhere that was easy and could be quickly arranged, so they got in touch with the Scottish Tourist Board and there you are." She leaned back in her chair, watching him. "I should think you'll be speaking to Angela Derringham?"

"Yes," he replied.

She gazed at him with her intelligent brown eyes. "Well,

in that case," she said, "I should think that you'll be hearing quite a bit about the Halls, particularly Edward."

Marion Ploughman stood. "I happen to know that Angela is at home this morning," she said. "Anthony is away for a few days at some design conference." She looked at Ross out of the corner of her eye as she walked to the door. "I'm going down front myself," she said. "I'll walk you out."

As they came down the broad central steps into the main lobby of the complex, Ross noticed a series of exhibition boards that had been set up beyond the bookstore. One caught his eye. Without intending to, he stopped and stared. The photographs on the board were publicity stills for an upcoming production. There were pictures of actors and directors, and sketches of the new set design. The colors and the layout were unmistakable. There were the familiar greens shot through with livid reds and oranges. In the midst of a wall of jungle, the face of a lion peered out, his amber eyes glowing.

Ross had seen a similar picture only a few months before in the studio of the artist who had painted it. It was the sort of thing she was well known for. Suddenly he remembered the suffusion of spring sunlight, the slight smell of turpentine, a field of daffodils blooming early in the balmy March weather. His eye traveled to the next board, and there she was. She was even wearing the same clothes, a pair of faded chino trousers and a black sweatshirt. Her hair was held back rather unsuccessfully in a clip, and her smile was crooked. Ten degrees off of a Botticelli angel, he thought. There were those who had been convinced she was a murderess.

Marion Ploughman watched him with some interest. To his horror, he realized that he was blushing.

"Kate Davidson," she said. "She's doing a series of designs for us. Do you know her?"

Ross continued looking at the picture. "Well, not really." He pulled his eyes away. "We have met, briefly."

Marion Ploughman smiled. "The divine Kate," she said. "Once met, hard to forget. Nearly as tall as you are, I should think, Superintendent. She's in the States now," she added, "but she'll be back in a month or so. I'll tell her I saw you."

Before Ross could object, she led the way across the lobby toward the main entrance.

The house was on a rather bijou square in Islington. Once this area around the Angel had been run-down, the sort of place where you found endless numbers of homes for unwed mothers, offices for third world aid associations, and small decaying parks ringed with wire fencing to replace the wrought iron that had been taken for munitions during the war and never restored. Then, about ten years ago, Islington had been rediscovered. The young and newly wealthy who couldn't afford South Kensington had noticed that there were some rather nice houses up here, some potentially pretty squares, and an awful lot of architectural features. The Beautification had begun, and Fiona, Charlotte, Peregrine, and Piers arrived in their Volkswagen Ghias and Vauxhall Astras with their paintbrushes and their Laura Ashley wallpaper. Now, of course, Fiona and Charlotte and Peregrine and Piers were all grown up and the cars along the squares were BMWs and the wallpaper had matured into Nina Campbell and this had become the land of literary parties, well-spoken children, skiing in Verbier, and polite divorce. Ross also wondered if it had become the land of obstructing evidence, misleading the police, and impeding an investigation through false testimony. The look on the face of the woman who now stood before him suggested that this just might be the case.

Angela Derringham's black dress accented her natural fairness, and for a moment she seemed so pale that she nearly dissolved into the grayness of the day beyond. Ross noticed her fine, long-boned hands. She held them awkwardly in front of her, half braced against the door, her fingers resting on the stained oak of the door panel. A heavy silver cuff encircled each wrist. The jewelry, her stillness, and the long lines of her reminded him of an Egyptian statue, a Nefertiti or a cat goddess.

"Superintendent," she said.

"Mrs. Derringham," Ross replied, standing outside the door.

"What can I do for you?" she asked.

"I thought that you might like to tell me the truth."

She smiled, as if he had made a particularly good pun, or said something very clever that only the two of them might understand. He supposed that was the case.

She stepped back and gestured to the interior of the house. "Perhaps you might like to come in."

20

The room was as graceful and well-proportioned as its owner. Three tall sash windows faced the back of the house, through which he could see rain falling across a large, well-manicured back garden. The gas fire was burning behind glass coals in a polished regency grate. An abstract portrait hung above the mantel.

"Lucien Freud," Angela said, lifting a cigarette out of a malachite box that sat on the windowsill. "It belonged to Anthony's father. Freud was a family friend. Gave it to Pa Derringham in thanks for some legal work he did. I don't think Pa thought it was much good, so he gave it to us." She leaned against the window jamb and smiled. "Someone's told you about it, have they? About us and the Halls?"

"Not really," Ross replied. He turned to look at her and thought again how very much like a black and white photograph she seemed, propped there against the grayness of the day. For the first time he noticed the lines that unhappiness had etched across the fine features of her face.

"I suppose I'd better," she said. "You're going to hear it from someone, and it might as well be me. Edward and I were lovers." She saw the look on his face and shook her head. "It ended a year or so ago. Until last week. Sorry, would you like a cigarette?"

"No, thank you. I don't smoke."

"Neither do I. Well, I'm supposed to have given them up. Mind you, I was supposed to have given up Edward as well."

"Had you?"

She nodded. "As a matter of fact, I had. Even before someone blew him to bits with a shotgun. I'd better tell you from the beginning."

"That might save rather a lot of time."

She smiled at him sheepishly and nodded. "I guess we all live in hope that we can keep our sins secret. It doesn't really happen that way, does it?"

"Often not," Ross said.

"Do sit down, by the way."

Ross settled himself on the sofa and watched her as she made her way from the window to the mantel.

"The beginning was a long time ago. At the Guildhall Drama School. Claudia and I were at the Guildhall together. That's where we met, and we stayed friends. I got out of acting when it became pretty obvious that I wasn't going to be the next Vanessa Redgrave. Besides, I'd married Anthony by then and all that. So I went into publicity for television, and eventually the theatre. Claudia was a different story. She was, well, you saw that bit in the car park at Gleneagles, you know what she was." Ross nodded. She put out her cigarette and went on. "In time Claudia and I both ended up at the National. We'd never been out of touch, as I said before. Well, during all that time Juliet was around, I mean, you didn't just know Claudia, you knew 'them.' And since Anthony and I have known each other practically all our lives, he knew them too. Juliet went into publishing, and at some point—oh, it must be six or seven years ago now—she met Edward Hall and married him. I absolutely hated him at first. And in the end too, I suppose. Anyway, I think Juliet was rather jealous of how close Clu and I were. I don't know, or she loved me or hated me or something, hard to tell with Juliet. But the Halls sort of took us over as friends. Lots of Sunday lunches at each other's houses and that sort of thing. A few holidays together as well. Claudia wasn't there a lot of the time because of work. I don't know when or how it happened, exactly, but after a while there was cocaine. We all knew Edward used it rather a lot, Juliet occasionally, Claudia, as far as I know, never. Anyways, Anthony used it a bit, and then I started to more and more, and then somewhere, somehow, in the middle of it all, Edward and I became lovers." She crossed the room to the window and picked another cigarette from the green box. As she bent to light it, Ross saw that her hand was trembling.

"I don't know if Juliet knew or not," she said, looking at him from across the room. "I should think that if she did, it would have amused her. It went on for two and a half years. During that time, Edward and Juliet borrowed about thirty thousand pounds from us as a down payment for a farm they wanted to buy in France. We were still spending an awful lot of time together, and finally, between the lying to Anthony and the cocaine, I thought the whole thing was going to kill me. Just over a year ago I went to Claudia for help. She persuaded me to tell Anthony, and I did, and we stopped seeing the Halls altogether. I went off to one of those places in the country for rich ladies and we were all right again. Sort of.

"Claudia and I got much closer, but we didn't see the Halls at all. Anthony and I were really working to make things better. Then, about three months ago, I was offered a job in New York. Anthony's looking into finding something over there as well, but it's difficult. We wanted to start again, and Manhattan seemed like the perfect answer. But we didn't want to sell this house, and in order to go and have Tony not working, we needed our thirty thousand pounds back. We decided to try to make peace and that was why we went to Scotland."

"And did you make peace?"

She stared out of the window for a moment and then looked back at him. "Apparently not," she said.

Ross leaned back against the pale green brocade of the Derringham sofa and thought about how often it was that one asked one question and got the answer to another. It was like a chain reaction, small explosions of information, each sparked by another that seemed, at first, unrelated. He had no doubt that what Angela had just told him was the truth, and there was no doubt that it was an interesting truth, but it was still not the truth that he had come here to discuss.

"Mrs. Derringham," he said, "I don't know if you're aware of the fact, but the investigation into the deaths has been reopened."

A fearful look flickered across her face for just a moment. "What do you mean?"

"New evidence has been uncovered which lead the police to believe that Danny Blaine may not have been solely responsible for the killings." He added, "He may not have been responsible at all."

She stared at him, and Ross stared back, thinking the alarm on her face was not due to the fear that she too would be murdered by crazed maniacs with guns.

"Mrs. Derringham," he said, leaning forward, "I am not here in an official capacity, as you're aware. And you have absolutely no obligation to speak with me. However, I was present when you made your initial statement to Detective

Inspector Callum, and I cannot help but wonder if there isn't something you might like to tell me? In all likelihood I can help you, if you'll let me."

"I don't understand what you mean."

"I think you do," Ross said quietly. "You see, there were visitors who were at the Carey farm at six P.M. In addition to that, I'm afraid that you were seen, in Edinburgh, shortly after five. Alone."

She stared at him for a moment before she sank down into an armchair on the far side of the room. The effect was similar to a puppet whose strings have been cut.

"Angela," Ross said quietly, "as I've said, you have no obligation to talk to me, and if you would prefer, I'll leave now. But I might be able to help if you tell me the truth."

"I don't know," she said. There was a faint edge of panic in her voice.

"What don't you know?" Ross asked.

"I don't know what happened," she said. "I just don't know."

Ross got up and collected the cigarette box from the windowsill, offered her one, and lit it for her. Then he sat down on the sofa again, rested his elbows on his knees and said, "You were in Edinburgh until sometime after five. You were on your own. Anthony had taken the car and he didn't lunch with you either, did he?" She shook her head. "What happened?" Ross asked.

"We had a row," she whispered. Ross could barely hear her voice against the steady patter of the falling rain.

"You had a row in Edinburgh?"

"In the morning, on the way. We went for coffee at the Balmoral when we arrived, and I told Anthony that I didn't know if I could go on any longer. With us, I mean. I said I thought it might be better if I went to New York alone."

"And then what happened?"

"He was furious. We decided to spend the day apart, to meet at four to go back."

"But he didn't turn up?"

"No. Not until almost half past five."

"Did you ask him where he'd been?"

She nodded. "He said he'd been driving. That's all. Just driving. I didn't think anything of it, really. Not until we got back. Not until we found—"

"Yes," Ross said.

"I had to protect him," she said suddenly.

"Is the rest of it true?" Ross asked. "The rest of the statement you gave them?"

She nodded. "Yes," she said. "All the rest of it except for the time."

"Angela, tell me about before. About the few days before the killings. What did you do? Tell me anything that you can remember."

She twisted around in her chair and looked out of the window toward the drenched garden. "We flew up on the Sunday," she said. "We were supposed to go on the Friday night and spend a week, but we didn't really want to stay all that long. So we put it off until Sunday afternoon. We got there in the evening and then we had supper, and after supper we watched this videotape that Tarquin had made of the holiday so far. Someone had given them a video camera for their wedding, and he was driving everyone mad taping with it all the time. So we watched that, 'Holiday at Grotty Cotty,' I think he'd called it. Then on Monday we did, you know, touristy things. We went to Stirling and climbed about on the castle in the morning, and in the afternoon we went to some sheepdog trials. That night we'd got some grouse from somewhere or other, so we did those up and had them at home. Then on the Wednesday, Claudia and I went shopping in the morning in Blairlochie. I'm not sure what the others did. And in the afternoon we went for a walk, and then Anthony and I went down to the distillery and bought some malt and did the tour thing at about teatime. The others didn't want to come because they'd already been. Then that night we decided we needed a treat, so we took ourselves out to Gleneagles. Claudia'd got herself a bit overwrought and I think everyone felt like a change of scene."

"Tell me about that," Ross said.

She looked at him, not understanding.

"About Claudia getting overwrought, I mean."

"Oh," she said. "It happens from time to time. She gets terribly overtired and then she gets a bit, you know. It's true, actually, all that bit about artistic temperament. I didn't pay much attention to it at the time, to be honest. I wish to Christ I had."

"Why?" Ross asked.

"Because of what she said." Angela looked away from the window and stared straight at him. Tears were welling in her large gray eyes, and she reached up with the side of her hand and brushed them away like a child might.

"What did she say?"

"She said that the place was haunted, that there was something in that cottage, that she could feel it and she was afraid. None of us paid any attention to her."

Ross sat in his unfurnished sitting room, closed his eyes, and listened to Chopin. He had been to Wheelers, which he didn't much like, for a fillet of sole, which wasn't much good. With it, he'd had a few glasses of mediocre wine. The whole episode had cost quite a bit. Not a particularly satisfactory experience. He opened his eyes and looked out of the window. His flat overlooked a small private garden that ran along the back of the block of the building. In it was a statue of a naked girl running about with a lot of doves. Ross rather liked it. One day, he thought, I shall do something about furnishing this flat. He'd bought the place in order to have a toehold in London, which he really didn't need. He wasn't altogether sure if he'd done it because he thought that one day he might be a very important policeman and thus need to be within moments of Westminster in the event of a crisis of national importance, or whether he'd done it for sentimental reasons, since he simply couldn't bear to feel as if he didn't have anything to do with London anymore. He had begun his career with the Metropolitan Police, and while Kendal had been alive their home had been in Knightsbridge, not far from her family house in Eaton Place. After she died, however, he lost the heart for it, just as he had lost the heart for the fast pace of the Met. He had sold up and moved to Kent and what was supposed to be a new and less harrowing career. Within a year, however, he'd bought this flat. It fed the illusion that he was still somehow connected to what had been, it now seemed, a so much better time. I shall buy a carpet, he thought, and a chair to go with this sofa, and perhaps even a desk; one to go under the large painting of his grandmother, which dominated almost the whole far wall of the little sitting room. He liked having this beautiful lady for company. She was always impeccably dressed, always smiling, always living in the romantic 1900s summer landscape of her background, in an England now gone forever.

He wondered about Angela Derringham. Would her painted portrait come out in black and white, or would a gifted artist somehow manage to find her well-hidden color? Something was not right! Something he'd heard or that he knew, or that he ought to know. His ruminations were interrupted by the shrill ringing of his telephone. The world, Ross thought as he went to answer it, would be an immeasurably better place if there were less communication. He knew before he picked it up that his caller was Owen.

"Hoi, master," Owen said, by way of greeting. "You have any plans for ever coming north again?"

"Tomorrow morning, I thought."

"Good thing," Owen said. "Why don't you make it

early? There's a six A.M. commuter flight I've booked you on. I'll collect you at Edinburgh."

"What's going on?" Ross asked. He could feel Owen's excitement running all the way down the line.

"All holy hell's broken loose, that's what all," Owen replied. "Your boy Danny Blaine had a good go at getting himself killed in a prison bust-up this afternoon, but you won't need to worry about that. He's in the infirmary and he's not going to be talking to anyone for a while. But that's not it. We've got a lead on Julie. We're meeting a Moira Lawrence tomorrow at nine A.M. in a lay-by up near St. Andrews. Or rather you are. She knows about you somehow, and she's told Callum you're the only person she'll talk to."

"How—" Ross started to ask, but Owen cut him off.

"Don't fret on it, master. I'll explain all when I collect you. Just don't miss the flight. It's Caledonian 68, from London City."

21

Owen was waiting for Ross at the barrier beyond the arrivals gate. He wore a pair of moleskin trousers and a tattersall check shirt, and at first Ross didn't recognize him.

"I see you've become a sporting gentleman," he said.

"And why not?" Owen asked, leading him out toward the car park. "I like this shootin' and fishin' lark as much as the next chap, just don't get much of a chance to practice my countryman's skills. Nanda told me to go play golf, the saucy kit, and when I wouldn't do that, she tricked me out like a country toff."

"Very becoming it is too," Ross said as they threaded their way through the car park. "I especially like the shoes." Owen gazed down admiringly at his feet: encased in a very new pair of Church's walking brogues.

"My wife's good." Owen flipped open the hatchback of

his rental car, noticably nicer than Ross's, and placed Ross's overnight bag in the boot. "Hop in, master," he said. "Your chariot awaits."

The chariot had cleared the ticket booths and turned due northwest on the roundabout by the time Ross had finished filling Owen in on his trip to London.

"Our friend Edward was into a little recreational coke, was he?" Owen said.

"It sounds it," Ross replied. "Possibly more than recreational. That would bear some looking into, I should think. Also, we ought to suggest to Callum that they run a search for priors on him, though I'm certain he's done that already. Have you spoken to him, by the way?"

"He rang this morning to let me know that our lady's changed the meeting place. You're having a rendezvous on the seafront now. You're to hang about on one of the benches. She'll find you."

"How does she know me?" Ross asked.

Owen shrugged. "I've no idea. Presumably your fame precedes you. You shall have to ask her. Oh, and Callum says can you ring him first thing you get back."

"Right," Ross said absently.

"So Angie has an affair with Teddy and the wife does or doesn't know about it. The husband doesn't know about it until she tells him, and then we can assume that he's not happy. In fact, it would be safe to say that he probably didn't like old Teddy Hall one little bit, seeing how he's turned his wife into a cocaine addict and been doing the dirty on her as well." He glanced at Ross and smiled. "Throw a thirty-thousand-pound bad debt in and it sounds like a motive to me."

"On the other hand, why kill all the others as well?"

"He got carried away? We can assume he's new at this and he got a bit panicky."

"Or he hired someone and they got it wrong."

"Could be. But then, where the hell was he all that

afternoon, if someone else was doing the job? If I'd gone and hired someone to kill my wife's lover and her best friend, etcetera, etcetera, I'd be damn sure that I was somewhere far away with a very solid alibi."

"True," Ross said. "So perhaps he hired someone to help him."

"Or it's one of those old school friend things. You know, anything for a chum?"

Ross looked at him. "I don't think even Eton's that bad," he said.

"You should know," Owen replied.

Ross was heartily affronted. "I went to Winchester."

"Oh, I beg your pardon," Owen said. "Mumbles Grammar and Comprehensive."

"Tell me about my date," Ross said, changing the subject before it further degenerated. "Who is she and where did they find her and why do we think she might know anything about Julie? Oh, and what the hell happened to Danny Blaine?"

"Last one first," Owen said, changing lanes and accelerating up the motorway toward St. Andrews. "Danny Blaine got himself into a very nasty prison scrape in the exercise yard. Somebody had a really good go at him with a knife. Some other good Samaritan decided to stop him, or else there'd be no Danny Blaine. He's in the infirmary and he's not going to be talking to anyone for a while." Ross was tempted to comment that that wouldn't make an awful lot of difference since he didn't do an awful lot of talking to start with, but he was too disturbed by the story to say much of anything. All he could think of was the look of utter passivity that hung about Danny Blaine. It was difficult to imagine him getting in a serious scrap with anyone, much less something savage enough to involve knives and near death.

"Do they know who did it?" Ross asked.

"What?" Owen said. "Oh, Danny Blaine. I think Callum said something about it, yes. They've got the geezer locked up, for what good that will do. Were you listening to me at all?"

"Sorry," Ross said. "Actually, I wasn't."

"Well, I was telling you about this girl, woman, whatever," Owen said. "And since we're all but in St. Andrews, perhaps you'd better listen more carefully, sir."

"I'm sorry," Ross said. "Go on."

"Glasgow's got rather a lot of squealers, use them for the drug trade, smuggling, that sort of thing. Anyway, Callum put out the word that we were looking for Julie, and 'Hey presto' one of them comes up with the goods. Says he knows this girl who he thinks knows her. The girl sends word back through the geezer that she can't talk to the police, but she'll talk to you. And no, I don't have a clue how she knew who you were or that you were up here."

"Well, the last's easy enough," Ross said, "it was in the papers that I'd been a witness and was assisting the police in their inquiries."

"There you are then," Owen said. "Perhaps she just fell in love with your photo. There was a photo, I take it?"

"Yes," Ross said sheepishly. "As a matter of fact, there was."

"Well," Owen said, "in approximately ten minutes you'll have a chance to ask her, because we've arrived in St. Andrews." And he swung the car up the exit ramp and headed for the waterfront.

The pier at St. Andrews is a sturdy stone structure that stretches only a short way out into the sea. This Sunday morning the day was bright and clear, and it appeared to Ross that the whole population of St. Andrews that was not playing golf was occupying itself by promenading up and down the pier. The only bench he could see was occupied, so he took his place amongst the strollers. He made his way to the end of the pier, where he stood for a moment looking out across the water. He wondered if the Vikings had come this way to make their landfall and then remembered that was supposed to be Lindisfarne on the Northumberland coast. John Knox had come this way, however, and as Ross turned and began to walk slowly back along the pier, he could see on the hill above him the great skeleton of St. Andrews Cathedral, which Knox had had demolished in his crusade of reformist zeal. Cromwell's men had finished the job and now all that was left was the stone outline of the apse, standing like a gray line drawing against the August sky's deep blue.

He was about to turn and begin his way back toward the water when a voice beside him said, "Are you Chief Inspector Ross, then?"

The woman who stood beside him was short and slightly dowdy. She had brown curly hair cut short and glasses thick enough to be the bottoms of beer bottles. He offered her his hand, and she shook it with a vigor that matched the determined tone of her voice.

"I'm Moira Lawrence," she said. "It's good of you to come. Shall we walk awhile?"

They had reached the end of the pier and stood watching the steady, foaming slap of the small waves before Moira Lawrence spoke again. "It's to do with Danny, isn't it?" she said. "The reason you're looking for Julie?"

"Not entirely," Ross said carefully. He looked down at the curly mop of brown hair that came barely to his shoulder. She stood beside him staring straight out over the Firth of Forth, her eyes fixed on some far point that Ross suspected was located more in memory than on the gray-blue chop of the water stretched out before them.

"She's in trouble, isn't she?" Moira said, looking up at him.

"Yes," Ross replied. "I'm afraid that she may well be. It is important, Miss Lawrence, that we find her as quickly as possible. If you have any idea, any idea at all where she is, or if you can get a message to her . . . She's not wanted by the police herself. It's for her own protection. So if you do know where she is—"

"Oh, I've no idea where she is," Moira said, cutting him off. "She's disappeared, hasn't she? When she didn't ring last Wednesday night, I was worried. Always rings on a Wednesday, right as rain for the last three years at least. So, when she didn't ring Wednesday, and then I saw on the news about the killings . . . well, I went to her flat, didn't I? And they tell me she's gone, and then another Wednesday goes by and by now I'm in a state I am. But not so bad, I'll tell you, as having Kenny coming into the shop and going on like a lunatic—"

"Kenny?" Ross asked.

"Oh aye, Kenny." She shook her head. "Like out of his brain, he was. Thank God I'd no customers there. It was just before closing, see. And he's going mad, shrieking and screaming and carrying on about Julie—"

"Miss Lawrence," Ross said. "I'm sorry. You'll have to fill me in. You see, I'm not following you. Who is Kenny?"

She looked at him as though he were a slightly slow child and said, "Well, he's her brother, isn't he?"

"That would be Kenny Taylor, would it?" Ross asked.

She didn't answer immediately, but continued to look up at him as though he was either out of his mind or intensely disappointing to her, or both. Then she smiled slightly. "Taylor," she said. "So she's still using that name, is she? Well, I should have known. No, her brother's not Kenny Taylor. MacDonald, man. MacDonald. That's her name."

Ross stared at her. It took him a moment to remember why the name Kenny MacDonald was familiar to him, and then he recalled Andrew Callum and the talk about a minor, or possibly not so minor thug, who'd skipped his parole.

"Are you telling me," Ross said slowly, "that Julie is Kenny MacDonald's sister?"

"You don't have a clue, do you?" she said.

"It appears that I don't." Ross said slowly.

She looked back up the pier toward the town and then she took hold of his elbow. "Come on," she said. "We'll go and have a coffee."

The café was almost empty. Its large plate-glass window looked down toward the water and had BAPS, SAUSAGES, CHIPS lettered across it in an arch of bright orange paint. Moira parked Ross at a linoleum table in the corner next to a large plastic fern in a wicker pot. She returned a moment later with two cups of coffee and two packets of biscuits wrapped in cellophane. Ross was still trying to digest what she'd told him. If Julie Taylor was the sister of some Glaswegian underground figure—what was it Andrew had called them? Our answer to the Kray twins?—and she was involved with Danny Blaine and had evidence relating to the killings, then what could the possible connection be to the Furnival twins and their husbands and Angela and Anthony Derringham? Assuming, of course, that she did have evidence. But if she didn't, why would she run? And why wouldn't Blaine talk? Assuming, of course, that they were all talking about the same person. That's it, Ross thought: we've got the wrong person. This is all a mistake. But even as he thought it, he knew that it wasn't true.

Still, just to be sure, when Moira sat down and started stirring her coffee, Ross put the snapshot of Julie and the little boy and the dog down on the faded red linoleum of the table and said, "That is her? That is the same girl? I want you to be quite sure."

Moira emptied a packet of sugar into her coffee and nodded. "Oh aye," she said. "That's her. That's Julie with little David. The dog's Danny's, is it?"

"You're certain, Miss Lawrence, really certain that this is the same girl?"

Moira looked up at him with a slight grimace of exasperation and said, "Call me Moira, everyone else does." She took a sip of her coffee and put it down. "Look, perhaps I'd better tell you the whole story."

"Yes," Ross said, "I think that perhaps you'd better."

"Well," she said, "Julie and I, we were in the same school, right? Julie's, oh I don't know, maybe two or three years younger than me. My family, we moved to Glasgow, didn't come from there. So it wasn't quite the same for us, as far as Kenny and Terry are concerned, I mean." She leaned back in her chair and extracted a package of cigarettes from her handbag. "How much do you know about the MacDonalds?" she asked.

Ross shook his head, turning down her offer of a cigarette, and said, "Not much. Why don't you tell me?"

"They're a nasty piece of work," she said. "Terry, he's the older one, he's pretty much your everyday bother boy. Got a few brains, more or less took over the family business from his dad. Got done a while back in a proper smuggling case that went to court and the lot. In the end they couldn't make charges stick. Kenny, the younger one, he's *really* a nasty piece of work. He's not right in the head, mean just for the sake of it, all twisted up. He's only about a year younger than Terry, idolizes him. So that's the two of them. There's a part of Glasgow they just about run, down in the Gorbals. There was a rumor that the old man, the one who started it all, that he was mixed up in some even bigger stuff, but that might've just been talk. Then there's Julie. She was born later, an accident, if you know what I mean, a good ten years younger than her brothers, and right from the start Kenny had this thing for her. Called her his princess, bought all her clothes, the lot. Like she was his little doll."

She shook herself and finished the last of her coffee. "Gives me the creeps, it does," she said, "even just thinking about it. By the time we'd moved there and I met Julie in school, she must've been, I don't know, ten or eleven. She was a weedy little kid, you know, skinny, small for her age, quiet. Anywhere else other kids might've bullied her, but not there, not where people knew who her brothers were. It's funny, isn't it, what kids know without being told? Like Julie. Julie knew that she wasn't to have friends. So we kept it a secret. No one ever said anything to us or anything like that, we just knew. Kenny brought her to school every morning and he was waiting for her when school finished every afternoon. Like I said, it was creepy. I don't even like to think about what it was like for her at home. If the teachers noticed, well, they weren't about to say anything, were they?

"Anyway," she went on, stubbing her cigarette out in the blue plastic ashtray, "I got out. More or less. After school finished I went to beauty school, worked as a cutter. I've got my own place. Samantha, it's called, down Anderson road. Julie stayed at home. Not that she had much choice. But Kenny liked her to look nice, if you get my drift. So he let her have her hair done regular every Wednesday afternoon. He let her have a little car, a little blue Metro, and she was allowed to drive herself to have her hair done, so I'd see her once a week. So one day, right after she's finished school, must be six, seven years ago now, she comes in and she looks different. I dunno, like they say, radiant or something, and that's the first time she tells me about Danny Blaine. She's met this bloke, she says, who works for her brother, but he's not like that, he's different and they're in love.

"Well," Moira said, looking at Ross, "I can tell you right

now, I knew there was going to be trouble. I mean, I couldn't see Kenny letting her have a boyfriend. I said to her, 'For Christ's sake, Julie, be careful.' And she sort of giggled. I remember that, you see, on account of she didn't exactly laugh much, our Julie. So about a year later she comes in and she tells me she and Danny are going to have a baby. Well, she seemed cheerful enough about it, and so I asked her, 'Does Kenny know?' 'Oh yes,' she says. And I ask her what Kenny thinks, and she doesn't answer me at all. She just looks at me and then she pulls up the sleeve of her jersey. Black and blue isn't in it. From the elbow to the wrist and I'm certain there was more. He was always careful, he never did it to her face, anywhere you could see. Apparently he'd almost killed Danny as well.

"That was the first time, that afternoon, that she started talking about how Danny was going to save her. He was going to take her away. They were going to go to New Zealand. He was going to work as a shepherd. After that, after she got knocked up, she and Danny started pretending like they weren't so keen on each other anymore, mainly so Kenny wouldn't kill them both. But they still saw each other. Kenny made a mistake, giving Julie that little blue car. After the bairn was born, he eventually set her up in her own flat, just around the corner, but still it was hers. The baby drove him mad. Sometime 'round then Danny went off south and he did do some shepherding. I don't think Kenny and Terry had much for him to do just then, or something, but you never get away from them, if you know what I mean. Still, it suited Kenny fine, because if Danny was down south, there was no way he could be seeing Julie, right?

"Well, a bit after that, I got the chance to have my own shop here. I couldn't leave Glasgow fast enough, I'll tell you. Julie somehow wangled the move to a new flat about then, a bit farther away, and even though she wasn't on the phone, she used to ring me, right as rain, every Wednesday evening. You see, other than Danny, I was the only outside world she knew. So she rang me every Wednesday until the last two. Until the night of the murders."

"And she was still seeing Danny Blaine?" Ross asked.

Moira nodded. "Regular," she said. "She told me that she'd got Kenny pretty much convinced that it was all over, that they didn't even think about each other anymore. But nothing was farther from the truth. Mind, they had to be very careful. You see, Danny'd gone back to working for Kenny and Terry, hadn't he?"

Ross stared at her. "You mean now? In the last year?"

"I think so," Moira said. "That's what Julie told me. Like I said, you don't leave people like that, you know? At least not unless it's feet first. They wait until they need you, and then they call, and when they call, you come."

"So they'd called Danny?"

"That's right, or so Julie said. Kenny was making her nervous. She wasn't totally certain he believed her about not seeing Danny anymore. He's a sly bugger, Kenny is. She told me that she thought he'd found some job for Danny 'cause he wanted to keep an eye on him."

"The car?" Ross asked. "Does she still have it? The blue Metro?"

Moira shrugged. "I think so, but I dunno. She might do."

"We know that she left the flat on Stephenson Road in a hurry on the night of the murders—"

"Wednesday week?"

"That's right."

"Well, I don't know about the car," Moira said. "Like I said, we mostly just talked on the phone. You might try minicab services in the area."

Ross looked at her for a moment, feeling like an ass for not having thought of it himself.

"And another thing," Moira said, "I think they might have had a plan."

"A plan?" Ross asked. She nodded. "Yeah, Julie and

Danny, for escaping, like. I'm not sure that the whole thing about New Zealand was actually such a lark. She did tell me once that he was sending her money, his salary. Well, most of it anyways. She had to keep that a secret, so she opened another savings account. That's when she first used the name Taylor. You might check the Giro accounts, Building Society, that sort of thing. Julie would have been intimidated by anything grand, and it would have had to be somewhere she could go regular without attracting attention. I'll tell you something else for nothing," she added. "Kenny's looking for her. So she's not run to the bosom of her family."

"You said Kenny came to your shop?" Ross asked.

Moira nodded and fished in her bag for another cigarette. "That about freaked me out," she said. "Like I said, Kenny's a sly bugger, and he must have put two and two together that she'd come to me for haircuts all those years so we might still be friends. Well, of course I pretended that I hadn't heard from her since I moved here."

"Did he believe you?"

"Dunno. He was out of his head. First he comes screaming through the door like a mad thing, yelling about do I know where she is and when he finds her he's going to kill her and she's betrayed him and all that. Then he practically breaks down and starts to cry, telling me about how she's the only good thing in his life and he wants his princess back. Well, like I said, thank God I'd no customers."

"When was this?" Ross asked.

"Three nights ago," she said, "Thursday, just before closing. I'm not frightened of that scum, but it shook me up, I'll tell you. So when that grass Neil Kennedy comes and tells my brother that he's heard the police are looking for Julie, well, I didn't have to think too long about talking to you. You see," she said, "the way I figure it, someone's going to find her, and it will be a whole lot better for her if it's you and not Kenny. But I'll tell you this," she added. "You'd better get a move on, because Kenny won't hang about. Christ, he'd probably kill me if he knew I'd talked to you."

"May I ask you something?"

She smiled at him. "What else have you been doing all morning?"

"True enough," he said. "I'm curious. I wanted to know how you knew I was involved in this, why you wanted to talk to me 'specially?"

"Read the piece in the paper, didn't I?" she said. "I don't like the Bill much, but you, well, you've got a nice face."

Ross felt himself smiling. "Moira," he said, "let me know if you ever want a job with the police."

22

Walking back toward the car park where he had agreed to meet Owen, Ross found himself indulging in a highly uncharacteristic fit of nerves. Twice he stopped in front of shop windows, studying the reflections of people who passed by him to see if any of them were the same. As he made his way back up through the town, he crossed the road several times, zigzagging and watching to see if anyone zigged and zagged with him. As far as he could tell, they did not, but still he couldn't shake the sensation that he was being followed.

Owen was in a phone booth on the far side of the parking lot, and as Ross approached, Owen gestured vigorously to him. A few seconds later Owen hung up and bounded out of the booth like a jack-in-the-box.

"That was the Tourist Board," he told Ross as he

unlocked the car. "The bit of it that's responsible for renting cottages. We've an appointment to see a Margaret Carruthers at noon, before she goes for the day. If we step on it, we won't miss her." He leaned across and unlocked Ross's door, and as he did, he said, "So, have you found Julie, then?"

"I'm afraid not," Ross said, "but I've certainly found out about her. What do the names Kenny and Terry MacDonald mean to you?"

"Scotland's answer to the Kray twins?"

"I do wish everyone would stop saying that," Ross said irritably. He was beginning to feel as if he was the only policeman in the U.K. who didn't know the intimate details of the MacDonalds' criminal history.

"Why?" Owen asked as he pulled out of the parking lot, narrowly missing a bakery delivery van. "What've they got to do with the time of day?"

"Not much," Ross said, "but they've quite a bit to do with Julie Taylor."

"Oh? And how's that?"

"Well, for a start, her name's not Taylor. It's MacDonald. She's their sister." The car swerved dangerously as Owen stared at him.

"Bloody hell," he said. "You must be joking? What the hell does that mean?"

"I'm not altogether certain," Ross replied. "But I have an uneasy feeling that we're going to find out." If he hadn't, at that moment, been almost totally preoccupied by the thought that Owen was about to kill them both in his attempt to pass a trailer truck, he might have noticed the maroon Ford Granada that followed them down the exit ramp and moved into the motorway lane behind them.

"It could be coincidence," Owen said when Ross had finished filling him in.

Ross gave him a long look.

"I know, I know," Owen said as he pulled into a parking

space that was almost in front of the Scottish Tourist Agency office. "You don't believe in coincidence."

"Only in cheap crime novels," Ross replied. And he got out of the car and fished in his pocket for a twenty-pence piece for the meter.

The office was new and modular. In this travel agency, the only destination was Scotland. Posters of Scotland, from coast to coast and John O'Groats to the border, covered the walls. Two plastic chairs sat next to a melamine table that held a profusion of brochures describing the possibilities and attractions of sheepdog trials, hurling matches, and salmon fishing. A glossy leaflet sang the praises of the festival production of *Macbeth* that was to be performed on the castle grounds. Owen rang the bell for service.

The woman who appeared behind the counter might have come out of one of the brochures herself. She was plump and jolly, with bright red hair. Her navy-blue pullover sported a name tag that read "Margaret Carruthers."

"Mrs. Carruthers," Owen said, "I'm Owen Davies and this is Superintendent Ross from the Kent County Constabulary. We're involved in a fraud investigation and we would be most grateful if you could give us a moment of your time." Ross wondered when it was that Owen had become such a charming and fluent liar.

"Oh, of course," Mrs. Carruthers said, positively beaming at any opportunity to be of assistance to the fraud squad. "You'd be the gentleman that rang earlier. Yes, I've pulled out the file already, so you can have a look at it. Of course, that was a terrible business," she added, her face becoming momentarily grave before springing back into its almost relentlessly cheery mold. Ross wondered if it was the very idea of people visiting Scotland that made her so gleeful. And he suppressed the desire to comment that "terrible business" certainly was one way to think of the shotgun massacre of four people. Perhaps she meant it in the literal sense, as in the fact that it might not be the best advertisement for a week in the bonnie highlands.

The blue paper folder Owen spread onto the counter contained a rental agreement, a contract, and copies of several letters. Owen handed Ross the contract and the rental agreement. Both of them were in the name of Edward Hall Esq. of Kensington Church Street, London. No other names were included.

"Did you deal with this rental yourself?" Ross asked, trying not to let his distaste for this rather silly and hopelessly happy woman creep into his voice.

"Oh yes," she replied. "I'm really the only one here, you see, half the time. Since we had to let Alice go, that is. Now that was a real shame. Such a nice girl—"

Ross smiled and nodded, effectively cutting her off before they could hear too much more about Alice's virtues. "And Mr. Hall arranged the rental himself, did he?" he asked.

"Oh yes," she said, "a most charming gentleman. Yes. He said he wanted to take his wife and her sister for a bit of a holiday. He chose the Balnacoil cottage. I must admit I did write to him and say that it wasn't the nicest we had available." She held up a photocopy of a letter, and clipped to it, a picture of a rather pretty little stone cottage that appeared to be next to the sea. "It was pushy of me, I know," she went on, smiling, "but I did send them the information on Dolphin Cottage. It's such a pretty place, and it was available for the two weeks they wanted. I'd just had a cancellation, actually. But he wasn't having any of it. He did write and thank me for being so considerate, but he said Balnacoil had struck their fancy."

"Oh well," Ross said, "I should think that Dolphin Cottage was perhaps a bit too small?"

"Oh no." Mrs. Carruthers was clearly scandalized that

he should think that she might make so gross an error as that. "Dolphin Cottage is rather larger and exactly the same price per week. No, Mr. Hall was simply most set on Balnacoil. But there you are. There's no accounting for taste, is there? That's why we have so many listed, after all. People come in as many shapes and flavors as cottages, I always say."

"Yes," Ross said. "I'm sure you do." He closed the folder and handed it back to her with his best schoolboy smile. "You've been a great help, Mrs. Carruthers, I can't thank you enough," he said. In an instant he was out the door, with Owen hurrying along behind him in his new Church's walking shoes.

Ross drove them back to Gleneagles. He was feeling rather old and tired, and he wasn't sure that his heart could take too much more of Owen's distinctive chauffeuring style.

"What do you make of that?" Owen asked.

"Edward Hall wanted to be at Balnacoil and nowhere else, it seems," Ross replied. He had turned off onto the back roads and they were winding their way through the hills toward Auchterarder. He glanced at Owen, who was reclining in the passenger seat and staring out of the window at the passing hills tinged purple with heather. "Do you still think the fact that Danny Blaine worked for the MacDonalds is a coincidence?"

"Nope," Owen replied. "Do you think the fact that he was nearly killed in prison just after you went to visit him and the announcement was made about new evidence was a coincidence?"

"Nope," Ross replied.

They drove for a while in silence.

"Kensington Church Street," Owen said a few minutes later.

"Hmmm," Ross said. "I thought the same thing."

"Pricey area, even if you are a solicitor and your wife's in publishing. I mean, I don't know that it's a particularly lucrative line, maritime law. Perhaps it is. Perhaps he worked for Onassis."

"Onassis is dead," Ross said.

"So's Edward Hall," Owen said.

Ross smiled in spite of himself and came to a stop at the crossroads in Auchterarder village. He glanced in the rearview mirror and thought, with a flash of annoyance, that the stupid red Ford was tailgating.

"Check into it," he said, pulling out and turning left toward Gleneagles. "Let's see if someone can't have a look at the state of the Hall family finances for us."

"I mean, it's entirely possible he was unwilling to pay the Derringhams back because he didn't have the money. Did you ask her about that?"

Ross nodded. He remembered Angela Derringham curled in her armchair, the sound of the rain on the wide sash windows of the sitting room in Islington. "She said that Edward said he would pay them, apparently within the year or something."

"Kensington Church Street, a farm in France, and a cocaine habit. I'm surprised they could afford to come to Scotland, even with a thirty thousand loan. Then there's brother Derringham rushing about in a jealous temper through the highlands. The only problem is a jealous temper doesn't fit with all the signs of premeditation. And if he hired someone, he must have known it was going to happen, so why leave yourself without an alibi? Unless he was one of the killers. Hell, for all we know, Angela could be the other. The powder room lady didn't see her until after three, according to Nanda. That gives her time to drive back to the cottage, do the dirty with him, drive them both back to Edinburgh and go through the hoopla of pretending she can't find him."

"Did anyone look into the mileage on that car, by the way?" Ross asked.

"I should think that's what Callum wanted to speak to you about. Be a good chap and ring him at home when we get in, will you? I gather he's stuck there this afternoon, something to do with a dog."

Ross nodded and turned in through Gleneagle's large gates. The dark red Ford narrowly avoided crashing into his tail end, and while he was relieved that its occupants were not tailing him up the drive on their way to a Gleneagles Sunday lunch, he still had a few eloquent words on his mind for local Sunday drivers.

The message light on Ross's phone was flashing when he reached his room, and as he guessed, the message was from Andrew Callum, asking him to ring him at home. Ross put his overnight bag back on the rack and sat down at the desk that faced the window. He looked out for a moment onto the slopes of Glendevon, and then he picked up the receiver and dialed. The voice that answered was instantly familiar. Harry Matchum's thick Yorkshire accent reminded Ross of the first time he had heard it, a few months before, when he had been working on a case at home. Matchum, a newspaperman in York, had been peripherally involved, and although Ross had never met him, he felt that their phone conversations concerning Ellis Martin had made them friends.

"Chief Inspector!" Matchum said after Ross had identified himself, "How're you keeping?"

"I'm very well," Ross replied. "How are you, Harry?"

"Oh," Matchum said, "the same, the same. Still giving up smoking, still trying to convince myself that running two miles a day instead is good for me, still waiting for Elizabeth Taylor to ring up and ask me to write her life story."

Ross smiled. "I'm sorry to bother you at home on a

Sunday at lunchtime," he said, "but actually, I was hoping that you might have some time to spare to do a job for me?"

"Now, Chief Inspector," Harry Matchum said, and Ross did not bother to tell him that he'd been promoted, "you know I'm always willing to put in a little time to help the forces of law and order."

"I'm grateful," Ross said. And then he told Harry Matchum what was needed.

23

It was late afternoon when Ross arrived at the Callums' home at Brae Farm. As he got out of the car, the collie came around the corner of the house, slithering on her belly and grinning at him. Andrew Callum followed close behind.

"It's good of you to come," he said. "I'm imprisoned here this afternoon for a bit. Sheila's taken Rosie off to visit her parents, and I've been given the job of waiting for the vet. Come 'round into the garden, why don't you?"

Ross followed Callum along the flagstone path that led around to the back of the farmhouse. They passed through a small gate in the picket fence that Andrew Callum referred to as an "antigoose device," then came into a large garden laid out in neat beds of mixed flowers and precisely trimmed shrubbery. A blue stand of delphiniums leaned like a gaudy streak of paint against the pale gray stone, and a circular bed in the center of the lawn was striped with roses in a design of coral pinks and whites.

"Good Lord," Ross said, pausing to admire what lay before him. "How on earth does Sheila have time for all this? Or do you have someone come in?"

"This isn't Sheila's bailiwick. It's mine," Callum said, smiling. "Even policemen have hobbies, Superintendent."

"I should think you'd better call me Ross," Ross said. He looked at the garden and wondered if he had a hobby. Did listening to Chopin and Bach count? Perhaps he ought to take up woodworking or raising impossibly rare orchids in his spare time. Andrew Callum was offering him one of the striped lawn chairs, and he sat down as the collie joined them, slinking under her master's chair and resting her long needle nose on her paws.

"Owen told you about Danny Blaine?" Callum asked.

Ross nodded. "Is there any chance at all, do you think, that it might have been a planned event?"

Callum regarded him for a moment and then said, "Why do you ask?"

"Because Danny Blaine's girlfriend is Kenny and Terry MacDonald's younger sister."

There was a silence in the garden. Ross felt the warmth of the August sun on his face, and somewhere, just behind them, he heard the faint hum of honeybees buzzing in a lavender hedge.

Callum got up and went into the house. He returned a moment later and handed Ross a sheaf of papers that had been stapled into a manila folder.

"You don't have to read it," he said, sitting down again. "It's a ballistics report, what I wanted to talk to you about as a matter of fact, on the bullet that you dug out of the armchair."

"Go on," Ross said.

"It's from a thirty-eight semiautomatic," Andrew

Callum said. "A thing called an M-25. They're a scopey, lightweight, extremely accurate semiautomatic handgun."

"Not your average Saturday night special?"

"Not by a long shot, pardon the pun. They used to be favored by the SAS."

"Used to be?"

"That's right. They're obsolete now. Obsolete and unavailable. Even at the time, they were army issue only. The bullets were made in Czechoslovakia, the last batch manufactured about five years ago. Now also obsolete. The tracer marks on this bullet are distinctive. It came from a batch that was distributed to one of three bases over the four years that the army was using them. None of those bases have reported any theft or irregularity in ordnance in the last five years. Now," he went on, "you may turn to page ten, at the back."

"You've done rather a lot of work on this in the last—what?—forty-eight hours." Ross opened the folder.

"As a matter of fact, I've been working on almost nothing else for the last ten days." Before Ross could comment, Callum took the folder and ran his finger down the list printed on the open page. "Item three," he said, handing the papers back to Ross. Ross looked at the line Callum had indicated. It read, "Five M-25 .38-caliber semiautomatic weapons with full ammunition clips."

Ross looked at Callum. "What is this?" he asked.

"That is the inventory list of the weapons cache discovered at Stirling ten days ago. We've narrowed down the batches of guns by serial number. We're now left with one of two bases that those could have come from."

"So you're telling me that the bullet that killed Juliet Furnival was probably fired from a weapon that came from, or was connected to, this cache discovered at Stirling. And in addition to that, those weapons could only have originated out of an ordnance supply from the armed forces?"

"Correct," Callum said. "And given the rarity of the weapon and the bullet, I can only assume that it either came from the cache at Stirling or from one of two army bases in the U.K. And I cannot, for the life of me, think of a reason why Her Majesty's Armed Forces would want to kill Claudia and Juliet Furnival. In addition to that, I now have a connection to the MacDonalds, who have previously been involved in smuggling, one of whom has disappeared altogether and the other of whom jumped parole within twenty-four hours and also disappeared. It's very hot out. I don't suppose you'd care for a beer?"

"As a matter of fact, I would."

Callum placed two very cold cans of Tartan bitter on the table along with two glasses and a large bag of peanuts. He opened the beer cans and tossed the peanuts to Ross.

"I can never open these bloody things," he said. "They're worse than child-proof aspirin bottles." Ross tried three times to split the cellophane neatly from the top and finally gave up and bit the top of the bag open. He took a handful of peanuts and passed the bag to Callum in exchange for a beer.

"There is nothing like beer, I don't care what anyone says," Callum announced. "And how is Danny Blaine connected to the MacDonalds?"

Ross swallowed his peanuts. "Worked for them, according to Moira Lawrence. She didn't think that it was anything heavy, but she really didn't know. Julie told her Danny Blaine was working on a job for them up here. She also says that Kenny MacDonald is looking for Julie."

"I think I'd better have Miss Lawrence in for a word," Callum said.

"Why would the MacDonalds want the Furnival twins and their husbands dead?"

"Damned if I know. We don't, actually, know that the MacDonalds themselves have anything to do with any of this, though I admit my instincts are fair twitching. But what the hell do I know about who killed them? I've got the bloody Derringhams on their way in to see me tomorrow morning. For all I know, they'll confess."

"What?"

"That's right," Callum said, smiling at the look on his face. "Apparently whatever you said to them had some effect. They're not waiting for me to call them. I had a call from Mr. Derringham this afternoon to ask if he could see me first thing tomorrow morning. He said there were several things he needed to 'clear up' with me. In fact, you'll probably run into them tonight. I believe they're staying at Gleneagles." There was the sound of a car in the drive, and Callum got to his feet. "There's the vet," he said. "I wanted to tell you about the bullet myself, ask you what you thought. I've no idea how the guns got out of the bases without being recorded as missing, but I'm talking to a fellow tomorrow morning who may be able to help. And then, of course," he added, holding the antigoose device open for Ross to pass through, "there's the fact that none of this draws us a wit closer to knowing why the Furnivals et al were killed."

"No, I suppose not," Ross said.

They had reached the front of the house and the vet was climbing out of his Range Rover, black bag in hand. "Andrew, there you are."

"Tom, this is Mr. Ross," Callum said. "Ross, Tom Weatherby, our local saw and bones man."

"Glad to meet you," Weatherby said, wringing Ross's hand. "Ah," he said, peering behind Ross, "there's my favorite lady. Let me give her her jabs, Andrew, and then we'll get to those sheep."

The collie was lurking behind Ross, and at the sight of the vet she flattened herself onto the gravel, as if hoping that she might fade into it and disappear altogether. Callum grabbed her by the collar and held onto her while the vet produced a syringe from his bag.

"I don't suppose they ever found those dogs of young Blaine's?" he asked. "From over at Angus Carey's?"

"No, we never did," Callum said.

"Damn shame that," Weatherby said, shaking his head as he let go of the collie, who stood up and gave herself a vigorous shake. "That was a fine bitch, and after all the trouble we went to to treat that puppy, I think we would have saved it."

"Was there something wrong with the puppy?" Ross asked. "Other than the broken legs?"

"Heartworm." Weatherby put the empty syringe into a plastic bag and turned back to his car. "Awful stuff," he said. "We'd just about finished treating it as well. The little fella was doing fine. Nasty treatment that, but not half so bad as leaving it undone." He turned and smiled at Ross.

"What happens if it's not treated?" Ross asked.

"Oh, they'll die," Weatherby said. "Particularly a pup that age. I was supposed to give it the last dose of stuff last week, but, well . . ." He shrugged and looked at Andrew Callum. "What about those sheep, then?" he asked.

"Would Danny Blaine realize," Ross asked, "that the puppy had to have the rest of the treatment?"

"Oh Lord, yes," Weatherby said. "That boy was good with collies. And devoted. It's a sad thing, isn't it, guns and violence?"

"Yes, it is," Ross replied.

Angela Derringham was the first person Ross saw when he walked into the bar at Gleneagles after dinner. She sat on a bench by the fireplace drinking a brandy. She was wearing gray this time, rather than black. Ross wondered if, after she told Callum the whole truth and nothing but the truth tomorrow, she would appear dressed in white.

"Superintendent," she said, "I was hoping we'd see you." She started to stand and he waved her back, sitting down in the armchair beside her.

"Mrs. Derringham, how nice to see you again."

"I wanted to thank you," she leaned toward him slightly, "for the other day. I—We . . . I mean I spoke to Anthony and we decided that by far the best thing to do was come up here of our own accord and speak to Callum about that day and, well, everything."

"He's a good policeman," Ross said, "I'm sure he'll appreciate it a great deal."

She relaxed slightly and smiled at him. "I feel very sheepish," she said.

"Mrs. Derringham," Ross replied, "life is full of people who make the elementary mistake of trying to protect something they love when it doesn't really need protecting."

She looked at him for a moment and nodded. "But noble motives don't really make it any better, do they?"

"Oh, I don't know," Ross said. "I'm a great believer in noble motives."

She looked up over his shoulder and smiled. "Here comes Tony. Tony, look who I've found."

Ross got to his feet and shook hands with Anthony Derringham. He noticed that Derringham looked, as they say, a new man. There was less of the haggard look about him and he seemed to have gained some weight.

"Superintendent, I'm delighted. Will you join us for a drink?" The waiter appeared at Anthony Derringham's elbow and they both asked for a single malt.

"You know," Derringham said, after their glasses had arrived, "I never did really like this stuff, but I think it might grow on you. I suppose it's fabulously expensive in Manhattan."

"I should think everything's fabulously expensive in Manhattan," Angela said. "You shall probably have to start drinking bourbon or Wild Turkey or whatever it's called."

"When do you leave for the States?" Ross asked.

"In a couple of months, I should think," Angela said. "I shall have to tie up my job at the National, and we shall have to find somewhere to live, and then—" She was about to finish her sentence when the waiter appeared beside Ross, holding a portable telephone.

"There's a call for you, Superintendent," he said, handing the phone to Ross.

"Excuse me," Ross said, taking the object with distaste. He had enough of an aversion to the regular telephones that sat quietly on desks and hall tables. These traveling things were utterly beyond him. "Hello," he said gingerly, as if he were not quite certain that a voice would carry through the other end.

"Ross," Andrew Callum's voice said, "I'm sorry to bother you, but its been a hell of an evening. The press have got hold of the story about the bullet and tomorrow's going to be a nightmare. Still, I thought you'd want to know."

"Thank you," Ross said, uncertain as to why, exactly, he might want to know. He asked if Callum needed help with the wording of a statement.

"No, no," Callum said quickly, "I didn't mean that. Sorry, I'm not making myself clear. When I got in here I decided to go about getting ahold of Moira Lawrence to come in and make a statement. I'm afraid I was a bit late."

Ross's blood went cold. "What do you mean?" he asked.

"She was found in a car park off behind her flat in St. Andrews. She'd been badly beaten, left for dead in fact. But she's a tough little lass. She's holding her own at the Royal Infirmary in St. Andrews."

Ross felt for his jacket pocket and his pen and realized he was wearing a pullover. "Do you have a room number?"

Anthony Derringham leaned forward and offered him a pen and a cocktail napkin.

Ross accepted them as Callum said, "Room 411, the Tallard wing."

"Thanks very much for letting me know."

"I'll be in touch," Callum said.

"Yes," Ross said absently, "of course." He dropped the pen and napkin into his trouser pocket and was left staring at the mobile phone, wondering how to turn it off. Finally he decided to simply put it down on the table and let the waiter worry about it. He was feeling curiously light-headed. The Derringhams were watching him.

"Are you all right, Superintendent?" he heard Angela say. "Can I get you something?"

"No." Ross reached for his glass and shook his head, as if he could shake away the image of Moira Lawrence's face, her bright robin's eyes behind her National Health glasses.

"Was it important?" Angela asked.

"No," Ross said. "It was just a message."

24

"I'm sorry, Ross," Miranda said. "He honestly is in the shower and I honestly will have him ring you the minute he gets out."

Ross hung up the telephone in his room feeling cross. What right, after all, did mere detective inspectors have to be in the shower when a superintendent wanted to speak to them? He dug his hands into his pockets and looked out of the window at the bright summer morning. It was eight A.M. and he wanted to be on his way, but he couldn't be on his way until he'd spoken to bloody Owen, who, it seemed, had chosen this very moment to make himself pristeen and beautiful. He glared down at his desk where he had written the single word HEARTWORM in capital letters on his telephone pad. Beside that was the cocktail napkin with Moira Lawrence's hospital address on it. Beside that was the rather fine gold pen that Anthony Derringham had loaned him the previous night.

"Oh hell," he said aloud. It wouldn't do to forget to return that. No reasonable man could get through the day without his pen, and Derringham had bought him a drink last night. The Derringhams' room was just down the hall and around the corner from his own. He could return it and be back here by the phone in the time it would take Owen to finish his ablutions.

The door to number 107 was ajar. Ross could hear the dull murmur of voices.

"Come in," Angela Derringham called as he tapped on the door. He stepped into the room and saw her staring at the television. The remains of breakfast was on a room service table set up in front of the fireplace.

"It's just there," she said, and as she turned she saw Ross. "Superintendent!" she exclaimed. "I'm sorry. I thought you were room service."

"I'm afraid not," he said, "but I have come to return the pen your husband so kindly lent me."

"Thank you." She took it from him and nodded toward the television. "Have you seen this? But I suppose you knew all along." Ross realized she was watching the morning news, which was, as Callum had both predicted and feared, carrying the story of the Balnacoil bullet. They seemed to have a good deal of information, and Ross imagined that there'd be hell to pay over this at Blairlochie police station.

"The bullet," the newscaster said, "came from a discontinued batch of ordnance that the army has not used in over three years. From the serial numbers of the Stirling weapons, it has been ascertained that the weapon believed by police to have fired the fatal bullet that killed Mrs. Edward Hall came from one of two army bases in the

U.K." The picture shifted away to the front of a large building that looked like a courthouse in a country market town. The newscaster appeared in front of it. "Early this morning," she announced, "ordnance officers from both bases were interviewed by police here at Blairlochie police headquarters, where the incident room on the Balnacoil killings has been reopened." At that moment the doors opened and four men, two of them in army uniform, started down the front steps of Blairlochie police station. One of the army officers was a youngish nondescript fellow, and the other was rotund and had a moustache. The newscaster was besieging both of them with no great degree of success.

"Oh, my God," Angela Derringham said suddenly. "Oh, my God, how funny, there's Colonel Blimp!"

"You're right, my darling," Anthony Derringham said. He had just joined them from the bathroom. "It is, isn't it."

"I'd know him anywhere," Angela said. "Isn't that funny." She turned to Ross. "He was on Tarquin's video-tape, of the holiday, the one I told you about. Colonel Blimp was on the bit about the distillery."

"Really?" Ross said.

"Yes," she said. "Actually, Edward was quite cross about it, wasn't he, darling, remember?" She turned to Ross again. "Apparently they'd all said they wanted to go for a walk, and Edward said he was going to stay home and have a nap. And so they took the car off to find a suitable walking spot and ended up at the distillery instead, and when they did, as they were leaving, who did they see sneaking out of a back office door, but Edward with these men. So instead of saying anything, Tarquin filmed them and then presented him with the evidence later. He was quite cross about it. It was funny, really, wasn't it, darling?" Anthony nodded, still watching the television.

"Hmmm," Anthony said. "One of the other men saw them at it and he didn't look so pleased about it either."

"Mrs. Derringham," Ross said slowly, "where is that film, the one Tarquin Lassiter made of the holiday?"

"What?" She looked away from the television and smiled at him absently. "Oh, I don't know," she said. "Come to think of it, I never saw it again after that night of the great screening. I should think the police have it, you know, along with the rest of the stuff from the cottage."

Ross nearly ran straight into Owen as he stepped from the elevator.

"I was just coming to find you," Owen said. "I—" He stopped when he saw the look on Ross's face. "What is it?" he asked, "What's going on?"

"Heartworm." Ross shoved the piece of paper that he had written the single word on into Owen's hand.

Owen looked at him as if he was out of his mind.

"Heartworm," Ross announced again.

"So you said."

"You're going to go to Edinburgh first. If you don't find anything there, go on to Aberdeen and then Dundee. Check every single vet clinic that treats dogs. You're looking for someone who's brought in a collie puppy with a broken leg, probably last week, for the final course of a treatment for heartworm. She'll be telling some story about having had to move quickly and not being able to reach her own vet, and I'd put money on the fact that she's using the name Taylor."

Owen had suddenly taken on the look that a terrier gets when it's on the scent of something particularly desirable. He turned back toward the elevator. "And when I find her?" he asked.

"Don't do anything," Ross said. "Don't approach her. Just keep an eye on her. I'll be here. Ring me and I'll meet you. If I'm not here, just leave a message telling me where you are, and I'll get there as fast as I can." And then, before Owen could say anything further, Ross turned on his heel and disappeared down the long corridor and around the corner.

The final list was almost fifteen pages long. Not really all that surprising if you took into account the fact that it was an itemization of every fork, knife, spoon, and bit of carpet fiber removed from the Balnacoil holiday cottage. He read through it slowly and methodically, applying the kind of concentration that can only be applied in moments where the excitement level verges on panic. Like a schoolboy with a treat, he was going very slowly, eking out the final moment of satisfaction or disappointment. It was almost eleven A.M. by the time he finished going through the list for the second time. He had not found what he was looking for. Ross leaned back in his chair and let out a sigh of satisfaction.

He sat in the interview room at the Blairlochie police station, just down the corridor from Andrew Callum's office. The building was a large, mausoleumlike Victorian structure with high ceilings and bars on the windows. Ross wondered if the latter was a precaution against interviewees throwing themselves to the pavement of the town square below in fits of despair over their guilt. The Victorians, he thought, not for the first time, were very peculiar people.

Ross gathered up the pages, realigned them precisely so all of their corners matched, wondered why he always bothered to do that, and shoved them back into their folder. Then he made his way down the corridor to Andrew Callum's office.

"Well?" Callum asked, looking up as Ross came through the doorway.

Ross shook his head and put the folder back on Callum's desk. "It's not there."

"Right." Callum got to his feet. "Let's go have a word with the Derringhams."

"What have you done with them?" Ross asked as he followed Callum down the corridor toward the stairs. He had a sudden image of Angela and Anthony Derringham sitting in a dungeon in the bottom of the building, writing "I will not tell lies to the police" five hundred times.

"Oh, they've had a long talking to about wasting police time," Callum said. "And they've given us detailed statements of their whereabouts. They're just waiting to have them typed up so they can read and sign them now. He says he charged some petrol on his Barclay card at a filling station 'somewhere on a back road about forty-five minutes north of Edinburgh.' So now I shall have to send some poor sergeant trudging about half the north of Scotland to find the bloody place and see if we can identify him. He thinks it might have been a BP station, but he's not sure."

They had arrived at a sort of visitor's lounge, the kind of place, Ross supposed, where you gave people a cup of tea while you were waiting to decide whether you thought they were worth questioning or not. The walls were a loathsome washed beige, and the carpet was of the "indoor, outdoor" type favored by Americans and airport waiting areas. There were two plaid sofas, probably chosen about fifty years ago by some superintendent's wife who was distantly related to the Murrays of Atholl. It was unpleasant enough to be intimidating and nice enough that you couldn't complain that you'd been badly treated.

Just before he opened the door, Andrew Callum said, "Oh, by the way, Moira Lawrence is conscious this morning. She's asked for you."

Ross nodded and they went into the lounge.

Angela and Anthony Derringham sat side by side on one

of the sofas as if waiting for a bus. They drank tea out of light green melamine cups.

"Mrs. Derringham," Ross said, "I wondered if you might be able to tell me something more about the tape, the videotape that Tarquin made of the holiday, the one you first mentioned in London and then again this morning?" He sat down on the other plaid sofa while Andrew Callum stood against the door as if to discourage any possible ideas of flight.

"Of course," Angela said, looking for a place to put her cup down and not finding one. "You remember it, don't you, darling?"

"Yes," Anthony said. "We had to watch the bloody thing the first night we got there. Apparently Tarquin'd been driving everyone mad with that bloody camera, fancied himself the next Bertorelli."

"Bertolini," his wife said, smiling.

"All the same, one ini or some such . . . what, Superintendent?" Andrew Callum cleared his throat.

"About the videotape," Ross said. "Anything at all that you can remember."

"Well," Angela said, "it started out with some footage of the cottage and the farm. And there was the shepherd and Mr. Carey bringing the sheep in, and then some rather pretty footage of the loch. They took that on a walk, I think, and there was a bit of Claudia larking about in the wood doing some of *All's Well* or something."

"Always hated that bloody play," her husband muttered. "All those damned twins."

Angela ignored him and went on. "Then there was some footage of the hotel; Tarquin loved the restoration job they'd done. He was fascinated by the Victorians, a real fan of the Albert Memorial. Let's see. And after that there was the footage of the distillery that I told you about this morning."

"Tell us again, if you would," Ross suggested.

"All right. Well, of course I wasn't there at the time, but apparently, on the Friday or Saturday, in the afternoon, they were all deciding what to do. You know, should they go to Pitlochry or should they go to the sheepdog trials? In any case, eventually they decided they should all go for a long walk. And they decided that they'd take the car and drive over to Lochearnhead and walk up some glen that Tarquin had read about. In any case, Edward begged off. He said he was tired or he was going to read or something, and told them all to go on without him. So they did. And I think they did actually go over to this glen, but it wasn't quite all it was cooked up to be, so they came away rather earlier than they'd planned, and on the way home they drove past the distillery and they decided to stop, as it was still open. I think they took the tour or something, you know, down to look at all those casks and vats and barrels or something, and then they came up and went to the shop. And then, after all that, they got in the car and were leaving, heavily laden down with malt, I should think. Have you been there?" she asked.

Both Ross and Callum nodded.

"Well then," she went on, "you know how you come in one drive and you sort of circle around and go out the other drive, back by the garages where all their lorries live?"

"Yes," Ross said.

"Well, they'd got in the car and they were going down the back drive, and as they got to the bit where the lorries were, they saw Edward. Well, they thought this was simply hilarious, since he'd skived off going for a nice healthy walk to sneak over to the distillery, so they filmed him."

Ross leaned forward. "Tell me about that bit of the film as precisely as you can," he suggested.

"Let's see," she said.

"Tarquin was sitting in the passenger seat and he filmed him through the window. It was rolled down, though. It wasn't a long bit. They just stopped the car long enough to get Edward and Colonel Blimp and two other men coming out of this doorway. And then they all looked up and saw them, and the others all waved and laughed and shouted 'Got you' or something and drove off. It was funny actually, but Edward seemed rather put out about it when they showed it."

"The other two men," Ross said, "what did they look like, can you remember?"

"Oh, I should think so," she said. "There was Colonel Blimp—"

"Are you certain," Callum asked, "that was the same man you saw leaving this station on the news this morning?"

"Oh yes," she said. "That funny little moustache. And in the film he had an overcoat on. And I thought that was a bit odd, you know, since it was August and it was hot out, but you could see his uniform underneath. The coat was unbuttoned."

"And the others?" Ross asked.

"Well, Edward, of course," she said. "And then there were the other two. Let's see. One had a suit on, I remember that. And the other—"

"Psychopathic rugby player," her husband said.

"What?" Ross asked.

"He looked like a psychopathic rugby player," Anthony Derringham said. "You know, short, dark, curly hair, built like a brick shithouse. Pissed off when he saw them, I'll tell you that much."

"Yes, that's about it," Angela said. "And then there was a bit more of some highland games or something that they'd been to on the Sunday, just before we arrived. And that was it."

"And this tape," Ross said. "When was the last time you saw it?"

"Do you know," she said, "I've no idea. We watched it that night, and then I really didn't think about it again."

"I don't know how you managed that," Anthony said. "Everybody else had to. Don't you remember? Tarquin spent most of the day on Monday whining about how he couldn't find it. I had to buy him some more of the bloody things when we went to drop the car off. Claudia said he was always losing things, and Juliet said the fairies had taken it. Shame the fairies didn't take the damn camera as well."

Callum and Ross left the Derringhams to reread and sign their statements.

"I wonder what the hell an ordnance sergeant from a Northumberland base was doing in the Balnacoil distillery with Edward Hall on the Saturday before last?" Andrew Callum said.

"And there've been no reported or recorded thefts of ordnance on either of those bases."

"No," Callum said, sitting down at his desk, "but I did learn something interesting this morning. Ordnance is pretty strictly watched over on those bases. A sergeant couldn't just make it disappear on his own, if you know what I mean. But things do break, even guns."

"Go on," said Ross.

"Let's say the clip or the trigger or something on a gun goes wonky. Well, that bit's broken, but the rest of the gun isn't, is it?"

"You mean what happens to all of the other bits and pieces. Guns can be taken apart and put back together to make other guns."

"Precisely," Callum said. "And I don't know how the broken bits and bobs are kept inventoried, if at all, but it might be worth looking into."

Ross glanced at his watch. It was nearly one P.M. "May I use your phone for a moment?" he asked.

"Of course." Callum pushed it toward him. He picked up an elastic band.

Ross watched him play cat's cradle while he listened to the Gleneagles switchboard tell him he had no messages. So much for that, he thought. Probably he'd been completely wrong and Julie didn't even have the damn dogs, and if she did, she couldn't care less if the puppy died of heartworm or not.

He hung up and said to Callum, "Tell me one more thing. What do the MacDonalds look like?"

"Well," Callum said, "Terry's tallish, not quite your height, and I should be very surprised if he's ever worn a suit in his life. Kenny, on the other hand, is short and stocky with dark, curly hair."

"A psychopathic rugby player?"

Callum held up a perfect cat's cradle and showed it to Ross. "Exactly," he said.

25

The flowers were yellow and white: snapdragons, roses, and fuchsias. Moira Lawrence smelled them as the nurse held the vase to her face. She smiled. The nurse put them on the night locker and sternly turned to Ross. "Only five minutes, sir," she said. "This young lady's lucky to be with us at all." She then turned and squeaked out the door, past the police constable who had been sitting there since Moira Lawrence was admitted the night before.

Moira watched her go and then turned back to Ross. Most of her face was bandaged. She had a very black eye. Ross could see the bruising creeping across the few patches of skin that were left exposed. One of her legs had been broken, as had quite a few ribs and some fingers.

"Thanks for coming," she said. Ross had to lean forward to catch the words. "It was Kenny. I couldn't tell him anything about Julie 'cause I didn't know." She stopped for a minute to gather her breath.

"Take your time," Ross said. "It's all right."

She smiled slightly and shook her head. "Not all right," she said. "He knows about you. He knows who you are and where you are. He knows I talked to you."

"And that's why he did this?"

She smiled again. "Mean bastard," she said. "Be careful."

"I will," Ross replied. "And we'll have someone here all the time. All you have to do is get well."

She closed her eyes and nodded. "The flowers are grand," she said.

The door opened and the nurse came back in. She glared at Ross as he got to his feet.

Moira opened her eyes and looked at him. "Julie," she said.

"Don't worry," Ross said. "I'll find her. I promise."

On the drive back to Gleneagles, it started to rain. The fine summer morning had been crossed with clouds, and now a thin highland drizzle fell steadily. It was almost the end of August. Autumn was coming and then winter. Ross found the idea matched his mood. He'd always found the glories of summer a little hard to live up to. As he drove he thought about Julie MacDonald and Moira Lawrence. His own sister, Lavinia, had grown up in a Queen Anne farmhouse on two hundred acres where the greatest tragedy of her young life had been the fact that she could not keep her pony in the field directly next to the house so she could see it out of her bedroom window immediately upon waking every morning. Kendal and her covey of sisters had considered themselves hardship cases if they weren't allowed to go sailing in the mornings as well as the afternoons all summer long. Ross himself, when not occupied by pulling Vinia's hair or finding dead things to put in her bedroom, spent most of his youth reading Hardy Boys mysteries that his mother had sent especially from New York. Missing one of the sequence would have been disaster.

Julie MacDonald, however, had had things on her mind that no one, much less a child, should ever have to contemplate. And Moira Lawrence now lay in a hospital bed and faced episodes of reconstructive surgery for her attempt to help her friend. It wasn't fair, but it was inevitably and inescapably true: some simply paid a higher price for life than others. As he turned into the drive at Gleneagles, he thought it unnecessarily long. He wondered if the game of golf, to which so many of these manicured acres were dedicated, really did the world any good. As he parked the car and walked toward the huge hotel, he was embarrassed to find himself admiring the proportions of the building and looking forward to coffee in front of the fireplace, followed by a hot bath.

As he walked into his room, the telephone was again ringing. He grabbed it and heard Owen say, "Where the hell have you been?"

"St. Andrews, why?"

"You could have checked for messages," Owen replied. "I've found her. I've found the bloody girl! Sixth clinic I tried. She brought the dog in under the name of Taylor. I've been sitting here outside this block of flats for over an hour now. Finally I thought I'd better ring and see what you were up to."

"Well, why didn't you ring and leave the address?" Ross felt a rising tide of irritation. He could have been there an hour ago. He wouldn't have gone all the way to St. Andrews.

"I left the address with the front desk over an hour ago. I had the girl read it back to me and the lot. I've been sitting here waiting for you to show up."

"All right. I'll be there in an hour or so. Where are you?"

"Outside of Queensgate Flats. It's in a development just east of the city, Edinburgh." Owen went on to give him brief directions.

"Don't leave," Ross said as he hung up. He hadn't even taken the key out of the door to his room. Now he yanked it out, slammed the door, gave up on the elevator and rushed down the wide, carpeted stairs toward the lobby. As he went past the desk, he stopped. The girl on duty, a bright, pretty redhead named Flora, smiled at him inquiringly.

"My name is Ross," he said. "Can you tell me if there are any messages for me?" Flora turned around and looked in the cubbyhole for his room. She shook her head. "Nothing for 709," she said.

"Are you quite certain?" Ross asked. "I believe that an address was left for me, perhaps an hour ago, by a friend who rang in."

"Oh," Flora said. "I've only just come on duty. Grace will have been here. Grace!" she called, sticking her head into the office. Grace appeared. She was a tall dark girl with remarkably even teeth.

"Oh, hello, Superintendent," she said.

"Grace," Flora said quickly, "Mr. Ross thinks a message may have come through for him about an hour ago."

"That's right," Grace said, smiling at him. "An address in Edinburgh. I gave it to your sergeant when he called for your messages."

"My sergeant?" Ross had a sinking feeling.

"That's right," Grace said. "He was here perhaps twenty minutes ago. He said you were held up and had sent him to collect your messages." A cloud of doubt crossed her face.

Before she could say anything, Ross said, "Could you describe the man for me?"

"Yes," Grace said, now seriously worried. "He was short, rather heavily built. Dark with curly hair."

"A psychopathic rugger player."

"I beg your pardon, sir?" Grace said.

"Nothing," Ross said. He took a pen from the registration book and copied out the address that Owen had just given him. "Ring Detective Chief Inspector Callum at Blairlochie police station," he said, shoving the piece of paper toward the girls. "Tell him that this is Julie's address and that I've gone there to meet Kenny MacDonald. Hurry!" And before they could say anything, he was out of the revolving doors and running across the gravel forecourt to his car.

Queensgate Flats was one of four multistory, concrete buildings that loomed over a tiny courtyard park like giant rectangular building blocks. They were short-let flats originally built to house workers for the huge power plant that lay just to the east of Edinburgh. Ross and Owen stood beside Owen's car, parked just down the street from a bus stop and a small news agent's. Behind them stretched a railway depot yard and a seemingly endless procession of council flats just like Queensgate, but not quite as nicely kept. Queensgate Flats had sliding glass doors that led onto tiny balconies and other such amenities that the council flats lacked, reflecting the comparative economic well-being of the power company versus the government.

He was still feeling rather breathless from his very fast drive into Edinburgh, as if he had run rather than driven the distance. The traffic light on the road changed, providing a gap in the steady stream of trailer trucks and buses, and Ross plunged across the road, dragging Owen in his wake.

"But you haven't seen him go in?" Ross said, dodging around a post in the center of the four-lane road and heading for the opposite curb.

"I haven't seen anyone answering his description, no," Owen said, "but there's been a lot of traffic and I haven't always had a clear view of the front doors. It's flat number 519," he added as they reached the door to the lobby.

Once, back in the days when the building was new, the security locks might have worked and it might have been necessary to be buzzed into the building. But those days were long gone, and Ross and Owen found themselves in a wide, rather grubby lobby with a fire door behind them and two elevators facing them. Owen punched the buttons on the elevators repeatedly, but neither of the doors opened. The two men exchanged glances and, without speaking, turned toward the fire door.

The stairs were damp and littered and the stairwell smelled of urine and stale cigarettes. Please, Ross thought as they climbed, let us be in time. He could hear Owen's breathing behind him, hear his own breath as, out of long habit, he counted the steps in his head, twenty-five, twenty-six, twenty-seven, turn, landing, fourth floor, one, two, three.

They reached the fifth floor and both men paused automatically behind the closed door. Ross waited until he was sure that Owen was right behind him, and then he pushed open the door to the fifth floor corridor. There was a total and eerie silence. For one of the very few times in his life, Ross wished he were carrying a gun. The two steel doors of the elevators faced them. They turned left and moved slowly down the hallway. The numbers on most of the doors were still intact. Ross tried to will his shoes to be quiet against the linoleum tiling, but they still seemed to squeak hopelessly. They reached 517 and paused. The door to 519 was ajar. There wasn't a sound.

Owen stood back as Ross approached the door and shouted, "Mrs. Taylor? Mrs. Taylor?" There was no reply. Ross pushed the door open slightly. There was a narrow hallway, and beyond it he could see the living room. He saw the leg of an upturned chair, clothes strewn down the hallway, a bathroom towel and a child's shoe lying in the living room doorway.

"Julie!" he called out, pushing the door open. "Julie!" He went down the hallway and into the sitting room.

"Blimey," Owen said, standing in the doorway.

There was a cheap sofa that had been overturned and gutted. A lamp lay broken on the floor. Two chairs had been tossed sideways and clothes were strewn everywhere. The sliding doors that led onto the tiny balcony were open, the cheap curtains not even moving in the still, August air. Ross crossed the room and stepped onto the balcony, peering over, half afraid of what he might see below. There was nothing. Owen came into the sitting room and then stepped into the tiny kitchenette.

"Same here," he said to Ross from the doorway.

Ross nodded. "This is what they did in Glasgow as well," he said. He stepped over a ripped open cereal packet and pushed open the door on the far side of the sitting room. The devastation in the bedroom was exactly the same. Two suitcases were ripped open and their contents tipped across the floor. The sheets and blanket lay in a mangled heap, and sitting on the bed was Julie MacDonald. She had a large red welt running across her cheek, her sweatshirt was ripped, and her lip, where she had been hit, was bleeding and already beginning to swell. Her brother Kenny was sitting beside her. He had his arm around her and he was holding a gun to her head.

"Hello, Superintendent," he said. "I ever so enjoyed being your sergeant."

Ross heard a noise behind him and he glanced back to see Terry MacDonald come out of the bathroom and stand in the door between the sitting room and the hallway. It was a very old trap, and Owen and Ross had walked, very nearly run, straight into it.

"Hello, Kenny," Ross said.

Kenny MacDonald was extremely unpleasant to look at. He was short and stocky. There was the high color that comes with excitement in his face, giving it a red, sweaty sheen. And his eyes were lit with a brightness Ross found extremely disturbing. Kenny was enjoying himself. When he spoke, his voice was high and almost girlish. Ross noticed that his soft, pudgy hands were unusually white, giving his nails a sluglike, almost manicured appearance.

"We've come to see our little sister Julie," he said. "Haven't we, Jules?"

Julie MacDonald didn't move. She had gone quite white, and Ross wondered if she were going to pass out.

"Julie's been ever so naughty," Kenny went on, "haven't you, darling?"

"Bring her into the lounge, Ken," his brother said. "I want to have a look in the bog, and I can't do that and watch these geezers."

Kenny MacDonald got to his feet, taking Julie with him. "Please, Superintendent," he said, "would you step into the other room? And don't be brave, now, will you? I'd hate to have to do anything silly."

Ross stepped back slowly until he was standing in the center of the lounge. Kenny stepped forward with his arm still around Julie, the gun still resting on her cheek. She started to move and stumbled. Kenny kicked her hard in the shin and she gave a little whimper of pain.

"Out of there," Kenny said to Owen as they got to the doorway. "Why don't you two boys stand over there, against that wall where I can see you?" Owen moved carefully across the small room until he and Ross stood against the wall at a ninety-degree angle to the sliding doors.

"Awright," Terry said, sounding bored with the whole ordeal, "that's good enough. Let me just do the bog and then we can get shot of this place." He disappeared and they could hear the sounds of the toilet tank being lifted, things being tipped over, a cupboard opening. No one spoke.

Kenny MacDonald stood with his sister on the far side of the room from Ross and Owen. With one hand he held the gun to her cheek and with the other he reached around her shoulder and played with a strand of Julie's disheveled blond hair. "It's not looking so good, love," he said. "When we get home we'll have your friend Moira fix it again, shall we? Would you like that?"

Ross looked at the distance between himself and the open door to the balcony. He could cover it in less than a stride, but it wouldn't do him much good. There was nothing out there of any use, and no one would survive a five-floor drop. Neither he nor Owen could get to the kitchenette, and even if they could get hold of a carving knife, Kenny would happily kill them all before they could do anything with it. He could feel Owen thinking the same thing. There was no trace of the little boy or the dogs, which, on the whole, was a good thing, perhaps the only good thing. He wondered how long it would take Andrew Callum to get there.

Terry MacDonald came back into the sitting room doorway. He had obviously finished tearing up the bathroom. He shrugged. "It's not bloody there," he said. His voice was slightly whiny. "Come on, Jules," he said. "Just give us the fucking thing and we'll be off out of it."

"I haven't got it!" she snapped suddenly. "I told you, didn't I? I don't know what you're talking about!"

"Liar," Kenny said matter-of-factly, and he hit her hard in the face with the pistol butt. Ross felt Owen flinch beside him.

"I'm getting pissed off with this," Terry said. "Give me the gun, Ken, an' you go have a look. I tell you, you hadn't let her get involved with that fucking loser in the first place and none of this would've happened, would it?"

"It's not my fault," Kenny said. "Not everything is my fault." He shoved his sister toward Terry and handed him the gun, and then stalked out of the room into the bedroom. Ross had the bizarre sensation of being in the middle of a rather ordinary group of adolescent siblings. They might have been fighting over the television controls in the living room of any middle-class home. Terry had Julie by the collar of her sweatshirt and was watching them while he lackadaisically held the gun to her neck. In the bedroom they could hear Kenny snorting about like a truffle pig. Julie stared at the floor, looking almost catatonic. Suddenly, like an animal scenting the wind, her head snapped up toward the entrance door. There, standing in the doorway, was a child holding two dogs on a leash.

It happened very fast. Julie Taylor screamed at the top of her lungs, "No, David! Run!" At the same time, she twisted away from Terry MacDonald and flung herself across the room toward her child.

David, seeing her, screamed, "Mum!" and ran toward her, letting go of the leash. At the same moment, Owen took advantage of the chaos to fling himself bodily across the small room and tackle Kenny MacDonald, who was about to step out of the bedroom. Owen had the advantage of both momentum and surprise. Ross, for his part, turned toward Terry, who had raised the gun and stepped backward. David ran toward his mother, who was on her knees in the center of the sitting room and trying to get to her feet. Owen was in the doorway to the bedroom, struggling with Kenny, and Terry was stepping back, holding the gun in both hands, raising his arms to fire. Ross had a momentary vision of the interior of the Balnacoil holiday cottage. He threw himself at Terry MacDonald.

Ross caught MacDonald in the stomach. The shot went wide and high, into the ceiling, as Terry staggered back. He started to lower the gun to fire again, and as he did, Ross straightened up and hit him as hard as he could. There was a startled look on Terry MacDonald's face, then he fell backward onto the balcony, moving fast with the momentum of the punch Ross had thrown. He was a big man and he fell back, hitting the old, none-too-stable railing of the balcony with full force. There was a peculiar cracking sound as the railing gave and then, very slowly, it sheared off the side of the balcony. Terry MacDonald grabbed for the falling railing, screamed and fell over the edge.

Kenny MacDonald let out a howl of pain, broke free from Owen and half ran, half stumbled to the edge of the balcony. For a moment Ross thought he was going to throw himself over as well. He knelt on his hands and knees, looking after his brother, and then he got slowly to his feet and stared at Ross. "You bastard," he said, in his girlish voice. "You son of a bitch, I'll make you pay for this."

And at that moment Andrew Callum walked through the doorway.

26

The tiny flat was crowded with people. A dog was barking. Andrew Callum was directing the removal of what remained of Terry MacDonald. Owen was giving a detailed statement to a detective sergeant. David Blaine was sitting on the kitchen floor talking to a police constable about his collies, who lay beside him. His mother, Julie MacDonald, sat on the bed where Ross had first seen her. A medic was treating the superficial cuts on her face prior to removing her for more comprehensive medical care. At the least, she had several broken ribs. The medic got up and went off to fill in some records. Ross stepped into the room and sat down on the edge of the bed beside her.

"Mrs. Blaine," he said, "my name is Ross. I've been speaking to your friend, Moira Lawrence, and she sends you her best." Julie moved her head slightly and looked at him for a moment.

"Is Danny dead?" she asked. "Kenny told me they'd killed Danny."

"No," Ross said, "Danny's not dead. He's in the infirmary at the prison, but he's not dead."

"Can I see him?" Tears began to well out of the corners of her eyes, flowing down over the newly treated cuts and bruises on her face. "I've waited and waited for him just like he told me. I've done everything he told me," she said. "I want to see Danny. He said he'd come. He said he'd come that night, and next thing I knew people are dead and they say he killed them. Danny never killed anyone."

"I know," Ross said. She looked down at her lap, where she was twisting her hands into the bottom of her sweatshirt.

"I told him not to go back," she whispered. "I told him. But he said he had to. He said that there was something that he had to find."

"Mrs. Blaine," Ross said, "other than the dogs, did Danny give you anything, anything at all, that night he met you at the phone booth?" She shook her head, still staring into her lap.

"No. He told me to take the dogs, and he said that he was coming. He told me to come here. He'd worked it all out, rented this flat, the lot. He said we'd get away finally. We were going to leave. He just had to go back for one thing. And then the next thing I knew . . ." Her voice trailed off and she sat for a moment looking at her hands, which gradually stopped their twisting and became still. She looked up at Ross, and for the first time, looking into her bruised and worn face, he realized how young she was. "When Ken and Terry came, they kept talking about it, about something Danny was supposed to have given me. I would have given it to them if I'd had it. I would have done anything to make them leave us alone. But I didn't have whatever it was. Danny never gave anything to me. Do you understand? That night, he never gave anything to me. Do you understand?"

Ross nodded. "Yes, I think I do."

The way didn't seem as long as it had before. Ross climbed steadily, hearing nothing but the sound of his own breathing and the wind chasing its way through the heather. It was a fine day. The clouds had cleared off of the hills, and above him he could see the steep granite crags. He paused at the spine of the ridge. Looking back, he could see the thin elongated strip of the loch as it snaked through the shadows of the glen below. He turned the other way and saw the moor open out before him, the dark dot of the croft sheltering under the edge of the rise. A sparrow hawk skimmed across the gorse and wheeled away toward Balnacairn.

This time she stood outside the door waiting for him. As he got closer he saw that her hair had been newly brushed and pinned. The hem of her black skirt was muddy, but her tiny black boots had new laces, and all of the buttons had been sewn onto her cardigan. The fox was nowhere to be seen. They were nocturnal, so perhaps it was curled in its basket, sleeping off a night of field mice and wild hare.

The rucksack he carried was stuffed with offerings. Without speaking, he took them and laid them out, one by one, on the bench beside the door: a brightly colored caddy of tea, the largest tin of assorted biscuits that the Gleneagles gift shop carried, two bottles of Robinson's barley water, a hairbrush and matching hand mirror, four brightly colored hair clips, two tea towels with red and white stripes, and, last of all, something he had seen in the Gleneagles shop window and had turned and gone back for. It was a cardigan of the softest, thickest double cashmere, which was a heather-blue so deep and vivid that when he saw it, he'd thought of the color of her eyes and, according to legend, those of her ancestor who had built this croft and walked these hills some two centuries before.

She watched him, her head cocked sideways, her eyes never leaving him for a moment. When he finished laying out his offerings and placed the empty rucksack on the bench beside them, she touched each one in turn, not picking it up, but studying the feel of it with her hands. She came to the cardigan last, and when she felt the softness of it, her face broke into something like a smile.

"Finn," he said quietly when she finished examining her gifts, "may I see the other things, the things you took from the cottage? Not Danny's cottage, the cottage where the people stayed, before the hunters came." She considered the request for a moment and then she nodded.

"The hunters killed them," she said.

"Yes, they did."

She turned and started to walk around to the back of the cottage, and for a moment Ross did not realize that he was supposed to follow. She stopped and looked back at him, puzzled, and waved him on. He joined her, and the two set off across the moor side by side.

They were walking directly toward the bottom of the crag. It loomed over them until it almost disappeared above, blocking out the sun and covering the ground with shadow. There was no path, but Finn followed the way as surely as if she were walking along a road. Once, Ross glanced back and saw the croft receding behind them. The next time he looked it was lost beyond the corner of the rocks. The face of the crag was damp, cold, and dark. Here and there bits of lichen and moss clung to the granite. A creek fell off of its face and ran away, lost in the peat.

Ross did not even see the opening in the face of the rock until Finn was in the process of disappearing through it. It was a narrow fissure, a crack that opened sideways on the face so the entrance was entirely concealed, unless you knew exactly where to look. No wonder Danny Blaine had been unable to find it. He was only the last in a long procession of seekers who had tried to unravel the secret over the last two hundred years. Rob Roy had chosen his hiding place well.

She turned to him as she stood in the entrance and held up her hand.

"Stay," she said, as one would to a dog.

As much as he would dearly have loved to see the inside of the cave, the treasures her family had hidden there since God knows when, he felt he had no right to trespass. He stood outside, watching the view, listening to the water trickling in the creek. High overhead two fighter jets streaked across the morning sky, heading northeast toward RAF Lossiemouth. They might, he thought, have been eagles or osprey, birds of prey, hunters flying home, two dark specks of menace against the endless blue.

A moment later Finn was beside him again, reappearing out of the rock as magically as she had vanished into it. She crouched in the rough gorse and pebble, laying a shoe box at his feet. Ross crouched down and watched as she opened it. It had pink letters along the side that claimed that it had come from Jenners of Edinburgh. Very carefully Finn unpacked her treasures and laid them out for his admiration. There was a glove of fawn-colored suede with a black cuff, six or seven matchbooks with brightly colored logos from London restaurants, an unopened pack of Rothman's cigarettes, a small pair of nail scissors, a head scarf with flowers on it, a pair of sunglasses, a black velvet headband, and a rectangular yellow box that had "Kodak" printed boldly across the front. When she had finished, Finn sat back on her heels, looked up at him and said, "These things?"

"Yes," Ross said.

He leaned forward, his elbows on his knees, and admired her cache. After a moment she picked up a matchbook and handed it to him. It was from the Café Royal on Regent Street. He held it for a moment and then shook his head and handed it back to her. She replaced it and picked up the sunglasses. Again he examined them, noted that they were not prescription and were made by Aziza, and returned them to her. This time she regarded him shrewdly. She replaced the sunglasses and cocked her head in her little birdlike motion, examining him. Very slowly he reached out and touched the Kodak box.

For a moment he was not sure how she would react, and then she nodded solemnly and picked up the box and handed it to him. Ross made a show of examining it. He removed the tape cassette, looked at it, noted the handwritten label that said "Balnacoil Holiday," and replaced it in its box, nodding. Finn smiled. She gathered up the rest of her treasures, replaced them in their box, and disappeared back into the cave. She returned a moment later and led him away again, back down onto the moor. He glanced back once, knowing that neither he nor anyone else would be able to find the cave again. If he hadn't been holding the souvenir of his visit in his hand, he might not even believe that it existed outside of the legends of the highlands.

As they came down the slope of the moor, the tiny croft appeared and grew larger before them, until they were standing outside of the door, the sun just beginning to warm the slate paving stones and fill the morning air with the summer smells of heather and earth. Ross sat down on the bench and Finn scurried into the cool dark of the croft. When she returned a moment later, she was holding the fox under one arm and carrying a packet of bourbon creams. She sat down next to Ross, the fox curled on her lap, and carefully opened the biscuits. She offered one to Ross, took one herself, and gave one to the fox. Ross leaned back against the stone wall of the croft, luxuriating in the warmth of the sun. He had forgotten how much he liked bourbon creams, and made a mental note to remember them the next time he went to Gateway. Beside him, on Finn's lap, the fox nibbled its biscuit with great delicacy, sniffing fastidiously around the edges before licking away the side of the chocolate with its quick pink tongue. Seeing that Ross had finished, Finn carefully peeled back the paper and offered him another. They sat, side by side, without speaking, the brightly colored ornaments of another world at their feet. The wind raced itself in ripples across the moor.

When the packet was empty, the paper remains carefully folded and put in Finn's pocket, they sat for a while longer. The fox dozed, his red-brown fur standing up and bristling in the warmth. When it was time to go, Ross stood and put the videotape in his Barbour pocket. Finn, sitting on the bench and stroking the fox, watched him. He wondered, not for the first time, how old she really was, and for a moment he thought that perhaps she wasn't old at all, perhaps she was eternal and had been here forever on this moor with her treasures and her familiar.

"Good-bye, Finn," he said. "And thank you."

She nodded. "Will he come again?" she asked. "The boy?"

"He will."

She looked at him, considering. "But not you," she said.

"No," he replied.

She nodded and then her face broke into a wide smile. She patted the fox. "Go now," she said.

Ross turned and walked away, the videotape heavy in his pocket.

When he got to his car, which he had left at first light at the end of the Careys' farm road, he could not resist looking back at the hillside that rose above the cottages. He stood for a moment and scanned the ridge. He supposed that he wanted to see the tiny black figure above him, wanted to see her black against the green-gray of the hills, this time topped by a patch of brightest, bright blue. But there was nothing there save the gorse and the rocks and the wind. He gave himself a small mental shake and got into his car. As he drove for the last time down the farm track and away from Balnacoil, he did not look back.

27

Juliet Furnival stood by the sign that read "Balnacoil Malt, Pride of the North," staggered slightly, and fell into a heap in the witch grass at the base of it. The front of the distillery, dramatic in the late afternoon shadows, loomed up, and the old brick appeared almost black and red, dappled in the shadows of the trees that lined the courtyard. Two men stepped out of a doorway into the light and were joined by two others. Edward Hall and a small rotund man with a moustache spoke for a few minutes while the other two listened. Then, suddenly, the short dark man looked up. He stepped forward in an angry gesture of threat. Edward Hall reached out and put a hand on his arm and for a moment all four men were caught full face as a voice-over said, "Edward and friends on an afternoon outing." Claudia Furnival filled the picture. Her dark hair lifted in the wind, and she stepped back slightly, framed by the silver water of the loch beyond her as she turned, her face fey and unearthly. Pointing her finger at the camera, she said, "Nymph in thy orisons be all my sins remembered!" Then the track stopped abruptly, echoing out in gray fuzz across the screen.

There was utter silence in the darkened room until Sheila Callum got up, turned the television off and switched on the lights, revealing her sitting room with the child's toys piled in a corner and a bouquet of late summer roses filling the neatly swept hearth.

"I still don't understand," Angela Derringham said.

The Derringhams, the Davies, the Callums, and Ross were spread across Andrew and Sheila's sitting room. It was Tuesday evening, and Kenny MacDonald had been charged, not twelve hours earlier, with the murders of Juliet and Edward Hall and Claudia and Tarquin Lassiter.

"I mean," Angela went on, "all right, Edward was short of cash, so he sets up this smuggling thing. But who were those men and how did he know this MacDonald person, and . . ." Her voice trailed off as she looked up at Ross.

"Come on, Ross," Miranda said, stretching out on the footstool where she'd been perched like a small cat, "you've got to explain it to them." She turned to Angela. "He's dreadful. He's frightfully vain. He's dying to tell you how he's worked it all out, but he won't unless you absolutely beg."

"Well, we've a good half hour before dinner," Sheila said.

"Please, Superintendent," Angela said, "you can't let us go on without knowing."

"In that case, I suppose that I shall have to."

"Good thing," Callum said. "You start talking and I'll start pouring. This is not a story that one can understand without a drink." He got up and began to make the rounds of the sitting room.

"Well," Ross said, "I suppose that one ought to start at the beginning."

"A stroke of brilliance, master," Owen said.

"I haven't understood a word of this bloody mess since day one," Anthony Derringham said, handing his glass to Callum.

"Edward Hall was short of cash," Ross said.

"I should say so," Anthony said. "Thirty thousand pounds short, in my case."

"Edward and Juliet were inclined to live well beyond their means," Ross said. "I should think that they'd been doing so for some time. It was probably a rather unfortunate marriage in the sense that there doesn't seem to have been an awful lot of balance, if you know what I mean. They were moving in a rather fast set, and what with the cocaine, the farm in France, and a new house in Kensington Church Street, they had to work hard to keep up, and even that wasn't going to do it. Years ago, at the beginning of his career, Hall worked for a firm in Glasgow. He was quietly let go over a matter of a few thousand pounds missing from a trust fund that he administered. It was a shame, really, because prior to that he had done well at the firm and worked quite hard, especially on a case called the Crown versus McCavert. Do you remember it at all?" He turned to Andrew Callum.

Callum shook his head.

"Neither did I," Ross said. "So I rang an old friend who's rather good at that sort of thing and asked him to look into it. He rang me back this morning, and what he told me finally made it all make sense. The McCavert case was about smuggling. It was a customs and excise tangle. Beyond that it's not important. The firm that Edward Hall worked for instructed the barristers for the defense. And they managed to get the defendants off, so that created quite a lot of good feeling between the solicitors and their clients. One of the named defendants was a young man called Terry MacDonald."

"And through all this time they'd remained friendly and we didn't catch it?" Callum asked.

Ross shrugged. "I doubt they were bosom buddies, to use the term. But Edward certainly would have remembered Terry, and I'm sure Terry remembered him. In any case, Edward went to London to a firm that did quite a lot of work in maritime law. I don't know who contacted whom or how the idea came up, we'll probably never know, but at some point he and the MacDonalds started talking. The idea was very simple. All of the weaponry that's used by the army is very tightly controlled, inventoried, etcetera. However, when something breaks, it goes into a sort of limbo and all the bits and pieces are disposed of and the weapon itself is put down and inventoried as having been destroyed. Well, what could be easier than to take the bits that aren't broken and build new weapons out of them? You never have to worry about accounting for missing inventory and there's no paper trail."

"Colonel Blimp!" Angela said.

"Exactly," Ross agreed. "The next thing to do is figure out how you're going to transport all this stuff. You can't really just drive it around in the boot of your car, at least not over borders. It gets to be a bit risky. What you need is a well-established and completely incongruous form of transport. Something that customs in, say, Northern Ireland, is entirely used to, full duty paid etcetera. Enter Balnacoil distillery."

"Of course," Miranda said. "I knew I recognized him. The fourth man, the slick one in the suit. He's on the brochure, the one with the map that has all the places in Britain and Ireland where those smart lorries deliver single malt from Balnacoil."

"Precisely," Ross said. "And I think that Andrew will affirm that they found rather a nice little inventory waiting to be shipped out down in the basements of the distillery. Perhaps in some of those lovely old oak casks? Am I correct?"

Callum nodded. "You are indeed."

"So where did Edward come into it?" Angela asked.

"There's a demand for weapons in both directions," Ross said. "People always think of selling out of Amsterdam and Germany, Hamburg, but it works the other way as well. There's a lucrative seller's market, but unfortunately Balnacoil malt doesn't go in that direction, at least not by lorry. And I think we'll find that they were actually using the lorries themselves, perhaps something in the undercarriage. Not whiskey crates, which is a bit obvious."

"Not to mention clichéd," Miranda said.

"Quite," Ross agreed. "So they needed to arrange to get the stuff going to Europe in by ship, and who better to do that than a shipping lawyer, especially one who had previously practiced in Glasgow and knew something about the ports. It was a very neat setup. They also decided that they'd better have someone around, in an inconspicuous sort of way, to make certain that everything was all right at the distillery and that the weapons were getting in and out all right and not attracting any unwanted attention. Well, the word was out on the grapevine that the Careys might need a new shepherd, as the wife of theirs was pregnant and wanted to return home to her family. Danny Blaine had tried to leave the MacDonalds, strangely enough, to become a shepherd. I'm sure, however, if a shepherd's job hadn't happened to come up virtually next door, they would have created one at a local pub or at the distillery itself. You see, Kenny MacDonald didn't quite trust Danny Blaine, and the idea of having him too far out of range made him uneasy. This way they'd know exactly where Blaine was and what he was doing all the time. That's where they started to go wrong. Danny Blaine wasn't quite so malleable and stupid as they'd counted on. Kenny was right not to trust him. He'd never stopped seeing Julie and he'd never stopped planning how to get himself and his family away from Kenny and Terry and Glasgow altogether. By the time he got to Balnacoil to watch over the distillery, he knew what he was going to do. All he had to do now was save up the rest of the money."

"And of course," Owen added, "shepherding was a perfect cover. You're off on your own on the moors the whole time, and virtually no one sees you for days. You could be doing anything, like watching weapons shipments."

"Or rendezvousing with your girlfriend," Sheila said.

"Which was, in fact, the case," Ross said. "Danny was smart enough to know they were being watched pretty closely by Kenny. People like that have a great instinct for what's going on around them, so as often as he could, for the post in particular, Danny used a go-between. Then, at some point, it was decided that the principals of this little organization had better get together and work out exactly what they were going to do with the money and how it was going to be split up, etcetera. I think we'll find that there was a bit of disagreement over this. So they agreed to meet. None of them wanted to be seen. What better place than the distillery, where they could each come and go separately, and what better cover for Edward than a highland holiday with family?"

"But they didn't," Angela said. "Leave separately, I mean."

"No," Ross said, "they didn't. And unfortunately, by a rather horrible coincidence, Tarquin and Juliet and Claudia not only saw them, they filmed them."

"Oh Christ," Angela said.

"Are you telling me," Anthony asked, "that that bloody video camera literally cost them their lives?"

"In a manner of speaking, yes, I'm afraid it did. You see, everyone saw Tarquin filming them from the car, so suddenly they all know that there's a videotape in existence that has all four of them coming out of the Balnacoil distillery on it. Of course, as in most cases like this, if they'd done absolutely nothing, there was a very good probability that nothing would ever have come of it. There'd have just been some footage of some strange men on this tape. In time, perhaps Edward could have got hold of it and erased it. But that's not what happened. Unfortunately, someone, probably Kenny, perhaps all of them, panicked. I'm sure that Edward tried to convince them that he could simply get the tape back, and I'm sure that's what he was planning to do, at an opportune moment. But before that moment arose, the tape, like so many other things in that cottage, disappeared. Now Edward has no idea where it is, so the MacDonalds, who may now suspect that Edward's double-crossing them, have Danny Blaine get into the cottage while everyone is away on walks, or whatever, and look for the tape. Of course he can't find it either, because it isn't there. Perhaps at that point he may have begun to suspect what had really happened to it, or perhaps he too may have thought that Edward had taken it to use against the MacDonalds. In any case, his antennae began to tell him that there was trouble ahead, and that even though he wasn't entirely ready yet to get his family overseas, now might be a good time to make a run for it.

"By now, the time's coming up when you are all getting ready to leave the holiday cottage, presumably taking the tape with you. The MacDonalds decide to take care of the job themselves. I suspect Danny knew that they were coming that afternoon. In fact he probably had told them what day the Careys were most likely to be gone. I doubt he thought they were going to kill them. I should think that the plan was more likely that they were going to terrify Edward into giving up the tape. In any case, he decided that he'd best be gone in case the trouble got way out of hand and the finger was pointed at him. So he called Julie and put their escape plan into action. In the meantime, the MacDonalds arrived at Balnacoil."

"But I still don't understand," Angela said. "Why did

Danny Blaine go back? And why didn't they kill us? We could have taken the tape to Edinburgh, for all they knew."

"To answer the last first," Ross said, "they didn't know about you. Remember, the film or tape, or whatever, was shot at the distillery before you arrived. So Kenny only recognized three people and that car. Danny, for some reason, didn't tell them. Or perhaps he didn't even notice. Remember, your car wasn't there. It was being serviced. And by the time they did know about you, it was too late. Danny'd been charged with the killings, and they were now quite certain that Julie, who had disappeared, had the tape. That Danny had given it to her, possibly to use as a lever if he got in trouble. So they were absolutely hysterical about finding her. Danny didn't say a word, for fear of exposing her; she was his alibi and he couldn't risk Kenny finding her. Unfortunately, when Kenny did find her, it was because I led them straight to her."

"None of that," Miranda said. "Explain why Danny Blaine dropped his dogs off with Julie, told her to run, and then went back to the farm."

"Well, I don't think he did go back to the farm, at least not for a long time," Ross replied. "He wasn't seen there until almost half past eight that night. I think that at some point that Wednesday afternoon, possibly while he was waiting for Julie, he realized what had happened to the tape. And he knew that whoever had it would be in serious danger from the MacDonalds. You see, Julie wasn't the only person that Danny Blaine was protecting. So he went to look for the tape, but he couldn't find the hiding place. In the end, perhaps he thought he was wrong after all. Perhaps he went back to the farm to see if it was hidden there. Perhaps he just went back to his cottage to think it over, or because he had nowhere else to go. In any case, when he arrived back, he found the police everywhere and himself framed very neatly for murder."

"Do you think that Kenny planned on framing Danny?" Owen asked.

"I don't really know," Ross said. "It was certainly a golden opportunity, with Danny's prints already all over the cottage. And of course you can't tell which shotgun a cartridge has been fired out of. All you have to do is leave Danny's gun, recently fired, and a few goods from the cottage in a very obvious hiding place, and Kenny's taken care of his archrival for life."

"So that's really why they were killed, then," Angela said. "Because Tarquin took those pictures?"

"That's right," Ross said. "I'm afraid it's that simple. Rather like getting hit by a bus, they were simply in the wrong place at the wrong time with a camera."

"Oh Christ," Angela said quietly. "It seems as if there ought to be some terribly profound reason for something as big as getting murdered. And there just isn't."

There was a silence in the room.

"Tell me one more thing," Miranda said, "because Sheila's giving us those 'come on you're ruining dinner looks.' Who is this mysterious 'go-between' who also, presumably, had the tape and the other things that 'disappeared'?"

Ross smiled at her. "One of *Macbeth's* witches," he said.

Miranda rolled her eyes. "Well, will you at least tell me where you found the bloody tape, after all that?"

"Of course," Ross said. "I found it in Rob Roy's cave."

"Oh, H. W. Ross," Miranda shouted in exasperation, "you are the most impossible liar!"

DIANNE G. PUGH
Author of *COLD CALL*

S L O W
SQUEEZE

AN IRIS THORNE MYSTERY

Available in Hardcover

POCKET
BOOKS

1006-01